The Flight *from*
INTIMACY

The Flight *from* INTIMACY

Healing Your Relationship of **Counter-dependency** — the Other Side of Co-dependency

Janae B. Weinhold, PhD & Barry K. Weinhold, PhD

Foreword by John Bradshaw

New World Library
Novato, California

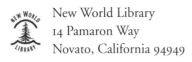 New World Library
14 Pamaron Way
Novato, California 94949

Text design by Tona Pearce Myers

Library of Congress Cataloging-in-Publication Data
Weinhold, Janae B.
The flight from intimacy : healing your relationship of counter-dependency, the other side of co-dependency / Janae B. Weinhold and Barry K. Weinhold; foreword by John Bradshaw.
    p.   cm.
Includes bibliographical references (p. 323) and index.
ISBN 978-1-57731-605-3 (pbk. : alk. paper)
  1. Intimacy (Psychology) I. Weinhold, Barry K. II. Title.
BF575.I5W45 2008
158.2—dc22   2007045300

First printing, February 2008
ISBN: 978-1-57731-605-3
Printed in Canada on 100% postconsumer-waste recycled paper

ℊ New World Library is a proud member of the Green Press Initiative.

10 9 8 7 6 5 4 3 2 1

We dedicate this book to all the lonely and wounded individuals seeking more intimate and joyful relationships, particularly those who have fled from intimacy because of struggles with counter-dependency issues.

Contents

Foreword by John Bradshaw   ix
Introduction   1

PART ONE. THE FLIGHT FROM INTIMACY

1. Counter-dependency: The Other Side of Co-dependency   19
2. Understanding the Counter-dependent Stage of Development   49
3. Getting Stuck in Counter-dependency   65
4. The Disease Model of Relationships   89
5. The Counter-dependent Culture   111

PART TWO. PATHWAYS TO INTIMACY

6. The Elements of Breaking Free   137
7. Empathy: A Path to Intimacy   155
8. Boundary Setting   169
9. Me and My Shadow: Reclaiming Projections   187
10. Self-parenting: Healing Your Inner Child   199
11. Conflict and Intimacy   217
12. Pillow Talk: Sexual Communication   237

PART THREE. BEYOND COUNTER-DEPENDENCY:
PATHWAYS TO PARTNERSHIP

13. Creating Partnership Relationships   259
14. Creating the Partnership Society   287
15. How We Created a Partnership Relationship   305

Acknowledgments   321
Notes   323
Bibliography   329
Index   333
About the Authors   341

Foreword

Counter-dependency is the untalked-about polarity of co-dependency. One reason many severely co-dependent people go without treatment is the failure to focus on counter-dependency. Many lonely, agoraphobic, rebellious, sexually addicted people are counter-dependent. Most of us who define ourselves as co-dependent exhibit some counter-dependent behaviors.

We need this book to fill a gap in our understanding of co-dependency. The Weinholds are experts in this field. I recommend their work as having the highest integrity. This is a crucial addition to the literature on co-dependency.

— John Bradshaw, author of *Bradshaw On: The Family, Healing the Shame That Binds You, Homecoming, Creating Love,* and *Family Secrets*

Introduction

*I have never known a patient to portray
his parents more negatively than he actually experienced them
in childhood, but always more positively —
because idealization of his parents was essential for survival.*
— Alice Miller

It had been a long day. I had been struggling with my doctoral program, orienting myself in a new life in a strange city, and worrying about how I would support myself financially during the next two or three years. Ordinarily I could talk myself out of my fears by using my well-practiced "be strong and act tough" program. On this night, however, I am feeling overwhelmed as I realize the magnitude of the commitments I have made by marrying Barry and agreeing to become a full partner with him. I'm afraid I will fail. I feel little and vulnerable. I go downstairs to find Barry.

He is watching the sports news on television. When I sit down beside him, he barely notices I am there. I sit quietly for a few moments, hoping he will notice my fragility. When he doesn't, I tell him how tired I am and ask if he is ready to go to bed. He says he will be there in a few minutes, if I want to go ahead.

I go upstairs and get into bed, waiting for him to come. In the dark my wall of toughness crumbles and my unspoken fears begin to consume me. I curl up in a little ball and start to cry. It's a half hour before Barry comes to bed. By this time I've gone deep inside myself, feeling abandoned and hurt by his delay. When Barry gets into bed, I move over onto my side and pull away from him. He immediately knows something is wrong and comes toward me. He asks empathically what is wrong.

By this time I have converted my unspoken fears into anger at Barry for not noticing my needs and for not hurrying to bed to take care of me. I try to make him into the bad guy by telling him he is unsympathetic, insensitive, and unavailable when I need him. I begin to lash out at him, telling him how awful he is, and forget all about what I originally wanted from him. He continues to talk softly to me, trying to get to the bottom of my anger.

My anger now has totally lifted me out of my fears and my vulnerability. In the strength of my anger, I hurl one last insult at him and leap out of bed. I put on my robe and slippers, find a blanket, and head into the living room to sleep on the couch. I lie down and pull the cover over me in righteous indignation and try to sleep.

The solitude feels familiar. It reminds me that I am the only one I can count on in my life. No one has ever been there for me when I really needed someone. For several minutes I run through my list of lifelong hurts and feel like a victim. The steam of my anger and resentments finally cools, and all I feel is the pain of isolation.

I begin to realize that even though my behavior feels familiar and justified, it doesn't get me what I want. What I really want is to be close to Barry and to be comforted by him. The next moments are some of the most difficult of my life, for in them I understand that I have a choice. I can choose to let down my wall of resentment and bravado and let him see who I really am underneath it, or I can keep up my wall and set in motion the breakup of another doomed relationship. It's difficult to acknowledge my pattern of isolation and abandonment and how I struggle to reveal my wounds and vulnerability.

In my first marriage, my husband seemed distant and unavailable. I was usually the one who took the part of pursuer and co-dependent partner. Barry, however, is very available. I see now that his desire for closeness and his availability as a partner is forcing me to look at my own fears and resistance to intimacy. The realization that I am now behaving like my ex-husband in my relationship with Barry shatters some illusions I have about myself. I feel ashamed and vulnerable.

From some deep part of myself, I feel a push toward wholeness and hope for a new life. This helps me gather my blanket and return to the bedroom. Barry is still awake. I ask him if he will help me sort through this episode. He is still hurt that I yelled at him and made him seem bad, but he, too, says he wants to be close. Out of our mutual commitment to make this relationship work, we begin to unravel the pieces of the conflict.

What I have come to understand is my lifelong pattern of looking good and appearing strong in the midst of crises and traumas: the emotional abuse and abrupt abandonment at eleven months by my mother; her suicide when I was twelve; her homicide of my brother when she committed suicide; my abusive first marriage; my divorce; and my decision to venture out into the world of work at the age of forty with fears of being single. The decision to finally reveal my counter-dependent side to Barry on this evening in 1985 was the first time I had ever opened myself up to the fears and rewards of intimacy. No longer could I play the suave, cool, capable person so many people saw me as. Breaking free of my counter-dependent patterns has been one of the most difficult tasks of my life. It has brought me to the depths of my psyche through two breakdowns, which have allowed me to remove most of the barriers, to a full, intimate partnership with Barry.

WHAT IS COUNTER-DEPENDENCY?

People with counter-dependent behaviors appear strong, self-confident, and successful on the outside. On the inside they are weak, insecure, fearful, and needy. They may function well in the world of business, but often they are failures in the world of relationships. Frequently they have poor relationship skills, are afraid to get close to others, and avoid intimate situations as much as possible. They are also very well defended against anyone seeing their secret weaknesses and vulnerability. In short, they keep very busy trying to show other people that they are okay and do not need anything from anyone.

Counter-dependent behaviors in adults often control and severely restrict the amount of love, intimacy, and closeness they can give and receive in their lives. These behaviors, many of which we've listed in the "Troubleshooting" sidebar on the next page, can create feelings of loneliness, alienation, and a sense of "quiet desperation."

TROUBLESHOOTING

Have You Ever Done These Things?

- Attempted to hide normal fears, anxieties, or insecurities from others
- Felt the inability to identify and/or express important feelings
- Attempted to always "look good" and always be "right"
- Felt a lack of trust in other people's motives
- Felt victimized by the actions of others
- Felt anxious in close, intimate relationships
- Been reluctant to ask for help from others when needed
- Preferred to work alone
- Been in constant fear of making a mistake
- Had low tolerance for frustration, marked by temper tantrums or fits of anger when frustrated
- Been unable to relax and had a constant need to be engaged in work or activity
- Felt afraid of being smothered or controlled by the needs of others
- Had little awareness of the needs or feelings of others
- Tended to sexualize all nurturing touch
- Been addicted to work, sex, activity, or exercise

HOW DOES COUNTER-DEPENDENCY DIFFER FROM CO-DEPENDENCY?

It's important to understand how counter-dependent behaviors differ from co-dependent behaviors, and that they are caused by very different experiences in early childhood. The "Behavioral Differences" chart on the following pages illustrates how they are different.

BEHAVIORAL DIFFERENCES

Co-dependent Behaviors	Counter-dependent Behaviors
• Clings to others	• Pushes others away
• Acts weak and vulnerable	• Acts strong and invulnerable
• Is overwhelmed by his or her feelings	• Is cut off from his or her feelings
• Is other-centered	• Is self-centered
• Is addicted to people	• Is addicted to activities or substances
• Is easily invaded by others	• Is "armored" against others' attempts to get close
• Has low self-esteem	• Has falsely inflated self-esteem
• Acts incompetent	• Tries to "look good"
• Has depressed energy	• Has manic energy
• Acts insecure	• Acts secure
• Acts weak	• Acts strong
• Feels guilty	• Blames others
• Craves intimacy and closeness	• Avoids intimacy and closeness
• Acts self-effacing	• Acts grandiose
• Has victim behaviors	• Tries to victimize others first
• Is a people pleaser	• Is a people controller
• Suffered neglect as a child	• Suffered abuse as a child

In addition, people with predominantly co-dependent behaviors often end up in relationships with people who have more counter-dependent behaviors. This can cause many conflicts and misunderstandings. Adults with counter-dependent patterns often have a series of relationship failures. They often form superficial relationships that they cannot sustain, or that they never allow to become very intimate. The following examples illustrate some of the difficulties encountered by adults with counter-dependent behavior patterns.

John is a hard worker who pushes himself and his co-workers; they see him as being as too hard on himself and others. Frequently, though, he has "rage attacks" when the smallest thing goes wrong. Despite his high job performance, he is passed over for promotion because of his poor relationship skills.

Sam is bright and seems to handle life easily. He's a sharp dresser and a likeable person, but inside he feels insecure and has low self-esteem. When he is asked to give a presentation at the monthly sales meeting, he has to snort some cocaine to get himself up for the presentation.

Joan always looks as if she stepped off the pages of a fashion magazine. She is witty and fun-loving but hard to get close to. Nobody knows her secret fear of sexual intimacy.

Susan always seems to be on the go, caring for her children, cooking for her husband and family, working for local charities, playing tennis, and exercising at the club. At home after all the work is done, she has trouble just sitting and relaxing. She has frequent migraine headaches that can send her to bed for days. Her husband complains that he never gets enough time with her, and finally, in desperation, has an affair with someone at the office.

WHAT ARE THE CAUSES OF COUNTER-DEPENDENT BEHAVIORS IN ADULTS?

Counter-dependent behaviors are caused by a failure to fully complete the two most important developmental processes of early childhood: bonding and separation. When these processes are not completed at the appropriate age, they are carried forward as excess baggage and affect each subsequent stage of development. If these processes are not completed during later childhood or in adolescence, people carry them into their adult lives and continue to seek to complete them. These incomplete developmental processes can lead to addictions, serious conflicts, problems with closeness and intimacy, victimization by others, and unfulfilling and unsuccessful relationships. From birth to about three years of age, children need help in completing these two important developmental processes, bonding and separation.

Bonding with parents and others, which usually starts at birth, allows children to develop a sense of basic trust and safety. It involves a deep attunement between parents and children that includes a lot of physical contact, holding and nurturing touch, and pleasant, reassuring messages to the child. Children need to know they are loved for who they are, and that they are wanted by their parents. Bonding provides a solid foundation for children as they to begin to separate physically and emotionally and to gradually move away from mother and father, exploring their world safely and securely and learning to become emotionally autonomous human beings. Children also need supervision and support in order to become emotionally separate from their parents. The stronger the bond, the easier it is for them to become separate. Ideally, children should achieve emotional separateness from their parents by about age three.

When children become individuated, they have the self-confidence and ability to rely on their own internal signals when making decisions. No longer must they rely solely on others to direct their lives. By the time they complete this important step, also known as the psychological birth,[1] they have developed a healthy sense of self that allows them to accept responsibility for their actions, to share and cooperate, to handle frustration in appropriate ways, to respond effectively to the authority of others, and to express feelings in healthy ways. But when their developmental needs during this period are not met, people remain stuck in co-dependent or counter-dependent behavior patterns that recycle throughout their lives.

What happens during early childhood that interferes with the successful completion of these developmental tasks? Often the child experiences the trauma of emotional, physical, spiritual, or sexual abuse, or in some cases, physical or emotional abandonment or neglect. We found in our clinical research, however, that the most common cause of co-dependent and counter-dependent behaviors is *developmental trauma* caused by subtle disconnects between parent and child involving the lack of, or loss of, emotional attunement. If these disconnects are not recognized and resolved, this creates a pattern of isolation and disengagement that can seriously affect intimacy in adulthood. Adults who, as small children, were abused by people they trusted often fear they will experience similar abuse or abandonment when they try to get close to other adults. Adults who have been abused learn to construct physical and psychological walls to protect themselves from encountering the feelings related to their unhealed childhood traumas.

Although people often don't remember many of these traumas, they are visible in their relationship histories. One reason people deny the impact of these early events is because they believe the abuse they suffered as a child was done to them for their own good by well-meaning parents. Children often believe they were the cause of any abuse or abandonment they endured.

Emotional abuse by a parent or other adult can take the form of withdrawal of love, verbal abuse, a lack of understanding or respect for the needs of the child, and attempts to overcontrol the child's activities. Symptoms such as fractured relationships, abuse of others, depression, divorce, and addictions are strong indicators of undetected childhood developmental traumas.

Physical abuse — physical punishment for wrongdoing — includes slapping, punching, hitting with a stick, and spanking and hitting on bare skin in ways that leave marks or bruises. Sexual abuse of children by parents or adults involves both intentional and unintentional activities, ranging from actual incest to giving a child incorrect or no information about sex. Adults who were physically or sexually abused as children have difficulty being close to and intimate with others. They often unconsciously reenact their abuse with their own or other children.

Abandonment or neglect may be physical, emotional, or spiritual. The wounds of physical abandonment or neglect, characterized by the absence of relationship, are sometimes easier to break free of than emotional or spiritual abandonment or neglect. With physical abandonment or neglect, people had a tangible experience that leaves them knowing "something happened." Emotional and spiritual abandonment or neglect are less concrete. They can result when a parent is physically present but emotionally absent, or when a parent neglects to support the child's emotional needs for touch, holding, and comfort. These types of abandonment or neglect are more difficult to identify because they are less visible, but they can leave deep scars.

IS IT POSSIBLE TO CHANGE
COUNTER-DEPENDENT BEHAVIORS?

Fortunately, people can break out of their denial about problems with intimacy. By reading books on the subject, doing various written exercises, talking to others who have had similar experiences, and undertaking therapy, they can begin to connect the problems they experience as adults to abuse in childhood. They can realize they were not the cause of that abuse. With help, they can overcome the effects of their early developmental traumas. Breaking free as adults is possible once they understand the relationship between their childhood experiences and their adult problems and use effective tools to help them become whole.

Recognition of counter-dependent behaviors is relatively new in the field of developmental psychology. Only a few other people, such as John Bradshaw, Pam Levin, Jean Clarke, and Jon and Laurie Weiss, have approached relationship addictions from a developmental perspective. Developmental psychologists Stephen Johnson, Erik Erikson, Robert Havinghurst, Jean Piaget, Margaret Mahler, and James Masterson contributed much to our understanding of how human development evolves. Our developmental approach offers much hope for people who want more intimacy in their adult relationships, because it provides a step-by-step program that does not require medication or long-term psychotherapy.

In addition, we have created a systemic developmental theory called Developmental Systems Theory (DST) that applies our four-stage model of individual development to other human systems. Through our clinical and heuristic research, we discovered that all human systems (couples, families, groups, organizations, cultures, nation-states, and the human species) go through four stages of development: co-dependence, counter-dependence, independence, and interdependence. They evolve by going through this sequence of developmental processes and stages entering into higher-functioning systems.

We utilize this four-stage model throughout this book to help you understand that everything and everyone is evolving. Most human systems are stuck at the counter-dependent stage of development. In this book, we also describe Developmental Process Work, the approach we use to help people and systems change by assisting them in completing their developmental processes.

The incomplete developmental processes of bonding and separation create predictable problems in adult relationships. Once you identify the traumas caused by bonding breaks during your early development, you can begin repairing these breaks through self-parenting activities. It's possible to complete these developmental processes and experience more intimacy in your life.

While co-dependent behaviors are related to traumas involving abandonment and neglect, counter-dependent behaviors are associated with traumas involving abuse. If you experienced both kinds of traumas, you will likely alternate between co-dependent and counter-dependent behaviors as an adult. This means that individuals who appear more co-dependent may also have counter-dependent behaviors that show up only in certain relationship situations. Most adults in our society have relationship problems directly caused by counter-dependent behaviors, co-dependent behaviors, or a combination of the two. Co-dependency issues have been identified, studied, and written about, while counter-dependency issues and co-dependent/counter-dependent combinations are still unidentified and unexplored.

> Counter-dependent characteristics are so pervasive in the United States that they seem like "normal" behavior.

This book shows you how to easily and quickly identify the sources of your counter-dependent issues and to identify the unmet developmental needs that keep you struggling with intimacy in your relationships. It also shows you effective ways to change these behaviors so that you can create more functional and sustainable intimate relationships. We estimate that over 99 percent of adults in the United States experience some dysfunctions in their relationships that are caused by incomplete developmental processes and unmet needs from early childhood.

These dysfunctions range along a continuum from mild ones, such as not being able to ask directly for what you want and need, to severe ones, such as addictions to alcohol, drugs, sex, work, or activity, that prevent sustained, successful relationships. We estimate that at least 75 percent of adults have moderate dysfunctions that have led to long-standing conflicts or a lack of sustainable intimacy.

It is evident that dysfunctions involving counter-dependent and co-dependent behaviors are influenced by more than simply our experiences within our family of origin. Most institutions in our society unwittingly support counter-dependent and co-dependent behaviors and victim consciousness. Moreover, these personal, social, and cultural symptoms demonstrate that our evolution as a species is stalled and contribute to reproducing the kind of parenting we received from our parents — which we then give to our children.

The goal of breaking free of dysfunctional co-dependent and counter-dependent behaviors is to recover our True Self. Neither our parents' nor our grandparents' generation recognized or saw value in having a Self. They saw those who wanted a Self as selfish, egotistical, and narcissistic, an idea supported by mainstream culture as well, including mainstream religions. They didn't understand that wanting a Self is not selfish but is an innate drive toward wholeness that is truly our natural birthright.

Ours is the first generation to understand that wanting a Self is a natural stage in human evolution. Slowly, this realization is making its mark on our society as new information from the field of developmental psychology is generated. Only in the last twenty years has new information been widely available regarding optimal parenting, birthing, and human development.

With this new information, it's now possible to see that many of the methods our parents used to raise us, and that we used to raise our children, were dysfunctional. From this perspective, it is not useful to judge, blame, or feel ashamed. We are slowly becoming more aware of what humans can be, and to have a new vision of wholeness that can free us from the traumas of our childhood.

Individuals in the baby boom generation were among the first to want a Self. Now many of their children and grandchildren are hungry for a message of hope that gives them permission to seek a Self and for tools to help them experience more intimacy. This is the audience we had in mind as we formed our Developmental Systems Theory.

WHAT IS UNIQUE ABOUT THIS BOOK?

Our book is the result of more than twenty-three years of intensive research. While many of its ideas may seem radical, we know they are valid and that the tools we offer are effective. Many elements make this book unique.

The story in it is highly personal. In our journey together as a couple, as professors, as therapists, and as parents and grandparents, we have committed to walk our talk. Our relationship, which has served as our laboratory, has been a primary source for learning about dysfunctional family patterns and for breaking free of them. In most instances, our personal issues have been catalysts for understanding deeper and more complex levels of human development.

We have applied what we've learned in our work as individuals and as a couple to our relationships with our parents, children, and grandchildren. We have also used this information in working with our psychotherapy clients, with our students, and with many participants in our workshops, seminars, and public lectures. Once we felt the material had become solid enough after applying it in these areas, we wrote about it. What we share with you in this book comes from our own journey. In fact, you will find our own stories in the final chapter.

We identify counter-dependency as the flip side of co-dependency. This book is the only one we are aware of that addresses the subject of counter-dependency, a term that may be unfamiliar to you. More than four hundred books and countless magazine articles about co-dependency have been published, and many interviews on the subject have been presented on talk shows, but the equally serious problem of counter-dependency has been virtually ignored.

DID YOU KNOW THAT...

Our approach to intimacy is unique. We redefine it to include all relational experiences, whether they are positive or negative; being in conflict with your partner can be as emotionally engaging as making love. In our model, we define intimacy as meaningful emotional contact with another person. The lack of emotional contact in close relationships is often experienced as indifference, which is more the opposite of love than is hate.

Our approach is unique because we recommend using committed relationships to transform developmental deficits such as counter-dependent and co-dependent behaviors when possible. It is our belief that wounds that occur in intimate relationships can best be mended there. Those who use their primary relationships to free themselves discover a kind of intimacy that would have been difficult to imagine at the beginning of their journey. As you break free of counter-dependency, you will experience new levels of closeness and a sense of spiritual connection.

When people help each other heal their wounds from childhood, they experience something we call depth intimacy, in which they have the sense that their souls touch. This happens when both individuals strip away the facades they constructed out of looking good and acting strong, and they experience the vulnerability that ultimately frees the Self. By helping each other heal the wounds from their childhoods, both partners (whether they are a couple or not) move forward developmentally and each becomes more individuated and psychologically separate.

This kind of intimacy is different from pseudo intimacy, which emphasizes having happiness and good times, or which focuses on rising above differences and conflicts. It has been our experience that people caught in the flight from intimacy often bury their problems, pretending they don't exist, until some small incident triggers the hidden issues and they erupt into a huge conflict.

There is a third kind of intimacy, which we define as transcendent intimacy. This form of intimacy requires individuals who are psychologically evolved and able to experience a high level of spiritual oneness without losing their awareness of their separateness. Advanced sexual practices such as tantric yoga involve moving into these states of ecstatic beingness by directing and controlling the flow of sexual energy.

A balanced relationship involves both transcendent and depth intimacy. It involves using the intimacy present in your daily life conflicts as a doorway to higher awareness. Here, in deep intimacy with yourself, you can discover and heal your brokenness and experience intimacy at a soul level. Clearing deep wounds can open you to transcendent experiences of spiritual connection. Once we discovered this phenomenon in our own work, we gradually came to trust that these wounds were opportunities to find greater intimacy. What most surprised us, however, was that transcendent experiences often opened up our deeper wounds. Without warning, we found ourselves quickly shifting from a peak spiritual experience into reexperiencing wounds that opened us to depth intimacy.

These two kinds of contrasting intimacy can create an energetic thrust similar to what pistons generate, and can move both partners forward in their evolution. Couples who develop skills in both kinds of intimacy can really use their relationship as a mechanism for soul evolution. Soul evolution requires a holistic approach. Breaking free of counter-dependent behaviors involves transformation at the physical, mental, emotional, and spiritual levels. People addicted to substances must first address their physical dependency before they can address the emotional issues related to their substance abuse. Our holistic program, which involves therapies for each of the different levels, presents a broad approach to helping you identify counter-dependent patterns that may be causing intimacy problems in your relationships.

In the addictions field, the terms *co-dependency* and *counter-dependency* are often used as disease diagnoses. We refrain from doing this, and instead offer a nonmedical, developmental understanding of the causes of counter-dependent behaviors and present a hopeful, developmental approach to help you experience intimacy. We identify the social and cultural roots of counter-dependency and their roles in social and cultural evolution.

Therapists working from a medical model have informed many individuals that they cannot recover from the "disease" of co-dependency and may even die from it. As a result, these people have been left with feelings of shame and low self-esteem. This approach has also caused people with co-dependent behaviors to deny their unmet needs so they wouldn't appear to be co-dependent. In many cases, their shame kept them from doing the deep transformational work necessary to get their needs met. Instead, they erected protective defenses and jumped into acting counter-dependent, which is seen as more socially acceptable. The disease orientation and people's reaction to it may have contributed to the sudden collapse of the self-help movement in the early 1990s and to the widespread erection of counter-dependent defenses against intimacy. In chapter 5, we show that millions of Americans have accepted a lower quality of life because they have passively accepted the judgmental, disease-oriented approach as the truth about addictive relationships.

This book does not diagnose you as being sick but instead provides a map for your journey to changing your counter-dependent behaviors. If you are interested in breaking out of the culturally imposed trance and achieving higher levels of intimacy, then this book can help.

Every individual, couple, family, and culture unconsciously seeks wholeness but lacks awareness and effective tools. In addition to looking at what is "right" about counter-dependency, we also include many self-help tools designed to help stop your flight from intimacy. Changing your flight patterns will help you develop healthier intimacy and fully recover your Self. You can eliminate counter-dependent behaviors without extensive therapy if you are willing to work on your intimacy problems by reading, participating in support groups, and creating committed, healing relationships.

In this book, we stress self-sufficiency and personal empowerment, providing you with essential skills for breaking free from the trap of counter-dependent patterns. We supply written exercises to help you identify counter-dependent patterns and move toward wholeness. We also show couples how they can work cooperatively to help each other break free of counter-dependent behavior patterns. We provide practical exercises that help you experience depth intimacy while assisting each other.

We offer a vision of life beyond counter-dependency and other kinds of dysfunctional behaviors. Many self-help programs do not provide people with a clear vision of what it means to recover your Self and be whole. We know that, without this kind of a vision, people cannot move forward and grow.

NOTE: If you are currently in therapy, please get your therapist's permission before doing the exercises included in this book. If you are not in therapy, we recommend doing the exercises with a nurturing and supportive friend or partner or in a support group.

Part 1
THE FLIGHT FROM INTIMACY

1. Counter-dependency
The Other Side of Co-dependency

But he's a human being, and a terrible thing is happening to him.
So attention must be paid. He is not to be allowed to fall
into his grave like an old dog.
Attention must be finally paid to such a person.

— Arthur Miller

In an earlier book, *Breaking Free of the Co-dependency Trap*, we identified the cause of co-dependency as a failure to complete the bonding process — one of the most important developmental processes of early childhood. We explained how to complete this process and eliminate co-dependency problems.

AN OVERVIEW OF THE PROBLEM

Co-dependent behaviors are rather easy to identify, much easier to identify than counter-dependent behaviors. Major signs of co-dependency are evidenced in some of the following ways:

• feeling anxious and insecure without knowing why
• constantly worrying that others will reject you
• feeling trapped in an abusive relationship

- not trusting yourself and your own decisions
- taking care of others instead of yourself
- trying to please others
- having few or no personal boundaries
- not knowing what you want or need
- acting like a victim or martyr

By contrast, hidden away in an office building somewhere is a person working late at night whose counter-dependent behaviors may be less apparent though just as dysfunctional. People who display counter-dependent behaviors probably have the same unmet needs for closeness and intimacy that people with co-dependent behaviors have, but these needs are hidden — not only from others but also from themselves, because counter-dependent people make judgments about needy people. These counter-dependent individuals do in fact have some justification for feeling this way. Previously, when they revealed their weaknesses and vulnerability, someone made fun of them or ignored them because of it.

How can you tell if an adult has counter-dependent behaviors? When you review the following list of characteristic behaviors, you will likely recognize some that remind you more of a two-year-old than of an adult. This isn't surprising, because people whose social and emotional needs aren't met in the first three years of their lives carry them around. These needs then emerge in adult relationships and interfere with intimacy. This is the chief cause of counter-dependent behaviors in adults. When individuals simply do not get their developmental needs met in childhood, they find themselves just "playing grown-up."

DID YOU KNOW THAT...

Developmental needs not met during childhood are dragged along as excess baggage. These needs continue to press for attention, causing conflicts that interfere with intimacy in adult relationships. Counter-dependent behaviors help you cope with having unmet needs. You are not bad or sick because of them. You are always doing your best to meet these needs in your current relationships.

Characteristics of Counter-dependency

As you read the list of characteristics, see how many of these behaviors you recognize in yourself. The first step in understanding your counter-dependent attempts to meet your vital developmental needs is to identify your compensating behaviors. Do you:

- have trouble getting close to people?
- have trouble sustaining closeness in intimate relationships?
- tend to view people as bad or wrong when you leave them or they leave you?
- have trouble feeling your feelings other than justified anger or sadness?
- have fears of other people controlling you?
- tend to say no to the new ideas of others?
- rebel against or move away from people who try to get too close to you?
- get anxious in close, intimate relationships?
- feel constantly afraid you will make a mistake?
- try to be perfect and expect others to be perfect?
- refrain from asking for help even when you need it?
- have a strong need to be right?
- have thick layers of muscle or fat across your shoulders, chest, or abdomen that create a kind of body armor?
- get afraid of being consumed by the needs of others?
- fear that others will reject you if you show your weaknesses or fears?
- get bored easily and need to seek new thrills?
- make high demands on yourself or others?
- tend to see people as all good or all bad, depending on how they relate to you?
- work long hours during the week and go into work on weekends too?
- keep very busy with hobbies, recreation, or other projects?
- find it difficult to relax and do nothing?
- have difficulty with free play or unstructured time?
- have fits of anger when you don't get your way?
- take outrageous risks in sports or business dealings that you secretly hope will make you rich and famous?
- believe you're entitled to have others treat you in special ways?

Like people with co-dependent behaviors, people with counter-dependent behaviors also have a sense that they are not whole without the help of someone else. However, they try to hide this fact from others so they can appear as if they really don't need other people. In order to maintain this deception, they often sink an enormous amount of energy into fooling themselves and others regarding the depth and range of their needs.

They often do this through an almost compulsive adherence to activities that others will value and reward, such as work, hobbies, recreation, exercise, or community activities, all of which serve to keep them busy and make them look good. In this way, they are actually hiding from themselves, hoping they won't have to feel their deep feelings of being rejected, abandoned, abused, or smothered by the people they were close to while growing up. These people may be their parents or parental figures like teachers, older siblings, or peers.

Causes of Counter-dependent Behaviors in Adults

There are three basic developmental reasons why adults behave in counter-dependent ways: (1) they did not bond sufficiently with their parents during the first year of life, (2) their parents were not able to help them become emotionally separate during the second and third years of their lives, and (3) they suffered developmental traumas as the result of various subtle forms of abuse and/or neglect. We estimate that only 1 or 2 percent of the adult population successfully completed bonding and separation, the essential developmental processes during early childhood. As a result, incomplete developmental processes show up constantly in adult relationships, preventing people from being intimate.[1]

With the appropriate parental and societal support and guidance, you should have completed your psychological birth by about age three. What often interferes with the completion of this very important developmental milestone is the presence of subtle forms of emotional, physical, and/or sexual abuse and developmental traumas during the first three years of life.

> Counter-dependent behaviors indicate that you did not fully complete your psychological and emotional separation from your parents during early childhood.

Repeated, early exposure to any form of trauma and violence desensitizes people to violence. When we give talks on counter-dependency, we typically ask members of the audience to raise their hands if they have personally witnessed violence or abuse, or if anyone has treated them violently or abusively. Typically, about one-third of the audience raises a hand. But never witnessing violence or abuse means never watching a violent television show or movie and never watching anyone in the family, workplace, highway, school, or neighborhood being violent or abusive. That any individual has been this sheltered is highly unlikely! So why don't more audience members raise their hands when we ask this question?

Perhaps they learned to dissociate during these moments in order to cope with their memories of trauma and abuse. They may also, however, remain in a constant state of hypervigilance to prevent being triggered by memories of past traumas and abuse. When people are in a persistent hyper-aroused state, they have adrenal hormones flowing through their blood-stream that trigger the fight, flight, or freeze response. This is particularly true when a current conflict in their relationship contains even the slightest hint of an earlier unresolved trauma or abuse. These classic adrenal stress reactions are wired into our brains to help us cope with situations we perceive as dangerous. We don't even have to think about them, we just react. Unhealed developmental traumas may be a major factor in why people own over 270 million guns in the United States. People just don't feel safe.[2]

Along with the fear of traumatic encounters, there is often a companion phenomenon that causes people to be attracted to and fascinated by trauma. The natural learning style of humans is to repeat behaviors until the lessons are learned or the trauma is healed. Freud called this the repetition compulsion. We are drawn to what we fear so we can heal the trauma. That is why so many people seem to enjoy watching violence in movies and seem to enjoy having the wits scared out of them. While people may appear to be addicted to violence, they are still trying to understand and heal traumas from their early childhood. When young children, who have not completed their psychological births, witness violence at home or on TV, they experience it as happening directly to them.[3]

The Role of Parental Neglect and Abandonment

In *High Risk: Children without a Conscience*, Ken Magid and Carol McKelvey state that severely abused and neglected children grow up to become violence-seeking adults, unless there is an intervention in their lives before age sixteen. They estimate that over 20 million adults fall into this category, and that their number is growing more rapidly than the general population's rate of increase. They advise us to do a better job of protecting our young children and intervening early in their lives. Magid predicts that, if we don't, "soon there will be more of them than us, and then we will be in real trouble."[4]

New research by Dr. Bruce Perry of Baylor College of Medicine says that it takes a special kind of family environment to turn a normal child into a killer.[5] He concluded that repeated abuse, neglect, or experiences of terror cause permanent physical changes in the brains of young children. He found that a constant flood of adrenaline causes the brain to reset its normal alarm system to a permanent hair-trigger alert.

Children who are constantly exposed to abuse or who witness the abuse of others, such as a sibling or parent, have high levels of adrenal stress hormones that shut down their brains. These are the high-risk kids that Magid talks about. They typically have antisocial personalities, low heart rates, and impaired emotional sensitivity, including a lack of empathy. They often will kill or torture animals.[6]

A profiler of the character-disturbed child, Foster Cline was one of the first to profile the characteristics of high-risk children who have attachment disorders.[7] According to Cline, high-risk children

- are unable to give and receive affection;
- exhibit self-destructive behavior;
- are cruel to others;
- employ phoniness or seductive "sweet talk";
- have severe problems with stealing, hoarding, and gorging on food;
- exhibit marked behavior control problems;
- lack long-term friendships; and
- display abnormalities in eye contact.

There are three types of maternal attachments: secure, avoidant, and anxious/ambivalent. Campos, Barrett, and colleagues, found that 62 percent of infants were securely attached, 23 percent were avoidant, and 15 percent were anxious/ambivalent.[8] The child's type of early attachment causes him or her to develop what is called an internal "working model" of the world.[9]

There are also three identifiable subtypes of avoidant children: (1) the lying bully who blames others, (2) the shy, dissociated loner who seems emotionally flat, and (3) the obviously disturbed child with repetitive twitches and tics who daydreams and shows little interest in his or her environment. And there are two subtypes of anxious/ambivalent children: (1) the fidgety, impulsive child with poor concentration who is tense and easily upset by his or her failures, and (2) the fearful, hypersensitive, clingy child who lacks initiative and gives up easily.[10]

The *Diagnostic and Statistical Manual of Mental Disorders*, fourth edition, published by the American Psychiatric Association, lists the characteristics that lead to a diagnosis of what the manual identifies as a "conduct disorder."[11] This diagnosis can apply to a child under the age of eighteen; in diagnosing individuals over eighteen, the same disorder is called an "antisocial personality disorder." The symptoms are summarized as follows:

- Acts aggressively toward people and animals:
  - often bullies, threatens, or intimidates others
  - has used a weapon that can cause serious physical harm to others
  - often initiates physical fights
  - has been physically cruel to people
  - has been physically cruel to animals
  - has stolen while confronting a victim
  - has forced someone into sexual activity

- Has destroyed property:
  - has deliberately engaged in fire setting
  - has deliberately destroyed others' property (other than by fire setting)

- Practices deceitfulness or theft:
  - has broken into someone else's house, building, or car
  - often lies to obtain goods or favors or to avoid obligations
  - has stolen items of nontrivial value without confronting a victim

- Has committed serious violations of rules:
  - often stays out at night despite parental prohibitions, beginning while under the age of thirteen

- has run away from home overnight at least twice while living in the home of a parent or parental surrogate
- is often truant from school, beginning while under the age of thirteen

Before being diagnosed as having an antisocial personality disorder, a person must exhibit a persistent pattern of three or more of these behaviors over a period of twelve months, with at least one of the behaviors exhibited once in the preceding three months. You can see that most of these behaviors are similar to those that Cline found in his study of the effects of poor bonding and attachment.[12] It's clear that parental neglect, abuse, and emotional abandonment play an important role in shaping children's brains. They also are responsible for shaping children's internal working models of reality, particularly concerning how — or whether — adults in their environments are going to care for them. In order to prevent bullying, school violence, and other antisocial behaviors in children and later in adults, parents need therapy to learn to repair the attachment disorders in their children.

Perry's research also indicated that children living with parents who are withdrawn and remote, passive or depressed, and neglectful suffer from delayed brain development. He found that neglect impairs the development of the brain's cortex, where feelings of belonging and attachment originate. According to Perry, these neglected kids desperately need positive adult attention to compensate for the lack of attention, or the negative attention, they received early in life from their parents or family members.[13]

Other research has confirmed that the internal working model of the world formed in early childhood persists into adulthood virtually unchanged. Krause and Haverkamp have summarized the research, saying, "Existing research does suggest that the bond between parent and child is likely to remain in effect across the life span and plays an important role in later life parent-child relations."[14]

Developmental Trauma

In our research on conflict resolution, we identified the occurrence of developmental traumas during early childhood as the main reason people flee from intimacy. These traumas are more often the result of neglect than abuse.

As a result, they are harder to identify, because "nothing happened," except that children's social and emotional needs were neglected by the significant adults in their lives.[15]

The Causes of Developmental Trauma

- Abuse, neglect, or emotional abandonment during the child's first three years
- Disruptions in the normal sequence of development
- Prolonged, repeated, or premature separations between mother and child during the early bonding period due to illness
- Daily small emotional disconnects between mother and child
- Repeated encroachment on the child's physical, psychological, and emotional boundaries
- A lack of understanding of the child's needs
- A lack of safe and clear limits during the exploratory stage

Developmental traumas can have a variety of effects on the subsequent development of the child. These effects can be physical, emotional, or cognitive. Many children are mislabeled as a result, and the true cause of their behavior is not recognized. Professionals and parents alike need to better understand the effects of early developmental traumas on children and, later, on adults.

The Effects of Developmental Trauma

- Developmental delays, which can create "late bloomers"
- Attachment disorders (ambivalent or anxious/avoidant)
- Adult deficit disorder (our definition of ADD)
- Cognitive impairment due to a lack of emotional interactions
- Primitive problem-solving strategies that involve the use of violence
- Dissociation in females
- Aggressive, impulsive, reactive, and hyperactive behaviors in males

William Pollack, author of *Real Boys*, says that "when parents or other adults disconnect from young boys, the boys learn to suffer in silence and, rather than crying tears, they eventually 'cry bullets.' "[16] This fits with the description of events in the lives of the Columbine killers, Eric Harris and

Dylan Klebold. They used violence to discharge their pent-up rage from childhood and from being marginalized at school.

Dr. Bruce Perry found from studying brain scans that neglected children have more damage to the cognitive functions of their brains than do abused children. According to Perry, the brain actually atrophies when it isn't stimulated enough. He also found that children who were traumatized early in life develop more primitive, less mature styles of conflict resolution. They tend to be more impulsive, more easily triggered by stimulus events, and less likely to consider the consequences of their actions. Bullying viewed through this lens can be seen as adapting to the effects of early trauma and as a protective mechanism employed in an attempt to feel safe again.[17]

Conclusions from Our Research

Many people show classic signs of post-traumatic stress disorder related to the neglect of their early bonding needs.[18] Adults who use violence or abuse to try to control children usually experience a triggering event that causes them to reenact an unhealed developmental trauma that occurred in their own childhood. Almost everyone could benefit from learning trauma reduction techniques and conflict resolution skills and from experiences that provide them with the positive attention they missed getting in early childhood.

The severity of early childhood abuse and trauma determines the severity of intimacy problems that people will have in adulthood. We all know individuals who have overcome their abusive childhood experiences and now lead fairly normal, intimate, and successful adulthoods. Unfortunately, this is still an exception. Most people are not aware of their childhood abuse or trauma until a crisis or relationship conflict brings it to the surface.

It should not be surprising that abuse is a factor in counter-dependent behavior. We live in one of the most violent and abusive cultures on earth. The targets for much of that violence and abuse are family members, especially children.

One nationwide study indicated that between 3.4 million and 4 million children per year have been physically beaten by a parent before they leave home.[19] This study indicated that as many as 1.8 million children per year are threatened by their parents with a knife or gun. This study covered only cases of known abuse, and we know that probably only about 10 percent of abuse in the family ever gets reported. The figures quoted above are for intentional child abuse only. Many parents abuse their children in the name of good parenting. In order to discipline them, they slap, punch, hit with a stick or belt on the bare skin, bruise, cut, scald, burn, torture, beat, and actually maim their children.

Parents also abuse their children emotionally, which doesn't leave visible marks. This may be even more widespread in families than physical or sexual abuse. Alice Miller has noted that most emotional and physical abuse is done by parents who think they are doing it for the good of the child.[20]

The ways parents discipline their children include the use of lies, subterfuge, manipulation, ridicule, shame, scorn, coercion, humiliation, isolation, abandonment, threats of violence, and threats or actual withdrawal of love. Some parents also abuse their children through habitual neglect of their children's basic needs. Physical and emotional neglect appear to be the most damaging forms of childhood abuse.

We can only imagine how much intentional and unintentional sexual abuse occurs in families. Susan Forward and Craig Buck write that the families in which incest occurs come from every economic, cultural, social, racial, educational, religious and geographical background.[21] The overall picture of child abuse in the United States is not pretty. Consider the following facts based on information found in *The Third National Incidence Study of Child Abuse and Neglect* and other national studies on this subject:

- Over 1.5 million children were harmed by child abuse and neglect (a 149 percent increase from 1986 to 1993).[22]
- Over 1.4 million children were endangered by child abuse and neglect (a 306 percent increase from 1986 to 1993).[23]
- Neglect was found to be the most common form of maltreatment (a 114 percent increase, to almost 2 million from 1986 to 1993).[24]
- Over 1,200 children died of abuse or neglect in 2000, 85 percent of whom were under the age of six.[25]
- Over 300,000 children were sexually abused (a 125 percent increase from 1986 to 1993.).[26]
- About 60 percent of girls and 45 percent of boys are sexually abused as children per year.[27]

- In a national survey published in 1999, 41 percent of parents reported having spanked their child; 38 percent reported that they had sworn at or insulted their child; and 51 percent said they failed to meet their child's emotional needs.[28]
- Over 530,000 children were emotionally abused (a 183 percent increase from 1986 to 1993).[29]
- Over 1,335 million children were physically neglected (a 163 percent increase from 1986 to 1993).[30]
- Almost 600,000 children were emotionally neglected (a 188 percent increase from 1986 to 1993).[31]
- About 1,000 people who were abused or neglected in childhood were followed up as a group in 1996 and found to have significantly lower IQs, to hold significantly more menial jobs, to have 1.6 times more criminal behavior, and to be significantly more likely to commit suicide or develop antisocial personality disorders than a control group who were not abused or neglected.[32]
- Almost all criminals report having been abused as children.[33]
- Among all black males in jail, 82 percent were abused or neglected as children.[34]

In many cases, adults with counter-dependent behaviors have little or no awareness of the abuse they suffered as infants and children. Others, as a way to tolerate having endured a high level of abuse, learned to believe that they actually deserved this abuse. We have seen clients with obvious abuse in their backgrounds who report that they had wonderful parents and very happy childhoods. Secretly, however, they suffer from low self-esteem and still inflict some form of abuse on themselves and others. With therapy, frequently these people begin to connect their adult struggles with intimacy with their childhood abuse.

As this connection happens, they begin to recognize some of their "normal" childhood incidents as experiences of abuse. When they have support in expressing their feelings, and support when they remember their experiences, they can begin to identify their unmet developmental needs. It is common for people who suffered abuse to believe they didn't deserve to get their needs met. Breaking through such denial and self-limiting beliefs is often a first step to recognizing the abuse and uncovering the deep wounds from childhood that they still carry.

A FOUR-STAGE MODEL OF HUMAN DEVELOPMENT

We created our Developmental Systems Theory to help us understand how the human species evolves.[35] We discovered that the normal development of couples, families, groups, organizations, and nation-states — and of the human species as a whole — follows the same four stages of development that individuals follow: co-dependence, counter-dependence, independence, and interdependence. Each stage contains essential developmental processes that must be completed in order for the individual to move on to the next stage. If a stage is not completed, this delays development and makes it difficult to move to the next one. Delaying your development is like putting your DVD player on pause while it is playing. Chapter 5 contains more information about our developmental theory.

Most people are stuck in the co-dependent and counter-dependent stages and are still struggling to complete the essential developmental processes of these two stages in their adult relationships. Because they want to appear grown-up, many adults hide, deny, or ignore their unmet needs that have existed since these stages of childhood. The table below, "The Developmental Stages and Essential Developmental Processes of Individual Evolution," briefly describes each stage and the essential developmental processes that should be completed at that stage.[36]

As you read these lists, ask yourself, "Did I complete this process successfully?" If you're not sure, you can do further research by asking your parents or other relatives questions about your early life. Other good sources are baby pictures or a baby book. When you look at photos of yourself as an infant, tune in to that little you, and ask yourself, "How is he feeling?" "Is she a happy child, or is she feeling anxious?"

THE DEVELOPMENTAL STAGES AND ESSENTIAL DEVELOPMENTAL PROCESSES OF INDIVIDUAL EVOLUTION

Stage of Development and Primary Task	Essential Developmental Processes of Individual Evolution	Suggested Experiences for Completing the Essential Developmental Processes of Individual Evolution
Co-dependency (Conception to Six Months) Bonding and Attachment	• **Mother** receives good prenatal care and support **Child:** • experiences a nonviolent birth with immediate interventions to heal any birth trauma • achieves consistent, secure bonding and attachment with mother and/or other adult caregivers • learns primal trust in parents through a consistent resonant connection • learns emotional resiliency skills • creates a secure internal working model of self/other • learns healthy emotional communication and social engagement skills with parents and others • bonds securely with siblings and extended family	**Mother:** • maintains a high-quality diet and reduces environmental stressors to prevent the risk of cortisol production during pregnancy • receives effective postnatal emotional and physical support • provides nurturing, respectful touch and eye contact; she gazes at, sings to, and speaks to the child in loving ways **Parents:** • plan for and want the child • build prenatal relationship with the child • use nonviolent birthing practices • nurse and room-in at the hospital and have prolonged skin-to-skin contact between child and each parent in the first 12–24 hours following birth **Child:** • gets timely emotional and tactile comforting to help heal developmental traumas caused by disruptions in resonant connection to parents • receives unconditional love from parents • receives authentic mirroring and validation of his or her essence from parents **Immediate and extended family members:** • provide consistent, nurturing, and empathic contact • provide comfortable and protective environment to meet the child's needs for safety and survival

Stage of Development and Primary Task	Essential Developmental Processes of Individual Evolution	Suggested Experiences for Completing the Essential Developmental Processes of Individual Evolution
Counter-dependency (Six to Thirty-six Months) Separation and Individuation	**Child:** • completes the psychological separation process with parents • learns to safely explore his or her environment • learns to trust and regulate his or her own thoughts, feelings, and behaviors in socially appropriate ways • internalizes appropriate physical and social limits • develops healthy narcissism • resolves internal conflicts between oneness and separateness (I'm okay, you're okay) • bonds with self • continues to build secure internal working model • completes his or her individuation or psychological birth process	**Parents:** • offer timely help in healing any narcissistic wounds or developmental traumas that interfere with resonance • give the child permission and support to safely explore his or her environment; they give the child twice as many yeses as nos during this time • rearrange environment to provide safety • understand and respect the child's need to develop internal regulation of emotions, especially shame • help the child identify self-needs, as opposed to the needs of others • model how to directly ask to have one's needs met • use nonshaming responses in limit-setting and discipline • give positive support for the child's efforts to develop an autonomous Self **Adult caregivers:** • help the child quickly reestablish the resonant connection with the mother when it's disrupted • offer empathy and compassion as the child learns to regulate his or her conflicting emotions, thoughts, and behaviors • offer authentic mirroring and validation of the child's essence • offer permission for the child to be a separate individual and to trust his or her internal impulses

THE DEVELOPMENTAL STAGES AND ESSENTIAL DEVELOPMENTAL PROCESSES OF INDIVIDUAL EVOLUTION (*continued*)

Stage of Development and Primary Task	Essential Developmental Processes of Individual Evolution	Suggested Experiences for Completing the Essential Developmental Processes of Individual Evolution
Independence (Three to Six Years) Mastery of Self and Environment	**Child:** • masters self-care • masters the process of becoming a functionally autonomous individual, separate from parents • masters object constancy • develops and trusts his or her own core values and beliefs • has secure bonding experiences with nature • learns effective social engagement skills • develops secure internal working model of self/other • bonds securely with peers	**Parents:** • rearrange home environment to support the child's mastery of self-care (eating, dressing, and toilet training) • support the child's development of effective internal limits and consequences • help the child learn appropriate deferred gratification of his or her wants and needs • help the child learn effective emotional self-regulation and control • help the child learn to trust his or her inner sense of wisdom and guidance • provide the child with experiences for the safe exploration of nature • help the child develop sensory relationships with nature • provide for reciprocal social interactions with other children • teach cross-relational thinking, including empathy and respect for others • help the child develop cause/effect problem-solving skills • **Immediate and extended family members** offer nurturing, supportive, and consistent contact • **Adults** model partnership solutions to conflicts

Stage of Development and Primary Task	Essential Developmental Processes of Individual Evolution	Suggested Experiences for Completing the Essential Developmental Processes of Individual Evolution
Inter-dependence (Six to Twenty-nine Years) **Cooperation and Negotiation Skills**	**Child:** • learns to cooperate with others • learns to negotiate with others to get his or her needs met • learns to accept responsibility for his or her personal behaviors and life experiences • experiences secure bonding with peers and other adults • develops a social conscience • bonds securely with his or her culture • bonds securely with the planet • lives his or her life as an authentic adult • bonds securely with own children • understands the influence of incomplete developmental processes on his or her life and how to successfully heal developmental traumas	• **Parents** model effective cooperative social engagement skills in couple, family, and peer relationships Child: • seeks to learn negotiation skills to get his or her needs met in healthy ways • seeks solutions to his or her conflicts that honor the needs of all parties involved • seeks adult validation of the importance of keeping his or her relationship agreements • seeks an adult model that can teach him or her empathy and compassion for others • seeks adults who can teach him or her intuitive language and thinking skills • seeks nurturing, supportive, and consistent contact from immediate and extended family members • seeks support from parents and other adults on how to build sustainable relationships with other adults and how to find a primary love partner • seeks adult input on the values of his or her cultural group and how to overcome any limits imposed by family and culture • seeks personal meaning and a personal mission within the context of the "global family" • seeks information and skills for healing his or her developmental traumas • seeks assistance in developing systemic and transsystemic thinking • **Adults** encourage the development of an internalized "safety parent" allowing safe risk-taking behaviors

Co-dependent Stage

This stage begins at conception and continues for the first six months after birth. We now know that during this period children must receive a lot of love, touch, and eye contact from their parents and other adult caregivers in order to meet their bonding needs. Children need to be physically held, sung to, touched, stroked, and spoken to in loving ways. When the mothers look at their children, they must "mirror" them — that is, they must see their children's essence. Children also need to have their feelings taken seriously, to be respected, and to receive positive support when they first begin to explore their world. Most of all, children need adults who can synchronize with them energetically so they can learn to regulate their brains and emotional states. Children who did not experience enough of these developmental processes often become adults with co-dependent behaviors who try to meet these needs in their adult relationships.

Counter-dependent Stage

The counter-dependent stage of development usually starts at about the age of six or seven months and lasts until about age three. During this time, children begin to physically and emotionally separate from the safety and security of their parents and develop a love affair with the world around them. Children are naturally curious about the world, so they gradually move farther and farther away from their parents as they learn to crawl and then walk. Sometimes, when they get hurt or scared, they dart back quickly for comfort and reassurance. During this important stage of development, as children learn they are separate human beings rather than part of someone else, they undergo specific kinds of developmental processes that parents must help them complete.

For example, parents can kid-proof the home to make it safe for toddlers to explore. Parents need to say yes to their children twice as many times as they say no during this period of exploration. They also need to set limits in loving ways without shaming and without physically or psychologically punishing their children. Children who receive this kind of consistent emotional support will experience their psychological birth, or the birth of the Self, and perceive themselves as emotionally separate from their mothers and fathers.

The counter-dependent stage is sometimes called the terrible twos and can be trying for the adults who care for children at this stage. The motto of two-year-olds is: "I can do it myself. I'll show you I don't need you." Most anything can turn into a power struggle: dressing, eating, simple rules for safety, riding in a car seat, taking naps, and going to bed at night. Parents learn to pick and choose their battles and avoid the power struggles. Most challenging, however, is that two-year-olds can change their minds in a flash and try the patience of even the most saintly parents. But the more complete an adult's own separation process is, the less difficult this adult will find it is to cope with a two-year-old's ambivalence. Aware parents learn to recognize when they are being triggered by their child's behavior, and work on themselves rather than getting upset with the child.

If emotional support is not consistently available during the counter-dependent stage of development, or if there is any emotional, physical, or sexual abuse or trauma during this period, children will not get important needs met and will not become emotionally separate individuals. As adults, they will learn to cope by using counter-dependent behaviors. Fearing further hurt or abandonment, they will act strong and successful and will focus on helping others whose needs appear to be greater.

Independent Stage

Between the ages of three and five, children begin to function autonomously. If their developmental needs were met during the first two stages, they are ready to run on internal power — they are able to trust their own feelings and instincts to guide them in the world. This is a crucial developmental process that, if completed on schedule, will enable them to evolve much faster than if they are hampered by co-dependent and counter-dependent behaviors. Independence is a time of coming back together for the child and the parents. The power struggles finally end and peace and cooperation slowly return to their relationship.

During the independent stage, children begin to move into more mature forms of intimacy, to master self-sufficiency skills, and to learn parallel play with other children. If the important developmental processes from the previous two stages were not completed, children will have difficulty learning to do things independently. Rather, they may cling, act out their anger and defiance, or pretend they are independent. In the latter case, they begin erecting walls around themselves that prevent the development of socialization skills.

Interdependent Stage

In this stage, starting about age five or six and ending at about age twenty-nine, people gradually develop compassion, empathy, and cooperation. Interdependence is a highly complex stage of development, because it requires being able to move fluidly and consciously among the three previous stages. This fluidity is possible only when children are able to clearly communicate their needs and successfully negotiate with others to get them met. The relationship between the bonding needs of the co-dependent stage and the separation needs of the counter-dependent stage is significant. The more completely a child's bonding needs have been met, the more effectively he or she will complete the separation stage. If the child's bonding was weak in any way, it usually means that he or she will have to limit his or her exploration. For an adult whose bonding needs were not completely met in childhood, it can be frightening to be alone or emotionally separate.

During the interdependent stage, children develop the skills necessary for effective adult living. Culturally, most people regard children as self-sufficient once they leave home. As our own children navigated this stage, we recognized this as a fallacy. Between the ages of eighteen and twenty-eight, children must establish themselves professionally, learn to manage their own money, find jobs, buy cars, rent apartments, secure mortgages, buy houses, and, sometimes, have children. These young adult children still need a lot of support from their parents during this complicated and challenging phase, which is usually completed by the time they enter their thirties.

COUNTER-DEPENDENT
AND CO-DEPENDENT BEHAVIORS

People who were prematurely forced out of the co-dependent stage by abusive or rejecting parents often develop counter-dependent behaviors to push people away. This means they do not learn some of the critical skills for experiencing intimacy. These people often associate closeness with hurt and pain. As a result, they have difficulty getting close to other people and staying close. They often develop compensating behaviors to help them hide their deficiencies from others and, more important, from themselves. They learn to be superficially pleasant, hardworking, highly successful men and women. Inside, however, they are afraid of intimate situations, feel insecure when they aren't in control, and are unable to form or sustain close relationships.

In relationships, opposites usually attract. The typical pattern in our culture is that women with co-dependent behaviors attract men with counter-dependent behaviors, although this pattern can be reversed. Frequently, the woman who has unmet co-dependent needs and the man with unmet counter-dependent needs have patterns of behavior that interlock perfectly. Because of this perfect match, it is often very difficult for a couple to recognize the real causes of their problems. In addition, the traditional social stereotypes and expectations for men and women also support this sort of match, which makes it even more difficult for them to either recognize the source of their problems or resolve them. Society programs men to be strong and independent and expects women to be more emotional and dependent. There is virtually no support for partnership relationships that encourage both men and women to be strong and vulnerable.

In either combination, relationship partners often find that their particular mix of counter-dependent/co-dependent behaviors leads to conflict and competition, more than to intimacy and cooperation. This sets up a competitive, warlike environment between the sexes, in which there are no winners, only losers.

DRAWING BATTLE LINES
IN THE WAR BETWEEN THE SEXES

The following scenario illustrates how people with co-dependent/counter-dependent issues are drawn into a relationship with each other and how their patterns interlock. It takes place at a singles' party, where Renee notices Mark across the room. Mark is talking to several other men, and they seem to be listening intently to what he's saying. To Renee, Mark looks powerful, strong, and secure. She waits for the right moment and then approaches him cautiously. (Does this feel familiar?)

RENEE: Excuse me, I'm looking for the hostess.
(Maybe he'll notice me if I ask him a question.)

MARK: She just stepped into the kitchen, I believe. Hi, I'm Mark. What's your name?

(She looks cute.)

RENEE: Uh, I'm Renee.

(He's so good-looking. I probably don't stand a chance with him.)
You seem to know a lot of people here. I hardly know anyone.
(Maybe he'll feel sorry for me and talk to me.)

MARK: Yeah, I do business with a lot of these people.

(She seems to think I'm important. Maybe I can impress her.)

RENEE: Really? What is your business?

(Maybe I can get him to talk about himself so he won't ask anything about me.)

MARK: I'm in stocks and bonds. In fact, I was just talking to the guys over there about some speculative stocks I thought they might be interested in.

(Hmmm. She seems interested in me, and she's kind of sexy. I can't tell her that I'm about to lose my job. I'll have to play it cool so she doesn't see how nervous and insecure I am.)

RENEE: I don't know much about investing and those things. How did you learn about all that?

(He seems so sure of himself. I wish I could feel that confident. He seems like he'd be an exciting person to be with. I feel a little flushed. I hope he doesn't notice.)

MARK: Oh, I've done a lot of things. Maybe I could tell you about it sometime and give you some stock tips. Let's have dinner some night.

(If she is really interested in me, maybe she'll go out with me. And besides, a good lay would get my mind off the problems I have at work.)

RENEE: Gee, that would be great. I get so confused about financial things.

(He wants to help me. I've been so lonely and depressed. I could use someone exciting in my life.)

MARK: How about dinner this week, say Tuesday evening?

(She looks easy. Maybe she'll invite me back to her place after dinner to talk further.)

RENEE: That sounds like a great idea. I think I'm free that night.

(He must like me and really want to get to know me.)

MARK: Fine. I'll come by about seven.

(Hope she doesn't back out now that I've stuck my neck out.)

RENEE: Here's my address and phone number.

(I'll have to call Laurie to reschedule our visit on Tuesday night. I wonder if he's married or has someone special.)

MARK: Your place isn't far from where I live. I'll ring the bell for you when I get there.

(She turns me on. Maybe she'll invite me in for a drink, and we can make out some before we leave. I could sure use some good sex right now.)

The next day all Renee can think about is her dinner with Mark. At work she can't concentrate and makes many more mistakes than usual. Mark is also having his problems. He worries that she may not like him, and that he might accidentally reveal his insecurities. He begins rehearsing his lines so he can look confident and be in control. Then he remembers how easy it was to deceive Renee, and anticipates letting his guard down somewhat with her. Finally, he begins to obsess about having sex with her, thinking about how she might be in bed, which keeps his mind off his problems at work for the rest of the day.

You can begin to see how the attraction between Mark and Renee is one of opposites. Renee appears weak, insecure, dependent, and passive as she seeks someone important to help structure her life. Meanwhile, Mark tries to project an image of strength, aggressiveness, success, independence, and power even though he's insecure and needy. The attraction of opposites is a very common pattern in relationships, one that can help set up a dysfunctional relationship in which two half-persons come together to make one whole person. This kind of relationship seldom leads to genuine intimacy. Eventually, the passive person, who is being dominated, gets tired of playing that role and wants to change the rules. Men with counter-dependency issues often discard a relationship if they feel their partner is no longer willing to serve them and be dominated. This pattern is changing today as women in our culture tire of being dominated and demand more equal relationships. Men too are seeing that these methods are not working for them.

Historically, women have shouldered most of the responsibility for making relationships work and, therefore, have shouldered most of the blame when relationships fail. However, as more women claim their power and find their own voices, they are able to speak out more clearly. They often refuse to take full blame for the failure of a relationship. This forces men to look at their own counter-dependent issues that may be responsible for their lack of intimacy or the failure of their relationships.

More and more men are taking courageous first steps, such as entering twelve-step programs or therapy. Unfortunately, this still happens only after a man's wife or partner has left him, or has threatened to leave him, and he is in a crisis. This puts many men in a reactive position, which makes it more difficult for them to grow and change.

THE ASSUMPTIONS OF OUR APPROACH

We present the following beliefs and assumptions about the causes of, and the elimination of, counter-dependent behaviors and problems in relationships.

Counter-dependent behavior is not a hopeless, lifelong illness. Counter-dependent behavior is caused by the failure to complete essential developmental processes related to bonding and separation. We have developed effective tools to help you identify these incomplete developmental processes. In chapter 10, we share some of our easy-to-learn corrective parenting skills to help you meet these needs in your current relationships. You can change your compulsive and addictive counter-dependent behaviors if you are willing to do the necessary physical, mental, emotional, and spiritual work. This includes finding the sources of your problems and developing effective methods for meeting your needs in your current relationships.

There is something right about having counter-dependent behaviors. They represent a transformation in progress. Rather than simply viewing them as dysfunctional behavior patterns, notice that they are actually unskilled attempts to meet the developmental needs not met in your early childhood. This approach prevents shame and the sense that you are diseased. Most people know much more about what is wrong with or unhealthy in themselves and their behavior than they do about what is right or healthy. Therapists can inadvertently heap shame on their clients by using labels and diagnoses that imply the clients are flawed in some important ways.

Incomplete developmental processes recycle in our lives. There is a natural drive in everyone toward wholeness and completion. As a result, any developmental process we didn't complete on schedule will continue to reappear in our relationships and press for completion. It is our natural learning style to keep doing something over and over until we get it right. If we don't pay attention to these processes, they will escalate until we do. Some people actually avoid dealing with their pressing incomplete developmental processes by getting physically ill, getting divorced, or quitting their jobs.

Because people with incomplete developmental processes don't understand where these processes come from, they feel ashamed that they don't know how to deal with them and instead try to hide them. After many aborted attempts at intimacy, people stop trying and begin living isolated lives of quiet desperation.

Changing these patterns requires learning new skills and reaching new understandings. When people decide to change, they need help in locating the causes of their counter-dependent behaviors. In this book, you will find written exercises at the end of each chapter to help identify the sources of your counter-dependent behavior patterns. You may need to learn skills to help you complete your incomplete developmental processes that have been recycling in your life. This book contains many skill-building exercises for learning how to identify and change your counter-dependent behaviors.

Counter-dependency is also a social and cultural problem. Any psychological issue as widespread as counter-dependency must also have social and cultural roots. When looking at the primary characteristics of counter-dependency, it is easy to see how our culture not only supports but also actually promotes them as healthy, functional behaviors. For example, many companies require their workers to put in long hours and ignore their family responsibilities in order to retain their jobs.

Being strong, hard, manipulative, dominating, self-made, and ruggedly independent are all part of the mythical hero of the American dream. Moreover, our throwaway culture says, "If it doesn't work, toss it and get a new one." Many Americans in the 1970s and 1980s applied this rule to their relationships as well. Only the threat of AIDS and a slowly growing awareness of intergenerational family patterns have slowed down this tendency. As a result, people are no longer divorcing in record numbers as they did the 1970s and 1980s. Now it is time to address the widespread social and cultural denial about the power of unmet developmental needs and begin addressing counter-dependent behaviors.

It is important to be nonjudgmental about people behaving in counter-dependent ways and to realize that such behavior points to where we are in our collective evolution. In chapter 5, we explain more fully an exciting way of looking at addictions and provide a broader understanding of the social and cultural causes of the problem, as well as what's needed for change. Given the social and cultural conditions that currently exist in this country, it would be difficult to grow up here and not have counter-dependent behaviors.

Counter-dependency issues require a systemic approach to recovery. The interrelatedness of the different levels of the problem, including the societal levels, indicates that we must look at counter-dependent behaviors very broadly, as they show up in all social systems. Individual therapy is limited when it doesn't use a systems approach, which is why couples, family, and group therapy, as well as support networks, are necessary elements of changing these behaviors.

It's possible to eliminate counter-dependent behaviors. There is a common perception in the addictions field that people can't recover from relationship addictions. We don't subscribe to this idea. Our experience in working with clients is that people who are willing to do their physical, mental, emotional, and spiritual work can break free of their relationship addictions and live more intimate, functional, and effective lives.

RESOURCES FOR BREAKING FREE FROM COUNTER-DEPENDENT PATTERNS

In your journey to clear away your counter-dependent behavior patterns, you may find certain resources useful. As you use these resources, it's important to remember that you need physical, emotional, mental, and spiritual support in breaking free of any dysfunctional relationship patterns. Authentic support can help you slowly lower your defenses and address childhood trauma. We recommend using the following resources.

Read books. Consulting books like this one will help you begin to understand the dynamics and possible sources of your counter-dependent behaviors. You may also want to attend classes and workshops that focus on intimacy and how to change your counter-dependent behavior patterns.

Join a support group. A group can help you begin to share with others who have the same issues. It's comforting to know that you are not the only person who has counter-dependent behaviors. In a good support group, you will get emotional support and encouragement. Keep in mind, however, that some Co-dependents Anonymous (CodA) groups tend to look at co-dependent behaviors as symptoms of a disease from which you can never recover. If you find this approach restrictive, you can take what you need from these groups and leave the disease model behind for those who want it. Also, shop around for a group that fits your needs. We have found that these groups can vary greatly in the kind of emotional support they provide. Some are very good, and some are not.

Seek out psychotherapy. You may find that you need help in moving through blocked or repressed feelings, and psychotherapy may supply it. We once heard the psychologist John Bradshaw tell an audience, "You can't do your feeling work in a twelve-step group. They are not set up for that." Individual psychotherapy is usually designed to help people remove emotional blocks and learn to express repressed feelings. We also recommend couples, group, or family therapy because of the systemic nature of the problem of counter-dependency. We frequently work with couples to teach them how to help each other.

Therapy is often the only place where you can develop the skills and understanding you need to create successful relationships. We usually do therapeutic work with a couple for three to six sessions, helping them develop their skills and understanding, and then, if they demonstrate that they can do it, we encourage them to work independently of therapy to see how well they do on their own. If they get bogged down, they can use us as consultants. They can also come back for a short series of sessions to refresh or advance their skills if they get stuck.

Facilitated therapy groups, particularly those that are time limited, are also an excellent place to work on co-dependency and counter-dependency issues. These groups often become very intimate, and members feel safe enough to let their defenses down. You will also find that the groups provide people who can mirror parts of yourself that you are not familiar with and a safe environment for trying out new relationship skills.

Work in a committed relationship. A committed relationship is one in which both people agree not to leave or to make each other into the bad guy when conflicts arise. Because counter-dependent patterns are the result of early child-hood relationship traumas, intimate relationships that offer safety and security are the ideal places to heal these wounds. You can form a committed relation-ship with anyone: a sister, mother, spouse, best friend, child, neighbor, support group member, therapist, minister, and even co-worker. Counter-dependent behavior patterns will begin to appear in all your committed relationships once you feel secure enough to let them come to the surface.

SELF-QUIZ

How Counter-Dependent Are You?

DIRECTIONS: Place a number in the blank before each statement to indicate the degree to which the statement is true in your life.

1 = Never   2 = Occasionally   3 = Frequently   4 = Almost always

_____ I feel a kind of free-floating anxiety when I have nothing to do.
_____ I look to other people, substances, or activities to make me feel good.
_____ I have a difficult time knowing what I want or need.
_____ I fear that I will be smothered if I get too close to my spouse or a friend.
_____ I have difficulty knowing how I really feel inside.
_____ I exaggerate my accomplishments a bit when I meet someone new.
_____ I get anxious when my partner wants to be intimate with me.
_____ I'm afraid people will find out that I'm not who they think I am.
_____ I demand perfection of myself and others.
_____ I work long hours and never seem to get finished with my work.
_____ I don't like to ask other people for help, even if I need it.
_____ I prefer to work alone rather than with others.
_____ I feel controlled by what others expect of me.
_____ I feel it is really important to have the "right answers."
_____ I get afraid of being consumed by the needs of others.
_____ I function best in structured situations where I am in charge.
_____ I feel important when someone asks me for my opinion.
_____ I find it difficult to form and maintain intimate relationships.
_____ I have trouble deciding if I want sex or nurturing touch.
_____ I have trouble relaxing, and I have chronic tension in my body.
_____ I enjoy being the center of attention at social gatherings.

_____ I don't like to admit to a mistake.

_____ I reject offers of help from others, even if I need it.

_____ I have thoughts about sex each day that interfere with my work.

_____ I see myself and others as either all good or all bad.

_____ I compare myself to others, feeling either better or worse than them.

_____ I am told that I am not aware of the needs or concerns of others.

_____ I like being my own person and fear being controlled by others.

_____ I feel hurt when an accomplishment of mine is not recognized.

_____ I deny my problems or discount the importance of my problems.

_____ Total score

SCORING: Add up the column of numbers to find your score. Use the following guidelines to interpret it.

102–120 Very high number of counter-dependent behavior patterns. Can have a serious effect on your functioning level.

79–101 High number of counter-dependent behavior patterns. Can have a moderate effect on your functioning level.

56–78 Some counter-dependent behavior patterns. This range has a minor effect on your functioning level.

30–55 Few counter-dependent behavior patterns. This range has little or no effect on your functioning level.

THE BOTTOM LINE

- Counter-dependency is not a disease but an indication of incomplete developmental processes and unmet needs.
- With persistence, you can change your counter-dependent behavior patterns and experience the love and intimacy you've always wanted.
- Counter-dependency is the second stage of four developmental stages. If you are stuck here, you are halfway to experiencing your True Self.
- You can take charge of changing your counter-dependent behaviors by using proven tools for clearing them away.

2. Understanding the Counter-dependent Stage of Development

Oh, what a tangled web do parents weave
when they think that their children are naive.
— Ogden Nash

While you, like most people, probably don't remember specific details of what happened during this period of your life, you can look at your present behaviors to see how they may be connected to past events. Your childhood history, combined with information about your needs that should have been met at that time, can help you identify what you missed during this period. In order to understand your adult counter-dependent behaviors, you must review your counter-dependent stage of child development and examine it more closely. This stage can be broken down into phases that the child must pass through successfully if he or she is to move into the independent and interdependent stages of development.

INDIVIDUATION: THE CRITICAL TASK OF THE COUNTER-DEPENDENT STAGE

In order to achieve individuation, or the psychological birth — a process identified by Carl Jung — a child needs good bonding experiences with his or her mother and father or other adult caregivers during the first six to nine months of life. Margaret Mahler, a researcher and child psychologist, did extensive observational research with mothers and their babies to better understand this developmental process. She found that holding, singing to, and talking to the child; mirroring back the child's essence; giving patient attention to the child's needs; and providing nurturing touch were essential ingredients for strong maternal–infant bonding. She described this normal state of infant–mother bonding as symbiosis.[1]

Both mother and child have an innate drive to enter a deep state of emotional attunement, and this is at the core of symbiosis. Mahler and others found that there are degrees of symbiosis, which depend on the quality of the relationship between mother and child. She found that the stronger the emotional attunement between the two, the more likely the child would complete the psychological birth and become emotionally separate. Mahler says that this occurs between ages two and three.

Mahler believes that the separation stage is prompted by the child's innate drive to explore the world and to become an autonomous person. These desires create an internal conflict for the child, who also enjoys the comfort and warmth of oneness with the mother and father. When a child begins to separate, the kind of bonding relationship he or she has with both parents is crucial. If the mother is depressed, tired, or not available emotionally because she is frightened by the intimacy or stresses of parenting, or anxious because the father is unavailable, this will affect the starting time and the pace of the process. If any of these obstacles are present, the child will actually delay these initial moves toward separateness, wanting more bonding before venturing out too far.

If this bonding need is not met completely, children eventually move on without the inner security they really need. Physical development continues forward to the next stage, even when children have not completed their social and emotional development. Some babies who are faced with this dilemma develop a "False Self" and pretend to be strong enough for the task. They project a false independence, characterized by "I'm strong and can do it without you."

Some children separate unusually early, particularly when mothers or fathers cling too tightly or are too intrusive, trying to control every facet of their lives. These babies may even prefer strangers and, as early as three months, may stiffen against their mothers' efforts to hold them. This can cause anxiety in the parents. A mother may wonder, "Why doesn't this child like me any more?" Depending on the mother's self-esteem, she may see the child's attempts to separate as a threat to her identity as a mother. A father may withdraw even further if the child doesn't want to be held or played with.

In either case, the move from bonding to separation is a delicate process requiring not only that mothers and fathers have good information but also that they have dealt with some of their own unfinished business regarding bonding and separation. Children's struggle between oneness and separateness creates the framework for the journey toward selfhood.

DID YOU KNOW THAT...

Anything not resolved in an earlier stage of your own development will come back to bite you during the first two to three years of parenting your own children. As your children grow, their development will trigger memories of what is not complete in your own bonding and separation. This can interfere with your ability to provide them with the social and emotional support that they need at this crucial period. This is also when you can see what you still need in order to complete your own developmental process and can begin it. This is called "regression-progression," which we discuss more fully in later chapters.

THE FOUR SUBPHASES OF THE SEPARATION PROCESS

Mahler and Stephen Johnson, another developmental psychologist, found that the internal conflict between oneness and separateness can be resolved if the child is supported in his or her efforts to successfully navigate the four distinct phases of the separation process.[2] A careful look at each of the phases may help you better understand which of your needs might not have been met, and therefore, why you are stuck as an adult in the counter-dependent, or separation, stage of development. If you can locate the specific unmet developmental needs in any phase of this process, then it will be easier to find ways to meet them now.

The following descriptions of the phases of the counter-dependent stage of development show some of the important developmental processes that must be accomplished at each stage. For each developmental process, there is a set of developmental needs. The writing exercise titled "The Sins of Omission and Commission" at the end of this chapter will help you identify your specific unmet needs from the co-dependent and counter-dependent stages of development.

As you read the following descriptions of these four phases of the separation process, ask yourself: "Knowing what I know about my parents, how did they probably treat me during each of these phases of development?" This might help you begin to remember what actually did happen to you and either what you might have lacked but needed, or what you might have gotten and didn't need.

The Early Exploration Phase (Six Months to Nine Months)

During the early exploration phase, you became aware that there is a world outside the oneness you experienced with your mother and father or other caregivers. At first, you looked at this world from the edge of your mother's lap or over your father's shoulder while being held or burped. You saw your mother smile and you smiled back. Imitation — watching and doing — helped you learn new responses. Also, you first began to notice strangers and may have reacted with anxiety.

However, if your mother's and father's relationships with you were strong, supportive, and nurturing, you eventually grew more curious about strangers, and less afraid of them. If the relationship was weak or you were not yet ready to separate, then your anxiety may have been stronger and you may have begun clinging to your parents when strangers approached.

In the early exploration phase, you had no way of holding onto an image of your mother or father when either one was out of physical sight. You may have coped with your fear of loss by trying to keep your mother or father always in view. Eventually you were able to imagine that your parents were with you even when they were not. You could sustain this only for short periods of time at first, but gradually you learned to tolerate longer periods of being physically separated from them.

If your mother was available, nurturing, warm, and secure, you could hold on to memories of these experiences when she was not present. Your mother may have assisted you in developing these qualities by being predictable and reliable. For example, when she had to leave, she would let you know in advance that you were going to be cared for by a sitter or by your father. She knew that the quickest way to destroy your newfound confidence was to sneak away when you weren't looking. Also, she knew any prolonged absence of several days while you were very young would leave you feeling abandoned.

During the early exploration phase, you moved away and back many times during the day to confirm that the bond with your mother or father was still intact. You may also have been given a touch, a loving smile, a brief snuggle, a bottle, or an opportunity to nurse on your mother's lap. Each time, however, you were lured back to exploring the world around you, because your drive to do so grew stronger by the day.

Your father knew that his role was to play with you, hold you, and help you move away from your mother. Soon you learned that your father wasn't just a part of your mother but a separate person. You saw these differences and similarities, and your mother let you know that she trusted your father, which also helped you trust him. If your mother tried to keep you from your father, you may have picked this up and feared him. You also needed other relatives and friends to bond with. Again, you learned to trust people your mother or father trusted.

One of the developmental tasks processes of this phase involved developing a specific smile of recognition for your mother, father, or other caregivers. During this period, it was also time for you to learn to discriminate between your parents and strangers. If the bond with your mother was strong, you showed more curiosity about strangers. If it was less strong, you may have felt anxiety and distress around strangers, especially when you were about eight months of age.

The Full Exploration Stage (Ten Months to Fifteen Months)

During this phase of counter-dependency, you began to walk and you ventured out even farther. Learning to walk was a celebration of your ability to master the world. This skill would lead you to the development of a "love affair with the world." Separation and exploration, coupled with occasional trips back to your mother's lap or your father's knee for comfort and reassurance, became almost a full-time occupation.

Teething and too many "don'ts" may have slowed you down, but elation over new discoveries could distract you. The inborn drive for separateness and wholeness was in high gear by the end of this phase, and you probably had some transitional objects such as a teddy bear, doll, or blanket that represented your mother when she was unavailable. You may have carried these comfort objects everywhere you went. Eventually, you abandoned these objects when you were able to develop an inner mother figure that you could use to soothe or comfort yourself when you needed to.

> Learning to walk was a celebration of your ability to master the world. This skill would lead you to the development of a "love affair with the world."

During this period, you loved the thrill of being mobile. In this expansive stage, you found you could explore a large area of your home and discover all kinds of new things each day. Your excitement often reached a state of euphoria, causing you to often forget about wanting to be close or even eating, unless something scary happened. Because your mother seemed so big and so powerful, you saw her as omnipotent. Because you were not separate from her, you often felt omnipotent yourself — able to do grandiose things and entitled to everything that crossed your path. Life seemed limitless to you.

The developmental processes for this phase involved learning that there were limits to mother's presence, energy, patience, time, and resources. Because you needed to learn about her limitations gradually, she gave them to you incrementally. When she had to leave you with another caregiver with whom you had bonded, she stayed away only as long as you could tolerate it. At first this was just for a matter of minutes. As you grew older, she expanded this to hours. She made sure you had a reliable person to care for you while she was gone, one who could support your feelings if you were unhappy about her absence. She also helped you learn how to take care of your own needs and to be self-sufficient while she was away. She provided you with transitional objects, such as soft animals, for comfort so that you could mother yourself in her absence. She knew that this is how you would develop a "nurturing parent" inside yourself.

Other developmental processes for this phase involved learning that mother's absence wasn't personal, and that she was a separate person with her own needs and interests. She or other caregivers helped you express your feelings of frustration when you weren't able to have things go your way all the time. You also needed a constant adult presence that could monitor your exploration and make sure you were safe. They helped you when you struggled with two seemingly contradictory fears: the fear of separation (abandonment) and the fear of oneness (engulfment).

When we look at addictive behavior, we see that alcohol, drugs, cigarettes, sex, and food can become transitional objects that provide a person with the comfortable, reassuring feeling that an available mother might provide for a child. The object can be used, set aside, and reached for when the fears or anxieties of being out in the world without enough love or support get too great. The first step in eliminating an addiction requires mourning the loss of the available mother and recognizing that substitutes can replace the feeling of connection to the mother only for a short time.

Dependencies can't be broken until you feel your sadness about losing your available mother and accept that there is no mother who will always be available, but that there are some people who sometimes can be available to provide nurturing love and comfort if you are willing to ask them for what you want or need. Other times, you may have to learn to feel your feelings alone and comfort yourself using your inner nurturing mother. Some men have difficulty in distinguishing between sex and love and wonder why they still feel empty after sex.

The Early Separation Phase (Sixteen Months to Twenty-four Months)

Near the beginning of this phase, you realized that you were a person totally separate from your mother. When you first understood this, you may have felt scared and returned to your mother to be cuddled. It may have looked as though you were regressing back to an earlier phase of development, but if you received the comfort you desired, it was probably short-lived. Again, your innate drive to become separate took over, and you returned to exploring and mastering your world.

Your mother and father kept encouraging your efforts to separate during this phase while providing you with support and nurturing when you needed it. You were likely to feel angry and frustrated when you were unable to master certain tasks or when your parents placed restrictions on you. Your parents accepted this anger and frustration and responded empathetically to you. They may have feared that, if they simply forgave your outbursts of anger and frustration, they would inadvertently encourage future tantrums. This wasn't true. A warm hug and some assurance that you were still loved was all that you really needed. Humiliation or punishment only set up further cycles of tension that you needed to discharge. Their repeated reassurances helped you develop a sense of your Self, feelings of being loved and accepted, and the ability to stay connected to your feelings.

Another important part of this phase is the phenomenon called "splitting." There were times when you mastered a task or returned to your mother and found a warm, receptive reunion. When this happened, you experienced your mother as "good," and everything looked and felt good during these times. However, there were other times when you were unable to master a task or when you needed a warm hug, and you found your mother busy cooking dinner or talking on the telephone. These times you experienced her as "bad," and this feeling was generalized to everything. Mother became either "good mother," when she was available, or "bad mother," when she was not available. The healthy resolution to this conflict occurred gradually as you learned two important things: Your mother had a mix of good and bad qualities and was basically a good person in spite of this. You had good and bad qualities and were separate from your mother, and this mixture of good and bad qualities was also okay. You were both okay.

If you did not resolve this good/bad split during this phase, you will continue to see yourself, other people, and situations in the world as divided into good and bad, black and white, right and wrong. If, as an adult, you can think of only two solutions (either/or) to problems and tend to use black-or-white thinking, you still have not completed the splitting stage of development.

TROUBLESHOOTING

How to Avoid Getting Caught on the Horns of a Dilemma

If you can think of only two solutions ("either/or" thinking) to a problem or conflict, you are caught on the horns of a dilemma. Force yourself to think of a third solution that is in between "the horns." This is "both/and" thinking and can help you get out of the dilemma and greatly improve your problem-solving skills.

The developmental processes for this phase included learning how to resolve your inner conflict between wanting to be separate and wanting to be close. You had to come to terms with the reality that your parents were not "gods" or perfect parents. And because you were becoming separate, you also had to come to terms with your own humanness. Here is where you learned the limits of your natural narcissistic sense of omnipotence, grandiosity, entitlement, and euphoria.

If you didn't complete these processes successfully, it is likely that you became stuck at this phase of your development, creating a reality for yourself that is split into polarities of good/bad, all/nothing, or always/never. You also may have maintained your narcissistic feelings of omnipotence, grandiosity, entitlement, and euphoria. As an adult, these may be expressed through behaviors involving manipulation, pride, self-centeredness, addictions to activities and substances that help you maintain your euphoria, and, if all else fails, rage attacks when you refuse to accept limitations.

This was the most critical point in completing your psychological birth. During this time period, you made a decision either to become separate emotionally from your mother or to stay co-dependent. If you chose to return to the safety of oneness, you developed more co-dependent behaviors and decided you would rather feel safe and meet your needs by being dependent on others.

If you had repeated experiences of emotional, physical, or sexual abuse; neglect; or repeated developmental traumas, you likely decided that oneness and closeness was unsafe and too scary. Out of a need to protect yourself, you might have prematurely chosen to separate emotionally from your mother or father and developed more counter-dependent behaviors. For example, you learned to wall off your feelings of vulnerability and fear, and your need for closeness, by creating defensive behaviors that pushed people away and/or showed people how much you didn't need them. You began creating a False Self that helped you look capable and act strong. You also developed the illusion of an inflated importance so that you would never have to let anyone see your vulnerability and wounds. If this happened during this phase, you may have become stuck in toddler development.

The Complete Separation Phase
(Twenty-five Months to Thirty-six Months)

If you had loving parents who supported your needs for emotional separation, you began developing an initial sense of separateness and identity by the age of three. The ability to hold yourself as an object of worth separate from other people is called "object constancy." As a three-year-old, you had enough object constancy to feel safe in the world as a separate person only if you had built up enough good-mother and good-self experiences. The struggle to maintain object constancy continues during the rest of your life in your encounters with new problems and crises that may threaten your sense of Self. We constantly have to reconcile our yearnings to return to paradise and the bliss of oneness with our intense longing to be separate, autonomous individuals. The resolution of this issue between ages two and three involves a complex set of developmental processes.

DID YOU KNOW THAT...

The role of the father is critical in developing a strong sense of Self. If you bonded well with your father, and he was emotionally available to you when your mother was not, it was easier to separate from your mother. If your father was physically or emotionally absent during your first three years, separating from your mother would have been more difficult. The father's presence and active involvement as a parent is even more important for a boy, who must disidentify from his mother in order to develop a healthy male self-image. Do you think your father was available for you physically and emotionally at this time in your life?

When you went to your emotionally present father and complained about your unavailable mother, he needed to know how to respond effectively. If he used your complaining as an opportunity to vent his own feelings about having an unavailable wife, you may have learned to devalue women and overvalue men. Fathers often feel abandoned when wives become consumed by taking care of their children's needs and do not pay attention to their husbands' needs. If your father took the side of your mother and criticized you for complaining about her, you learned that there was no emotional support to help you become separate from your mother. You may have felt betrayed and defeated if any of these things happened repeatedly. What your father needed to do was support your feelings without agreeing or disagreeing with your definition of your mother's "badness." ("I see you are really upset that Mommy's gone, and until she comes back I am here to play with you.") This response does not blame anyone and acknowledges your feelings, and it can be difficult for men who never learned to express emotions.

Some fathers get scared and feel helpless when they find themselves in the middle of the intense separation struggle between the mother

> You cannot separate emotionally from someone by viewing him or her as "bad."

and child. They find reasons to work longer hours or have an affair or even leave the relationship altogether. Without the support of your father or another bonded caregiver to help you, completing your psychological birth between the ages of two and three would have been difficult.

So what about single-parent families? No research has been done on whether other caregivers who have bonded with a child, such as a babysitter or grandparents, can fill the father's role. However, if this person is a woman, a male child will have difficulty disidentifying with his mother, causing gender identity problems later. This area certainly needs much more research and study.

At the end of this chapter, complete the writing exercises listed in the awareness activity titled "The Sins of Omission and Commission." You can also check the awareness activity at the end of chapter 6, "How to Identify Your Incomplete Developmental Processes."

You can see from the descriptions of the four phases of the counter-dependency stage of development that individuation is a series of intricate processes. Successful completion of this stage requires educated, aware parents who have completed enough of their own psychological birth process that they can guide and support the child through his or her own process. Since most parents are not taught these skills before they become parents, they often fall short of this goal, making it necessary for the child to finish this process later in life.

It's now possible, for the first time in the evolution of the human species, to create functional families that can raise healthy children able

> It's important to stress two things: Parents do the best they can with what they have. And our developmental approach can be used to parent young children and to reparent yourself.

to experience emotional intimacy. This book gives you the information and skills necessary to make this happen in your life.

THE DEVELOPMENT OF HEALTHY NARCISSISM

As a child you needed to be seen for who you really were, to be understood, to express your feelings and needs, to be taken seriously, and to have your feelings and needs respected by your mother and father. These are normal narcissistic needs. If they were filled adequately during the co-dependent and counter-dependent stages, you probably have healthy self-esteem. One of the initial ways you could meet your narcissistic needs during the co-dependent stage was through your mother's mirroring of your essence while you gazed up at her face.

This is how infants learn who they really are. If your mother mirrored back her desires for you to be a certain way, perhaps to take care of her unmet narcissistic needs, this may have twisted or distorted your self-image. You may have stayed fused with her in order to be loved and cared for. Mothers must be able to meet their own needs with other adults rather than with their children. Children who are mirrored correctly during this bonding stage develop healthy narcissism that they eventually outgrow. Once they establish a strong sense of Self, they move on to become true humanitarians able to serve others without losing themselves. This is essential for the completion of the counter-dependent exploration stage of development.[3]

Alice Miller lists the ways that parents can help their children develop healthy narcissism.[4] As you read this list in the sidebar "What I Needed from My Parents When I Was a Young Child," ask yourself, "Can I imagine my parents doing these things for me when I was a child?"

With this kind of parental support, children develop a healthy sense of narcissism and grow up without unmet narcissistic counter-dependent needs. The only truly unselfish, genuine people in the world are those who were able to meet these healthy narcissistic needs at this stage of their development. If you didn't get this kind of support, it is likely that you have "narcissistic wounds" with defenses around them to protect against any further wounding. Alice Miller describes people who did get their narcissistic needs met in childhood this way: "Children who are respected learn respect. Children who are cared for learn to care for those weaker than themselves. Children who are loved for what they are cannot learn intolerance. In an environment such as this, they will develop their own ideals, which can be nothing other than humane, since they grew out of the experience of love."[5]

WHAT I NEEDED FROM MY PARENTS
WHEN I WAS A YOUNG CHILD

I needed my parents to

- react calmly and reassuringly to any of my aggressive impulses;
- support my attempts to become separate and autonomous instead of being threatened by them;
- allow me to experience and express my natural feelings and urges such as rage, fear, jealousy, and defiance;
- allow me to develop and follow my natural curiosity safely during each developmental stage, rather than overprotecting me or requiring me to do things to please them;
- be available both physically and emotionally when I needed them;
- permit me to express conflicting or ambivalent feelings and treat those feelings seriously and with respect;
- see me as separate from them, as someone with my own needs, wishes, fears, dreams, and accomplishments.

THE PSYCHOLOGICAL BIRTH

The successful resolution of the conflicting drives for oneness and separateness occurs between the ages of two and three if the normal, healthy developmental needs of the child are expressed and met by caring, self-assured, aware, and psychologically whole parents.

DID YOU KNOW THAT...

The psychological birth is the single most important developmental process for a person to complete. Completing it is essential if people are to listen to their own rhythms. Most likely, less than 1 percent of the world's population has completed this important milestone.

If you did not have parents able to help you complete this stage successfully, you had to develop a False Self to make you look strong and independent. You hoped this False Self was more to their liking than your True Self, and that it would help you survive in your family. As an adult, you may have retained aspects of your False Self that now interfere with intimacy in your adult relationships.

People with co-dependent behaviors generally develop a deflated False Self, one that looks weak and helpless, while people with counter-dependent behaviors generally have an inflated False Self. Those with co-dependent behaviors are more prone to depression, while those with counter-dependent behaviors are more likely inclined to grandiosity to avoid feeling depressed. To complete your psychological birth later as an adult, it is necessary for you to master your internal struggle between two seemingly opposite forces: the natural drive toward oneness and closeness and the equally powerful drive to be an emotionally separate, self-determining individual.

If you have not completed your psychological birth, the drive toward oneness will bring up intense feelings of being engulfed or consumed. This experience can feel like death and dismemberment to you. The counterforce of separation can produce intense fears of existential alienation, aloneness, and abandonment.

To navigate these intense experiences requires spiritual courage. Carl Jung says that such experiences are necessary before the individual can complete individuation. Jung sees this as both a psychological and a spiritual process that can be completed only in midlife or later. He says it's necessary to move beyond the conventional wisdom in order to discover "gnosis," or the knowledge of the heart that renders human beings free. Jung also realized that humans cannot fulfill the promise of their potential if they become too attached to the trappings of the external world. The Gnostic worldview is that people need to be "in the world, but not of the world" in order to feel free.[6] He urges people to find their spiritual truths inside themselves and not in established religions. Spiritual rebirth is, he says, a necessary prerequisite for the completion of the individuation process by adults.

In either case, by understanding what happened in your childhood and developing new relationship skills, you'll be able to complete your psychological birth. You may ask, "How will I know if I have completed it?" You will have a keen sense of who you really are, and will handle life's challenges and conflicts with a minimum of stress while feeling good about yourself and good about others. You will be able to maintain your object constancy in the midst of most life challenges. You will be able to be both close and intimate, and separate and alone, when you want to. Only the person who has prepared psychologically and spiritually can expect to complete this developmental process successfully. You will find more information later in the book on how to prepare yourself psychologically and spiritually for this work.

AWARENESS ACTIVITY:
THE SINS OF OMISSION AND COMMISSION

This exercise, which involves making two lists, will help you discover where to begin your search for counter-dependent behavior patterns in yourself. Get a large sheet of paper and divide it into halves, one on top and the other on the bottom. On the top half, list all the things you wish your parents had said to or done for you that they didn't when you were growing up. (Examples: "I wish they had told me they loved me," or "I wish they had given me birthday parties.") On the bottom half, list all the things your parents said to you or did to you that you wish they hadn't, things that were in fact hurtful and harmful to you. (Examples: "I wish they hadn't humiliated me when I got pregnant in high school," or "I wish they hadn't punished me by calling me names and hitting me.")

Make your lists as long as you like. If you had parent substitutes, such as older siblings, stepparents, or grandparents, as caregivers in your childhood, you may include them, as well as teachers, scout leaders, or any other significant adults who had a hand in parenting you.

What do the lists mean? The top half, the sins of omission, identifies the incomplete developmental processes from the co-dependent stage. These are the things that leave lifelong patterns of co-dependent behavior. These are the things that the small child in you is still waiting for: the perfect parent, the princess or the knight in shining armor, someone who can read your mind and who knows what you need without you asking. Learning how to complete these incomplete developmental processes represented by the items on this list requires that you take charge of them by finding ways to meet these needs in your life now. The most important skill to learn is to ask directly to get your needs met.

The bottom list, the sins of commission, identifies the incomplete developmental processes that helped create your adult counter-dependent behaviors. These items indicate things that the small child in you still fears, and events that contained invasive, hurtful behaviors from the past that now cause you to flee from intimacy. Learning how to complete these incomplete developmental processes represented by the items on your lists involves releasing unexpressed feelings associated with these early experiences and giving back (forgiving) the things you took on that you no longer want or need.

The approach we describe in this book shows you how to complete what is still unfinished about your childhood developmental processes. Generally, the experiences you placed on the two lists are also linked to your unmet developmental needs. These two lists can help you quickly identify which developmental processes did not get completed in your childhood and what developmental needs were not met. Knowing this can help you complete these processes and get your needs met in your current relationships.

THE BOTTOM LINE

- The completion of the psychological birth at about age two or three is crucial to the development of interdependence and humanitarian consciousness.
- Developmental traumas and other abuse or neglect in early childhood interfere with the completion of this important milestone.
- Fathers play a critical role in the successful completion of the individuation process.
- It is never too late to complete this important process, once you clear away the things from childhood that block it.
- People reexperience their own development while parenting their children.

3. Getting Stuck
in Counter-dependency

Humans are condemned to be free;
because once thrown into the world,
[they] are responsible for everything they do.
— Jean-Paul Sartre

There is almost always a series of events, or core traumas, in the first year or two of life that interrupt the developmental processes. These may be a difficult birth, an early illness for either the child or the mother, the birth of another child, or other unexpected events that cause a break in the bonding process between the mother and infant. In addition, there are other everyday events involving emotional or physical disconnects between mother and child that usually go unnoticed.

HOW CORE TRAUMAS DISRUPT INFANT DEVELOPMENT

The nature and timing of these developmental traumas become critical, for they often determine how a person's life unfolds. The dynamics of these traumas, along with feelings, memories, and perceptions about them, create a pattern of disturbed relationships and a flight from intimacy. Unless these early traumas are identified and healed, they will continue to recycle throughout life.

Where in the developmental process the traumatic breaks occur determines the set of symptoms you will develop. If they occur before age nine months, you will likely develop more co-dependent behaviors as an adult. If they occur only between ten and thirty-six months, you will likely develop counter-dependent behaviors that you carry into adulthood. If they occur over the whole period between birth and thirty-six months, you will probably exhibit both co-dependent and counter-dependent behaviors as an adult.

IDENTIFYING YOUR DEVELOPMENTAL TRAUMAS

Many people fantasize that life in the womb is paradise — simple, uncomplicated, peaceful, and harmonious — and that everything came without effort. However, we now know that this may not be true. What happened while you were inside your mother imprinted you in certain ways.[1]

Because of the transfer of hormones and other substances through the placenta, gestating babies have experiences that parallel their mothers'. If a mother is low on dopamine and other brain chemicals, a circumstance associated with depression, so is the baby. If she drinks alcohol, smokes, or is emotionally stressed, the baby has the same biochemical experience. For this reason, many prenatal psychologists encourage mothers to keep their stress levels low, listen to soothing music, and create experiences of joy, all of which produce dopamine and other mood-lifting brain chemicals. These experiences form the biochemical foundation of your neural wiring and wire the brain for your life experience here on earth.

Then came your birth process. Just being born was a traumatic experience. You traveled slowly for hours down the birth canal, experiencing contractions that put your body (particularly your head) under tremendous pressure. If you were born via caesarean birth, you may have experienced the trauma of being jerked quickly out of paradise. If there were drugs administered to your mother, if forceps were used on you, or if there were difficulties with the delivery, you may have been even more traumatized. The birth process is an abrupt change that was made easier if your parents became attuned to you while you were gestating and could communicate with you while you were in the birth process.

If your birth was easy and you were born in a warm atmosphere with soft lights and soft music, *if* you were laid immediately on your mother's belly, *if* your umbilical cord was cut only after it quit pulsating, *if* you were allowed to nurse soon after your birth, *if* you were placed in warm water and provided with a gentle massage to heal any birth trauma, and *if* you were kept constantly with your mother, then there was only a brief disruption in your connection with her. The first few moments of your life were a window in time during which you could quickly reestablish the connection with your mother.

If your birth was difficult, however, and you were born in a cold, sterile hospital room with harsh lights, were held upside down and slapped on the bottom, were laid on a cold scale to be weighed, had your eyes medicated with harsh chemicals, were circumcised, were wrapped tightly in clothes that shut you off from tactile contact with people, and were hurried down the hall to a nursery away from your mother and left there for many hours, then you probably experienced a traumatic disruption of your paradise state and were left with more severe birth trauma.

Birth trauma or any disruption between child and mother during these early weeks and months can fracture the delicate process of development. If you suffered unintentional abandonment and/or abuse either during your birth or afterward — by being left with strange caretakers for extended periods of time during the first three years of your life — then you are likely as an adult to have serious unfinished business from this period.

It has been established only in the last few decades that infants who are not drugged are born in a heightened state of sensitivity.[2] Because of human ignorance about this, you may have been treated as though you were an undeveloped lump of clay. It has been commonplace for newborns to have surgery and circumcision without anesthesia, to have needles stuck in them for tests, and to be isolated in incubators and nurseries. Until recently, parents believed it was all right to leave infants in the care of nurses, nannies, grannies, and babysitters for extended periods of time during the first two or three years of life, thinking that the child was not aware enough to know the difference in caretaking. Our work with clients indicates that children remember everything and, for the rest of their lives, carry deep scars from trauma caused by such treatment.

> Newborn infants see, hear, and feel, and thus are acutely aware of everything going on around them.

Violato and Russell conducted a Canadian meta-analysis of eighty-eight published research reports on the effects of nonmaternal care on the development of infants and young children.[3] They found that the absence of a mother for more than twenty hours a week can seriously affect the social-emotional and behavioral development, and the maternal attachment, of infants and young children. Lero and colleagues found that 70 percent of Canadian mothers with children less than six years old were working full-time. In the United States the figure is estimated to be 75 percent.[4] This form of unintentional neglect has serious implications for our national policy of federal and state support for child care.

Experiences of physical or emotional abandonment between the ages of ten and twenty-five months are particularly damaging to a child, as they can arrest development and leave children with many co-dependent and counter-dependent behaviors. A child stuck at this stage will grow up seeing the world as split into good and bad, and will see problems as always having either/or solutions. Solutions involving both/and will not be available as options in problem solving.

As a way of compensating for this split, a complex set of dysfunctional adaptive behavioral patterns gradually emerges. For example, intense anxiety and abandonment fears may surface whenever someone leaves, even for a short time. Many adults find themselves starting fights with their loved ones who are going out of town on a short business trip.

HOW CORE TRAUMAS BECOME A LIFE PATTERN

When and how the bonding process gets interrupted is critical. When a break occurs, it is almost as though the child's world stops. Like when the tape in a videotape player pauses, everything freezes. If this happened to you, you likely assessed the situation and identified it as your personal reality. In these frozen moments, a child creates his or her core beliefs, values, assumptions, and expectations about how life is going to be here on Earth, and about what kind of experiences life will bring. These experiences imprint the child deeply and help shape his or her brain and reality.

As we have worked with clients to help locate the sources of their early childhood traumas, we have come to think about people's lives as being layered like onions. In the center of the onion are the traumatic core experiences involving pre- and perinatal trauma. These traumatic experiences are stored as beliefs ("There must be something wrong with me"), as values ("It's okay for people to hurt me, because I'm not important or valuable"), as assumptions ("Adults are people who hurt you and can't be trusted"), or as expectations ("Starting new things in life will be difficult and painful for me"). These beliefs, values, assumptions, and expectations form a matrix, or internal working model, that shapes your perception about your life experiences.

Sometimes, complex family dynamics help create the traumas before you are even born. Perhaps your parents had a lot of conflict with each other and feared that their relationship wouldn't last. At this point they had three choices: they could try to get closer by working through the conflict (which few people have the skills to do); remain distant and avoid the conflict; or (more commonly) decide to have a child. Children are often conceived to buffer conflict between the parents.

If you were born into this kind of family situation, you may have made an unconscious agreement with both your parents either to become the receptacle for all their unexpressed feelings or to play the role of peacemaker. After leaving your family and entering adult life, you unconsciously attracted people who would help you reenact the early developmental traumas you experienced as a child. The family drama frequently looks something like this:

Here you served as a fulcrum to preserve your parents' relationship. You may also have become the target of your parents' conflicts so that they didn't have to get mad at each other, or you may have served as a surrogate partner for one or both of your parents to meet the needs left unfulfilled in their relationship with each other.

HOW YOUR LIFE PATTERN BECOMES
A SELF-FULFILLING PROPHECY

Eventually these traumas form an internal working model or life pattern that you reenact in many variations. Each time it is replayed, the trauma ends the same way: it confirms your early beliefs, values, assumptions, and expectations and adds another layer around the core of the onion. With each new layer, new players are drawn into what has now become your life drama based on the original trauma. The "trauma drama" often becomes a self-fulfilling prophecy or pattern.

It is also possible to use these people to help you identify and clear your early trauma so that you can become a whole person. If, for example, the physician who delivered you used forceps, you may attract people who jerk you around or physically abuse you like your doctor did. If your mother was drugged during birth, you may be attracted to drug use. If your mother died or was killed during your early childhood, you may find yourself in relationships where you get close and are then physically or emotionally abandoned. If no one shows up from "central casting" to act out parts of your drama, you act out all the roles internally. You can persecute yourself when you don't meet your own expectations, and then use that as an excuse to drink too much and feel hung over the next day. You unconsciously set up the drama and then switch between roles until the reenactment is complete and you end up the victim again.

> If life gets too sweet and too comfortable, or if your capacity to receive good things gets stretched too far, you may unconsciously sabotage the flow of good things into your life.

You may find times when life is going too well, and you begin to anticipate that something bad must be about to happen (as it happened at your birth). The expectation that something bad is about to happen when you believe everything is going well is also part of your life drama. As a result, most people set an unconscious quota on how much happiness they can have.

The Role of Unspoken Psychic Agreements

The moments when you experienced the original traumas were also points where you probably made unconscious psychic agreements with your parents. The creation of traumatic events is often the result of a crisis between your parents or between you and your siblings. If you are the oldest or an older child, one of your traumas may be related to the birth of your next sibling. Your parents, especially your mother, may have had to leave you for several days or a week while giving birth to your brother or sister. Depending on how that event was handled in your family, you felt abandoned. Or, if you were left with relatives because of a crisis in the family, you may have experienced an abandonment that elicited a survival fear. Out of this fear, then, you may have created an unhealthy psychic agreement with your parents as a way of self-preservation, such as "If I put your needs before mine, you will agree not to abandon me."

You may have unconsciously agreed to take care of one or both of your parents ("I will try my best to keep my parents together so I won't be abandoned"). This required you to fulfill some behavioral expectations that your parents had for you to help the family maintain its balance. By unconsciously agreeing to this and other, similar expectations, you may have given up some important aspects of your True Self. We've found that this kind of psychic agreement is common among the clients we've worked with. We also discovered that people play out their original psychic agreement in other, subsequent relationships in which they fear being abandoned or abused.

Psychic agreements are never conscious and never spoken. Some of the most common parent-child psychic agreements we've found in our clients are "I will take care of your feelings and be responsible for them if you agree to pay attention to me" and "I will take your abuse if you will let me live in this family." To openly acknowledge such agreements is absolutely taboo. Most people are unaware of the kinds of agreements they made as infants, until they begin, as adults, to do the work necessary to complete the process of separation from their parents, described in chapter 10.

As you created layers on your onion and attracted new players into your life drama, you also found people you hoped would help you break free of it. For example, a boy who unconsciously agreed to take care of his mother's feelings, and to be quiet and passive and not threaten his father's masculinity, may choose a partner who wants someone else to be responsible for her feelings and who will not be very successful in life. Once a person recognizes the presence of agreements from his or her original trauma drama, it's possible to find these same agreements running through each layer of the onion. When our clients do this, they often see their whole life flash before them, and they can actually trace the overlaying pattern from infancy as it is repeated again and again in all their relationships.

What keeps the life trauma drama recycling in adult relationships is the presence of unexpressed emotions. Small children are not able to verbalize their pain or feelings of abandonment. Adult caretakers typically are not aware when babies and small children are experiencing a trauma, and they don't know they need to provide comfort and nurturing support. This leaves children feeling abandoned and left alone to deal with the trauma, which makes it even worse.

Each time the life trauma drama is replayed with the same kind of traumatic ending, it adds another layer of unexpressed feelings to your onion. These unexpressed emotions act as a magnet to draw similar experiences to you to help create the next act in your trauma drama. Each time the drama replays, people seem to unconsciously hope they will get what they really wanted as small children: they will get their needs met.

There are several things you can do to complete the unfinished business in your core trauma drama. These are listed in the "Troubleshooting" box.

TROUBLESHOOTING

How to Heal Your Childhood Trauma Drama

- Identify your core traumas.
- Express the feelings connected to them.
- Receive comfort and support for your feelings.
- Have your experiences validated.

Once you complete this unfinished business, you take the "charge" out of the traumas and they can be healed. We frequently ask clients to act out their trauma drama while role-playing. Here, for the first time, they are able to speak the truth about their traumatic experiences and have caring people witness this original wound and support and validate their feelings and experiences. This often releases the energy they have been using to repress their emotions, and they feel freer and optimistic about the future.

THE DRAMA TRIANGLE AND VICTIM CONSCIOUSNESS

A family dynamic known as the drama triangle involves three interchangeable roles: persecutor, rescuer, victim.[5] First identified by Steven Karpman, the drama triangle entails a series of convoluted power and control games between the persecutor, rescuer, and victim that allows people to meet their needs only by being a victim. In some families, asking for something brings accusations of being selfish or self-centered. As shown in the following figure, there is often no direct communication link between the persecutor and the rescuer.

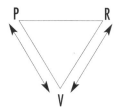

Drama-triangle dynamics are a primary cause of trauma in families. Children who are victimized repeatedly during family conflicts, or who witness others being victimized, internalize these experiences. Specific pictures, words, and feelings related to drama-triangle conflicts create modules of traumatic memories. The sensory triggers or cues related to these traumatic experiences can quickly catapult people from present time into a flashback or regressive experience related to past traumatic events. This also describes symptoms of post–traumatic stress disorder.

Dysfunctional drama-triangle experiences also imprint children cognitively, creating in them the belief that they can get their needs met only by becoming victims. Children with parents who use the drama triangle to meet their own needs find it almost impossible to complete their own splitting subphase of the counter-dependent stage and complete the task of separation. Rather than developing a strong sense of internal power and self-directedness, these children take cues from others and display passive, "other-directed" behaviors characteristic of the victim role. They remain developmentally stuck and cycle back and forth between the co-dependent and counter-dependent stages of development.

An Example of the Drama Triangle

This example of drama-triangle dynamics involves two parents and three children. The father comes home from work to find his children watching television and eating snacks and his wife in the kitchen drinking a cup of coffee and reading the newspaper. This scene does not match the one he fantasized as he was driving home, in which the children were doing homework in their rooms and his wife had dinner waiting. When he opens the front door and finds things are not as he fantasized, he erupts with the feelings of frustration he accumulated while dealing with problems during his workday.

His frustration comes flying out at the children: "Why aren't you in your rooms doing your homework? You all know this is the rule!" His children look up from the television, stunned by his sharp tone. They look cautiously at their mother when she comes into the living room. At this point in the conflict, the father is in the persecutor role and the children are victims. Mother picks up the rescuer role when she defends the children against what she perceives as an attack on them and addresses the father. "Why do you have to come home every night and yell at the children? They were just relaxing after being at school all day!"

As in theater, the next scene of the drama soon emerges. When the mother attacks the father in defense of the children, she assumes the role of persecutor and the father rotates to the victim role. Then the children quickly take up the rescuer role. They turn off the television and say, "We're going to our rooms now to do our homework." This is the end of the second act of the family drama.

In the next scene, the father attacks the mother, "Why don't you have dinner ready? I'm starved!" Father again plays the persecutor and the mother becomes the victim. When the daughter hears her mother and father arguing in the kitchen, she comes running in as the rescuer: "I'll help you get dinner ready, Mom." This is the end of the third act.

The merry-go-round nature of the drama triangle could let the game go on forever. Even though the dynamics seem benign, this communication style can be difficult to eliminate. The first step requires making a commitment to stop meeting your needs by being a victim and to ask directly for what you want and need. The second step is to refuse to rescue others. When you do these two things, you can eliminate the drama triangle from your relationships.

How to Recognize a Rescue

As shown in the example above, the drama triangle can begin from any of the three positions. Individuals who work in the helping or healing professions typically act out the rescuer role. Counselors tend to attract clients whose issues match their own. The counselor's own post-traumatic cues create a drama that both the client and the counselor can act out together. This professional pitfall is known as countertransference. Counselors and other professional helpers can easily become engaged in mutual dramas with their clients that traumatize the clients. For this reason, it's critical that those in the helping professions work diligently to clear themselves of their own unresolved issues.

The behavioral dynamics of the drama triangle relating to the rescue position can entail:

- doing something for someone that you really don't want to do;
- trying to meet other people's needs without being asked;
- consistently doing more than your fair share of the work in a counseling or helping situation;
- feeling so uncomfortable with receiving that you find it necessary to seek out relationships with others in which you only give;
- trying to fix other people's feelings or talk them out of their feelings;
- speaking up for other people instead of letting them speak for themselves;
- not asking for what you need and attending only to the needs of others;
- feeling rejected when your help is graciously refused; and
- trying to help others without an explicit contract. (This does not include acts of kindness and compassion when help is legitimately needed.)

Children who experience trauma during the counter-dependent stage have a more developed sense of self than those who experience trauma during the co-dependent stage of development. Older children, who have more defenses for protecting themselves, are more likely to use the "I'm good" identity and "one-up" defenses. For an example of a one-up defense, think of a two-year-old child whose mother goes to the hospital to have another child. The two-year-old decides that the mother is not trustworthy and refuses to bond with her when she returns home several days later. This "I'm okay, you're not okay," or "one-up," defense encourages inflated self-esteem and supports the persecutor and rescuer roles in the drama triangle.

Splitting behaviors, as indicated in the example in the previous paragraph, show that a person lacks object constancy — that is, lacks the ability to hold the self as an object of worth when feeling rejected or unworthy or when someone says unkind or unpleasant things. Splitting behaviors also form the foundation for "lose-lose" and "win-lose" styles of conflict resolution in adulthood.

Breaking Free of the Drama Triangle

One of the critical factors in the drama triangle is a differential in power between the victim and the persecutor, and the victim and the rescuer. Dominated individuals or groups typically play victim roles, while those who dominate play the persecutors. Drama triangles include the following characteristics:

- the strong dominating the weaker
- unequal rights
- a lack of clear boundaries
- belief in scarcity
- indirect communication
- secrets
- win-lose conflict resolution
- suppression of feelings

Drama-triangle dynamics get reinforced through power plays designed to intimidate those perceived as weaker. Some common power plays are:

- shaming others
- escalation ("rageaholic" behavior)
- sandbagging (dragging in old issues)
- asking why instead of how
- blaming others
- pulling rank
- labeling and name-calling
- leaving in the middle of a conflict
- avoiding responsibility for a conflict
- playing martyr
- using money or sex to control others

Changing the power balance in drama-triangle dynamics can be difficult, because much of the industrialized world operates on this dominator/dominated system. Individuals who are highly committed to changing this cultural system risk being viewed as strange or weird. Before they can become change agents in larger systems, such as nations, they must clear their own patterns related to dominating and being dominated. In order to transform systems into partnership models of relationship, participants must possess or experience the following:

- an attitude of abundance
- legislated equal rights
- social systems constructed to share power
- negotiation skills
- direct lines of communication
- open expression of feelings
- cooperative, win-win approaches to resolving conflicts
- a commitment to tell the truth and to seek intimacy
- respect for the boundaries of others

If you are willing to follow the guidelines presented here, you can successfully move out of victim consciousness and complete the separation process in the counter-dependent stage of development. Once you understand the dynamics of this game and its goal, you'll see it being played out everywhere you go. It's the only game in town in most family, social, and work relationships.

THE FUNCTIONAL FAMILY TRIANGLE

The drama triangle as it gets played out in families creates a *dysfunctional family* triangle. The alternative is the creation of the *functional family triangle*. When both parents have agreed not to play out the drama-triangle dynamics with each other, they can work cooperatively on parenting their child in a functional way. With this kind of support, eventually the child learns that he or she can get his or her needs met without resorting to the drama triangle. This also helps the child heal his or her internal split between good and bad and as a result, be able to hold a unified "I'm okay and you're okay" image of both him- or herself and his or her parents. This is the essential marker for the completion of the individuation process, also referred to as the psychological birth.

When this developmental process is completed, the child goes on *internal power*. This allows the child to use feelings and trusted inner resources to direct his or her life and get essential needs met. With the support of a functional family triangle, the child will be able to effectively regulate his or her emotions and move forward into independence, the next stage of development, without having to drag along incomplete developmental processes from the previous stage. Below is an example of the communication guidelines that parents can use in helping their child complete the individuation process.

GUIDELINES FOR COMPLETING THE INDIVIDUATION PROCESS

In chapter 2, we talked about how the psychological birth and individuation process require the support of two caregivers to whom the child has bonded, in order for him or her to become emotionally and psychologically separate. Here are some guidelines you can use to help children — large and small — complete the individuation process.

1. When one of the caregivers is not available to meet the child's needs, and the child complains or gets upset, the available caregiver should do the following:

    *   Support the child's feelings.
        (*"I can see that you are upset because your daddy left."*)

    *   Refuse to participate in the child's judgment about the "badness" of the unavailable parent, but offer empathy to the child.
        (*"It's hard when you don't see your daddy all day. You'd like him to stay here with you."*)

    *   Reassure the child that his or her needs will be met.
        (*"I'm here to take care of you while your daddy is at work today."*)

    *   Inform the child that the missing caregiver will return.
        (*"Your daddy will be back at four o'clock to pick you up and take you home."*)

    *   Inform the returning caregiver about the child's reaction to the separation.

("*Kevin was sad today when you had to leave. He wished that he could be with you all day today.*")

2. The returning caregiver should do the following:

    *   Ask the child if this is true.
        ("*Were you upset today that I had to leave? Did you want me to stay with you all day?*")

    *   Support the child's feelings and offer closeness.
        ("*You were sad and mad today. Do you need anything from me right now?*")

    *   Express his or her own feelings about separation to the child.
        ("*I miss being with you too. I feel sad when I have to go to work and leave you.*")

    *   Give the child reasons for the absence.
        ("*Daddy has to go to work to earn money to pay for the things we need.*")

3. When the child has a conflict with one caregiver and brings the conflict to the second caregiver, the second caregiver should do the following:

    *   Support the child's feelings.
        ("*I can see that you are upset with your mother. You look angry. Are you angry?*")

    *   Do not agree or disagree with the child's judgment about the first caregiver's "badness," but instead offer empathy to the child.
        ("*You are angry because your mother made you clean up your toys. You don't like to pick up your toys just because she told you to.*")

    *   Support the child in dealing directly with the first caregiver to resolve the conflict.
        ("*Are you willing to talk to her and tell her how you feel?*")

    *   Help the child talk to the first caregiver.
        ("*Do you need any help from me when you go talk to your mother?*")

    *   Let the child know that it is not okay to triangulate and have family secrets.

("If you are not willing to tell her how you feel, I will tell her that you are upset about your conflict with her.")

- Let the child know that you will not resolve his or her conflict with the first caregiver, and that you are available to support both the child and the first caregiver when they are ready to resolve it.

  ("I do not want to get in the middle of this conflict between you and your mother. I will not go to your mother and speak for you. I will only let her know that I am aware you are angry with her. If the two of you want to talk about this, I am available to support both of you.")

- Inform the child that, if he or she resolves the conflict without you, you would like to know the outcome.

  ("When you and your mother talk about your feelings about having to pick up your toys, please let me know what happens.")

At first, you may feel awkward using these unfamiliar kinds of responses. This is normal when you are in a learning curve. The truth is, we are all in a learning curve in understanding the kind of support children need to successfully complete the individuation process. Very few people have ever experienced this kind of communication.

When you do use it, however, you will see how effective it is in helping your children feel accepted and understood. There are also some guidelines about what *not* to do in the above situations:

- Do not contribute to making anyone into a bad guy.
  ("He is never here when you need him.")
- Do not take sides.
  ("You are right. He doesn't care about you. He doesn't care about anyone.")
- Do not ignore or discount feelings.
  ("Don't cry. Here, have a cookie.")
- Do not discount the importance of the child's situation.
  ("I'm busy. Go play.")
- Do not create secrets.
  ("I won't tell her you are angry at her.")
- Do not rescue.

("I'll talk to your mother and tell her that you shouldn't have to pick up your toys.")
- Do not play "two against one."
("Let's go talk to your mother. We'll tell her that you shouldn't have to pick up your toys.")

Using both sets of the above guidelines is critical for completing the individuation process of the counter-dependent stage of development. If you find yourself using the incorrect responses, you can always go back and change your responses. It is never too late to use the correct ones. Since most of us still have unresolved issues about wanting to be separate, the communication guidelines above are also useful for resolving conflicts in adult relationships where these same dynamics are present.

THE QUEST TO COMPLETE YOUR CORE TRAUMA

People with co-dependent behaviors attempt to cover the wounds of their early traumas by seeking out a series of special people on whom they can project the image of the "perfect parent," expecting that these individuals will fulfill their unmet narcissistic needs. These special people might include a religious or spiritual figure, a teacher, a boss, or a love partner. In these relationships, the co-dependent person projects his or her infantile need for blissful bonding in order to fulfill the need for bonding. The intense need to attach to another person and reexperience bliss through addictions to "perfect" people is a key element of co-dependency.

If we look at what is right about this behavior, we see that people instinctively know they must return to being dependent in order to break free of their co-dependent behaviors. Once adults have been able to satisfy their bonding needs in healthy ways, it's easier to complete the task of separation in the counter-dependent stage. Research shows very clearly that the more bonded a person is, the easier the task of separation.[6]

Other people with counter-dependent behaviors attempt to satisfy their need for symbiotic bliss in the opposite way. Rather than risk being rewounded through intimacy, they seek the bliss of bonding through addictions to activities or substances. They get their "high" through work, drugs, alcohol, sex, exercise, religion, meditation, or intense emotional states such as rage. We come to believe that, through these dysfunctional adaptive behaviors, we can break free of our core childhood traumas. But there are effective ways to break these patterns that can be easily learned. We discuss the two pathways in the next section.

TWO DIFFERENT PATHS TO WHOLENESS

The path to wholeness for people with counter-dependent behaviors is far different from the path for those with co-dependent issues. The following chart shows the qualities that each type needs to develop.

Those with Co-dependency Issues Must Learn to:	Those with Counter-dependency Issues Must Learn to:
• become more independent	• become more dependent
• focus on the self	• focus on others
• build boundaries	• remove walls
• cope with strong feelings	• identify and express feelings
• identify personal strengths	• identify personal weaknesses
• be intimate with the self	• be intimate with others
• be autonomous	• be cooperative
• defend against projections	• take back projections
• avoid unhealthy commitments	• make commitments
• master the world of work	• master the world of relationships
• develop compassion for the self	• develop compassion for others
• create sexual boundaries	• separate sexuality from nurturing

STEP-BY-STEP PROGRAM FOR CHANGING YOUR COUNTER-DEPENDENT BEHAVIORS

Identify your counter-dependent patterns. Only recently have people recognized the role of counter-dependent behaviors in addictions. It has been easier to see co-dependency addictions related to food, alcohol, "downer" drugs, and other people. We now recognize another whole spectrum of "upper" addictions that help people flee from intimacy, such as exercise, work, shopping, cocaine, amphetamines, multiple sex partners, and travel. Most people have some addictions from both categories. Many therapists are puzzled about why addictions are so difficult to change. We believe it's because counter-dependency issues are often ignored in treatment programs.

Use the step-by-step holistic approach presented in this book as a map for breaking free from your counter-dependent behaviors. This map identifies the key steps in the process and helps you discover where you currently are on your journey to recovery of the Self. These steps involve transformation work at the physical, mental, emotional, and spiritual levels. It's easy to get lost without a map to provide direction.

The Steps to Recovery of the Self Include:

- remembering what happened to you as a child;
- identifying the characteristics of counter-dependent behaviors;
- feeling your feelings;
- learning reparenting skills;
- becoming an autonomous person;
- learning to take charge of your body;
- developing a spiritual life; and
- learning to live interdependently.

Learn about your unmet developmental needs. This approach will help you identify the missing elements from your early developmental history that are causing counter-dependent behavior patterns to recycle in your adult relationships. The various written exercises in this book can help you identify your unmet developmental needs. Once you understand what is incomplete and where you might have missed completing it, you can use our easy-to-follow instructions to meet these unmet developmental needs now in your adult relationships.

Learn the skills needed to break free of counter-dependent behaviors. We devote an entire chapter in this book to each of these core skills. You can first read about why each skill is important and then use the chapter's skill-building exercises to learn how to use the skills more effectively. This self-help approach allows you to work on your counter-dependent behaviors without therapy or as an adjunct to therapy. We chose these particular skills because we've found that they help people create more satisfying, intimate relationships. The skills needed for recovery of the Self are listed in the sidebar "Six Skills for Changing Your Counter-dependent Behaviors."

Six Skills for Changing Your Counter-dependent Behaviors

- Developing empathy
- Setting boundaries
- Reclaiming projections
- Parenting yourself
- Resolving conflicts
- Communicating about sex

Create committed relationships. You can create safe environments in which to meet unmet needs from the counter-dependent stage of your development. We've found that people, particularly couples, who commit to helping each other break free of counter-dependent patterns discover a doorway to deeper intimacy. Some even experience a sense of soul connection.

Develop a broader view of your counter-dependent behaviors. The social and cultural aspects of counter-dependent behaviors provide a larger context for understanding these developmental deficits in adults. We live in a culture that has collectively evolved to the counter-dependent stage of development. This means that your counter-dependent behaviors are not wrong or bad but reflect the environment in which you live. Because of the structure of our social and cultural institutions, it would be almost impossible for you to grow up without having some counter-dependent behavior patterns. Therefore, we see the society and culture as part of the problem as well as part of the solution. Understanding that counter-dependent behaviors are both an individual issue and a social-cultural problem can free you from feelings of shame about having them.

Create a vision of life beyond your co-dependent/counter-dependent issues. This is a necessary and often ignored ingredient in breaking free of dysfunctional behavior patterns. You cannot recover from the limitations caused by co-dependent or counter-dependent issues unless you first develop a vision of what your life could be like without them.

Do the practical written exercises in the book. This will help you apply the concepts in this book to your own life. We urge you to take the time to write out the exercises we present, because they offer powerful opportunities for you to deepen your understanding of your counter-dependent behaviors and learn how they affect your life. These practical exercises, which we've used widely in our workshops, in our therapy practice, and with our clients, can help you break free of counter-dependent behaviors.

AWARENESS ACTIVITY:
IDENTIFYING YOUR CORE TRAUMAS

When you enter a relationship, each of you is hoping to develop a sense of primal trust. This involves creating a limited "all good" view of each other. You each may tend to see the other as kind, loving, and available to meet your needs. This view is similar to the blissful state of paradise the child experiences in infancy. Then, at some point, something happens that ends paradise, leaving one of you feeling betrayed, abused, or abandoned.

Later in childhood and even into adulthood, we continue to attempt to re-create primal trust in our close relationships as a way of meeting our need for bonding. Each time we do, however, we usually find our innocent, child-like trust shattered again by betrayal when our partner in this relationship fails to play the perfect parent. Betrayal can become a useful growth experience if we learn to look at what is right about it.[7] It can also help us identify elements of our trauma drama, as described in the exercise below.

I. Begin by making a list of the significant traumas or betrayals you've experienced in your life. These can be the times you were betrayed by others, as well as the times that you were the betrayer. You can make a chronological list, beginning with the most recent event, and then work backward to your earliest childhood memory of a betrayal experience. Use a few sentences or short phrases to describe each trauma. Then put them in a chronology that begins with the earliest betrayal event.

2. Review your list, asking the following questions. Write out your answers to these questions.

    *   What similarities are there between these traumas?
    *   What was my role in each trauma or betrayal?
    *   What were the circumstances that set up my betrayals?
    *   How did I feel in each betrayal or trauma?
    *   What beliefs, values, assumptions, and expectations have I formed about myself and about the world as a result of these traumas or betrayals?
    *   How does my earliest trauma replay in each of the other traumas?
    *   What dramas seem to replay over and over in my life?
    *   What was unfinished about each of the trauma or betrayal experiences?
    *   What do I need to do to finish each of these experiences?

3. Now write "The Story of My Life." Encapsulate your list of traumas into a mythic or metaphoric tale. Let your story reflect the relationship you see between your early traumas and your life drama.

4. Look at your life drama to see what isn't finished. Examine each event or betrayal to see what you need to do to complete it. Write a second story, "My New Life Story," which reflects what would happen if you completed the unfinished elements of your trauma drama and healed the effects of the betrayals you experienced.

5. Then construct experiences for yourself to do on your own, in therapy, in a support group, or in committed relationships, that would enable you to actually do the completion work necessary to end the cycle of betrayal. At the end of chapter 10 in this book is a completion exercise that will assist you with this task.

THE BOTTOM LINE

- New research is helping us better understand what children really need from adult caregivers in order to fully develop. The next step is to implement this new information.
- While parenting your own children, you will likely come face-to-face with your own childhood wounds. Be ready!
- Any developmental trauma not identified or healed will interfere with intimacy in your adult relationships.
- Unconscious agreements made in childhood can destroy intimacy in adult relationships.
- Victim consciousness, based on drama-triangle dynamics, can wreck your adult relationships.
- The step-by-step process to recovery of your True Self is well established and the goal is attainable.

4. The Disease Model of Relationships

*In every generation there has to be some fool
who will speak the truth as he sees it.*
— Boris Pasternak

While conducting a workshop in California on conflict resolution, we discovered that many of the workshop's participants were not in primary relationships. When we mentioned this to the group, several people spoke up, saying that they were told not to form relationships because they were sex and love addicts. They told us that, if they had an urge to begin a relationship, they would go to their sex and love addicts' twelve-step group for support to resist the urge. This view of relationships disturbed us, because we believe that a relationship is not something to avoid but a primary means for conscious people to heal any co-dependent or counter-dependent behavior patterns.

THE MEDICAL VIEW OF AMERICAN LIFE

It is big business today in America to label any compulsive behavior related to food, drink, sex, relationships, or activities such as gambling, smoking, working, or shopping as a disease. The expensive residential treatment programs that stand to benefit most from the disease model have been successful in getting almost all addictions or compulsive behaviors labeled as diseases, even though there is very little research evidence to support this disease model. Moreover, there is almost no solid research evidence to support the claims that participating in these treatment programs leads to recovery.

The National Council on Alcoholism says that you cannot recover from the "disease" of alcohol addiction, and that you will always have to identify yourself as an alcoholic or an addict. Alcoholics Anonymous (AA) also supports this widespread notion, which was originally developed to counteract the moralistic judgments against alcoholics or problem drinkers who were cured by staying away from alcohol.

While there is some research linking alcohol and genetics, it is mixed and contradictory. What's clear is that some people cannot metabolize the sugar in alcohol and should stay completely away from it. These people have an allergy to sugar, not to alcohol itself.

George Vaillant, a physician and a strong supporter of AA, argues that "alcoholism is not, strictly speaking, a disease — [but] calling alcoholism a disease . . . is a useful device both to persuade the alcoholic to admit his alcoholism and to provide a ticket for admission into the health-care system." However, he concluded, "in the long run, it [the disease concept] is not effective."[1]

Vaillant also conducted the largest comparative study of the effects of AA support versus no AA support on long-term abstinence by former alcohol abusers. He found that 81 percent of those who quit on their own were still abstinent after ten years, while only 32 percent of those who attended AA meetings regularly remained abstinent after ten years.[2]

The popularity of the disease concept of alcoholism has been spread by AA and the National Council on Alcoholism. In 1956, the American Medical Association determined that alcoholism was a disease, even though there was almost no research evidence to support the claim. As noted earlier, the founders of AA used the word "disease" metaphorically, meaning that they believed alcohol addiction resembled a disease. Certainly, this concept was useful at that time because of the widespread moral condemnation of alcohol abusers. The American Medical Association, however, began to see how useful and profitable it might be to drop the metaphoric use of the term, and stretched its diagnostic categories to include alcoholism. So definitive and authoritative was this pronouncement that, by 1987 (according to a Gallup survey), almost 90 percent of Americans believed alcoholism was a disease.

Besides helping more and more medical specialists become wealthy, the disease model has dramatically changed the insurance industry. Once co-dependency and counter-dependency were diagnosed as mental diseases, practitioners were able to collect third-party payments from insurance companies for treating co-dependency and counter-dependency. Between 1978 and 1984, the number of for-profit residential treatment centers increased by 350 percent, and their caseloads rose by 400 percent.[3]

Typical twenty-eight-day, in-patient programs (twenty-eight days is the usual maximum length for in-patient care that most insurance plans will pay for) cost the patient's insurance company from twenty thousand to forty thousand dollars. Many ads have played on people's fears that their undetected disease would eventually kill them or a family member if they didn't seek immediate treatment.

This excess was a major influence on the managed care model of mental health that limited treatment of mental illnesses and severely reduced the liability of the insurance industry for mental health coverage. As noted, cost containment procedures in most insurance companies now limit the number of days of inpatient care; they also limit the number of sessions of outpatient care, or the dollar amounts for both. Unfortunately, the short-term approach now in use, because of the cost-containment policies of insurance companies, has replaced the client-therapist relationship with prescription drugs, which do not, and will not ever, address the developmental issues inherent in addictions.

Once alcoholism became widely accepted as a disease, so was the concept of co-alcoholism (now called co-dependency). Co-alcoholism was defined as a disease that a person "caught" by growing up in an alcoholic family. This diseasing of alcoholism and co-alcoholism led to labeling other compulsive behaviors as diseases, including sex, gambling, eating, worrying, smoking, shopping, rage, religious beliefs, and being in an abusive relationship. The only compulsive behavior so far to escape the disease label is compulsive working (workaholism). Using the current medical approach, almost any set of behaviors engaged in excessively or compulsively that might have intermittently harmful effects on a person or on others whom this person relates to is defined as an addiction, which (and now for the biggest leap) is then automatically defined as a disease.

WHAT IS AN ADDICTION?

Deciding what qualifies as an addiction can be difficult. The bottom line is that some medical experts decide that a group of people are "out of control" or unable to exercise reasonable control over their behaviors, and these experts give them a medical diagnosis. This diagnosis may be based on a subjective judgment influenced by the diagnosed group's socioeconomic status. In the last half of the twentieth century, this medical definition of addiction replaced the former definition of an addiction, which, before circa 1900, meant a particular enjoyment found by engaging in a habit. This habit could be related to ingesting certain foods or drink (alcoholic or nonalcoholic) or to taking certain medicines such as herbal tonics or diuretics. For example, as late as 1906, large, potent doses of cocaine were part of the popular drink Coca-Cola.[4]

OUR APPROACH TO ADDICTIONS

Our approach to addictions is much different. We correlate addictive behaviors with trauma and regard them as ways of avoiding pain or unwanted feelings, and we see addiction as evidence of a "feeling dysfunction." Addiction helps minimize the reexperiencing of traumatic memories and the feelings associated with them.

Reexperiencing feelings associated with traumas that happened at birth or in our first year of life may be so overwhelming that we feel as though we may not survive. Not wanting to feel that scared again, we try to avoid anything that might trigger these traumatic memories and the feelings connected with them.

DID YOU KNOW THAT…

No one ever died from feeling their feelings, but millions of people have died from taking drugs, alcohol, and other toxic substances to help them avoid or repress their feelings.

If you look closely at your own addictive or compulsive behaviors (something that you probably really don't want to do), you'll likely find that they help you avoid some scary feelings. Addicts who finally bottom out often realize the futility of their efforts and finally surrender to the feelings, recognizing that this can't be any worse than the situation in which they find themselves. Much to their surprise, they discover that they don't die from feeling their feelings. This dispels their illusion about feeling their emotions and puts them on the path to recovery. Many addicts have wept when they finally realized how many people they have hurt and how much time, money, and energy they have put into avoiding something that would actually help them.

People with counter-dependent behaviors often use "uppers" — substances and activities that allow them to avoid feeling the feelings connected with some early relationship trauma they are trying to avoid. The problem is that close, intimate relationships often trigger memories of early relational traumas. This is why many people are in flight from intimacy. Like individuals with addictions, they eventually bottom out and find themselves leading isolated, lonely lives. Eventually they become motivated to face what they have been avoiding: the developmental traumas and the feelings that go with intimacy.

ADDICTIONS AS DISEASES

Defining an addiction as a disease is an ethical issue we want to address. The first thing to know is that there are three categories of diseases. The first category consists of disorders known by their physical symptoms and caused by microbes or viruses. These include polio, malaria, influenza, AIDS, tuberculosis, and so on. This list once included cancer, heart disease, and stroke, which are now recognized as related to lifestyle choices involving diet, exercise, and stress. The standard medical approach for treating diseases on the first list is to identify the specific microbe that causes the disease and then develop antibiotics to kill it or prevent its spread in the body. Also in this group are diseases thought to be inherited, which include diabetes, cystic fibrosis, Down syndrome, and hemophilia.

The second category of disease includes mental, or emotional, illnesses. A person with an illness from this group is usually diagnosed not through blood samples or brain scans but through an analysis of his or her thoughts, feelings, and behaviors, leading to a judgment that his or her social symptoms and behaviors are outside the "normal range" of accepted social norms.

How far outside the social norms a person is judged to be determines whether he or she is said to have a neurosis, a personality disorder, a psychosis, or a character disorder.

The third category of (so-called) diseases is addiction. Addictions are even further removed from the microbe- or virus-caused physical diseases in the first group. The addiction-as-disease theory contends that (1) you inherit a genetic disposition to the addictive behavior; (2) the genetic disposition takes over your body and brain and causes addictive behaviors that exist independently of the rest of you; and (3) addictions are progressive and irreversible and will lead to death if not treated.

The logic behind this all-encompassing theory breaks down quickly when applied to specific situations. For example, when people addicted to smoking cigarettes give up smoking, they are no longer seen as addicts. According to addictionology (the study of addictive behavior), this is not true for people addicted to activities, relationships, sex, food, and substances. These people are told there is no known cure for their disease, and that they will never get much better. In fact, they are told they could get progressively worse and die. The best they can hope for is to not get any worse. In the meantime, medical research money is being spent to look for chemicals that will bring relief to the countless millions of so-called addicts. According to estimates, 96–98 percent of the population has at least one addictive disease, and many people are diagnosed as having multiple addictions.[5] Those who promote this idea about addiction usually describe it according to a specific disease model, outlined in the sidebar "The Disease Model for Addictions."

THE DISEASE MODEL FOR ADDICTIONS

- The disease is marked by a loss of control over one's behavior.
- Education and training do not enable the sufferer to gain control of his or her behavior.
- The disease will get worse regardless of any lifestyle changes.
- The disease is a permanent flaw or trait, and the sufferer must adjust to this reality for the rest of his or her life.
- The disease will eventually kill the person if long-term treatment is not used.

TYPICAL APPROACHES TO TREATING ADDICTIONS

- Sufferers are encouraged to join support groups organized by and for those who share the disease.
- Sufferers receive medical treatment in hospitals or clinics, under the supervision of physicians or trained specialists.
- Addiction is framed as a moral issue, and people with this "disease" may be shamed for not living up to the moral standards or codes of conduct of those who don't have the addiction.
- Friends, family members, bosses, therapists, and ministers vigorously attempt to identify people with addictions and to force treatment on them, even against their will, because they deny having the disease.

This set of criteria has allowed 20 million Americans to be diagnosed as alcoholics and another 80 million as co-dependents. In addition, 80 million have been diagnosed as having eating disorders (if you count obesity), 50 million as being depressed and anxious, 20 million as gambling addicts, and about 25 million as love and sex addicts. Add to this number the countless workaholics, religious addicts, shopping addicts, addicted smokers, and spectator sports addicts who aren't generally counted in the official statistics.

Even without counting the unofficial addicts, the total number of people diagnosed as addicts in this country is over 275 million.[6] This means there are enough cases of addiction to allocate one to each man, woman, and child in this country. Yet as noted earlier, only alcoholism research shows evidence supporting the disease theory, since it involves an allergic reaction to sugar rather than to alcohol itself. Other addictions that show no evidence of physical symptoms should not be labeled as diseases.

I AM MY DISEASE

One of the biggest problems with the disease approach to addictions is that it encourages people to identify with their disease or addiction. They are told to say to people, "I am an addict," or "I am co-dependent." They are also told they will always have to identify themselves this way. They are further told that if they make progress, their twelve-step group or therapist may allow them to claim to be "a recovering addict" or "in recovery." This is offered as the best they can hope for in their lives. They are not allowed to identify themselves as having recovered from the disease, and therefore, their disease becomes a primary identity for the rest of their lives.

Identifying with a disease is disempowering and creates another form of co-dependency. How can people break free from addictive behaviors if they aren't given a vision of potential change? It's understandable that identifying with an addiction might be a necessary first step for some people in overcoming their feelings of shame, but the concept needs to be reframed. It's much healthier for people to describe themselves as "having addictive behaviors" related to some kinds of activities — for example, to a certain kind of relationship, to sex, or to some foods or substances — or as being vulnerable to certain kinds of authority figures.

This approach offers a more comprehensive picture of the problem and helps people associate their addictions with unprocessed developmental traumas. It also offers a vision of becoming "someone who has recovered from an addiction," or "someone who is no longer addicted to relationships, sex, food, or substances." These concepts are consistent with our developmental definition of addictions, which allows individuals to reclaim their power and to control their lives. The approach also provides an essential vision of wholeness.

Identifying as an addict or a co-dependent individual encourages a shame-based identity. Shame is different from guilt. Guilt is about something we have done — a behavior. Shame says there is something wrong with you — you are inherently flawed at the soul level and cannot change. Remember that the original purpose for labeling alcoholism as a disease was to remove the shame and moral judgment associated with it so that people would seek treatment. Identifying people as co-dependents or addicts reinforces the shame and drives traumatic memories even farther from our conscious awareness.

Turning co-dependency into a disease encourages you to give your personal power over to medical experts, who take control of your recovery. If you feel powerless and cannot recover, the disease diagnosis becomes a self-fulfilling prophecy. In fact, psychologist Stanton Peele says the research indicates that more people recover from alcoholism on their own than by attending Alcoholics Anonymous meetings or by going through expensive twenty-eight-day treatment programs in private hospitals. Peele quotes a long-term study of more than forty-two thousand Americans, whose results showed that "the vast majority of alcohol-dependent Americans, about three-quarters (of those in the study), never underwent treatment. And fewer of them were abusing alcohol than were those who were treated."[7]

Another study, by Steve Rollnick and William Miller, shows that the most successful treatments were nonconfrontational ones that allowed self-motivated change. These treatments were followed by a motivational enhancement approach that allowed the individual to decide whether or not to quit treatment. Other successful approaches included self-help manuals (thank goodness) and a community-reinforcement approach that allowed for subtle social pressures on the addict to change, as well as offered skill training for the individual.[8]

THE DISEASE MODEL OF RELATIONSHIPS

Since this book is about counter-dependency and co-dependency behaviors and how these two issues appear in relationships, we'll look next at how this disease concept is now being applied to relationship problems and then offer a more hopeful view.

The concept of co-dependency grew out of the alcoholism-treatment field, and so it naturally inherited the disease tradition, even though there is no research evidence to support the idea that co-dependency is a disease. Most of the books on co-dependency, however, have accepted the disease model. The disease orientation poses several problems.

Most experts on co-dependency say that 96 to 98 percent of the population has co-dependent behaviors. If one were to recommend the same disease-oriented tactic for treating co-dependency behaviors that is used for treating alcoholics — abstention from the addictive substance — then it would be unsafe for anyone to be in an intimate relationship. As developmental psychologists, we believe that this disease orientation scares people and encourages them to flee from what could be a primary source of recovery: committed, conscious relationships.

Besides offering almost no hope of breaking free, the disease model of co-dependency has created another disturbing reaction. It has encouraged more and more people to escape into counter-dependent behaviors to help themselves look good and prove to themselves and others that they don't have a disease. These behaviors include avoiding relationship commitments and avoiding becoming very close and intimate with anyone.

Finally, the disease model has permeated the twelve-step community's Sex and Love Addicts Anonymous recovery group by turning the concept of relationship itself into a disease. It labels those who want close relationships as love or sex addicts. As a result, many people avoid relationships altogether to prevent being diagnosed as addicts of this kind. Sex and Love Addicts Anonymous has become very popular in certain parts of the country. Granted, there are addictive and compulsive behaviors related to love and sex, but these behaviors are anchored in developmental trauma and not caused by a disease.

As we indicated earlier, we take a developmental view of addictions: all compulsive and addictive behaviors are attempts (sometimes desperate attempts) to avoid certain repressed feelings from childhood trauma. Mood-altering substances, certain activities, and focusing on taking care of other people allow only a temporary reprieve from experiencing these old, scary feelings.

THE DEVELOPMENTAL VIEW OF ADDICTIONS

Addictions are:

- ways to avoid deep unresolved feelings and issues associated with not experiencing consistent unconditional love and nurturing during the co-dependent and counter-dependent stages of development; and
- unskilled attempts to meet these bonding and separation needs as adults.

Sex- and love-related addictions, including pornography addiction, have become a big issue because most of the adult population in this culture has severe early-developmental deficiencies in bonding. When people lack the necessary skills for creating nonsexual intimacy and bonding, they use sexual behaviors to meet those nurturing and bonding needs. What they actually want or need is nonsexual touch and nurturing.

This is difficult, because most men and women in our culture cannot separate sexual touch from nurturing touch. Women who have borne children may have learned how to discriminate between sexuality and nurturing during the intimate bonding experiences of breastfeeding, holding, touching, and caring for young children. Most men, however, don't spend as much time in this kind of close contact and are less likely to develop this important discrimination.

One of our clients was a classic example of this. He grew up in a family in which there was no nurturing touch. He described his mother as cold and unavailable. When he married, his wife too was cold and unavailable. After the birth of their first child, he felt his wife was even less available to him. His need for nurturing touch became more desperate. Because he couldn't sort out nurturing touch and sexual touch, he ended up sexually molesting his daughter when she was six. He got her to stroke his penis while he stroked her clitoris. After a couple of weeks, he realized the inappropriateness of his behavior and stopped it.

He was overcome with tremendous feelings of guilt and shame, which he began covering with addictions to alcohol, sex, and work. He finally entered therapy, thinking he was a despicable sex addict and child molester. Through therapy, he discovered that he was experiencing a touch deprivation because of severe bonding deficits in childhood, and that he didn't know how to meet his needs in nonsexual ways. Over time, he learned to discriminate between sexual touch and nurturing touch and began rebuilding his life.

Men and women who have not learned the difference between sexual touch and nurturing touch often seek physical closeness and touch in the only way they know, through sex. Our developmental perspective looks at what is right about the phenomenon of sex and love addiction instead of labeling it as a disease. It may involve "looking for love in all the wrong places," and it usually doesn't satisfy the need for nurturing and bonding, but, for many people, it seems to be the only option.

Sadly, many people in Sex and Love Addicts Anonymous groups are cautioned against entering into relationships and told that to enter one would be like an alcoholic taking another drink. Meetings are often filled with confessions from people who had the urge to get into a relationship, but who called a group member instead or attended an extra group meeting.

The most direct way people can address such problems is by discovering their unmet developmental needs and finding ways to directly meet these needs in their current relationships. We tell people not to avoid relationships unless they're in ones that are physically or emotionally abusive. In fact, we support the idea of using all relationships (work, social, romantic, friend, family, spousal) as sources for meeting these important developmental needs in healthy ways. From this perspective, relationships become an important supportive environment for changing counter-dependent and co-dependent behaviors, rather than the cause of the problem.

BREAKING FREE OF COUNTER-DEPENDENT BEHAVIORS

In order to break free of counter-dependent behaviors by getting into therapy, attending a support group, or changing your relationship patterns, you'll need

- a strong desire to change;
- the recognition that you experienced developmental trauma during the first three years of your life;
- appropriate identification, acceptance, and expression of repressed feelings;
- new life skills and resources to support your desired change;
- improved communications skills in work, personal, and family relationships;
- support and encouragement from others;
- new values and beliefs; and
- a vision of life beyond addiction.

It's possible to eliminate counter-dependent behaviors if you incorporate these elements into a personal change program, whether it involves therapy, support groups, or committed relationships. Those who wish to use therapy to help overcome addictive or compulsive behaviors can combine the short-term therapy with nontherapy support systems that we describe later in this chapter. First, let's examine some of the problems present in the therapy industry.

THE DISEASE MODEL OF THERAPY

Other factors also contribute to the popularity of the disease model among therapists. Being aware of these factors can help you make intelligent, informed decisions if you decide to seek psychotherapeutic help for changing any of your counter-dependent or co-dependent behaviors.

Therapists' Family Histories

Therapists themselves are not the most stable lot, often suffering from burnout and other stresses. Interestingly, they have a common profile of unprocessed developmental trauma. Many therapists are firstborn or only children who were pushed through childhood too quickly and without the warmth, nurturing, protection, and love that they needed. They frequently became little adults who took care of their parents. They grew up believing that hard work and taking care of others were the best ways to meet their own emotional need for intimacy. They also have low self-esteem and are often loners; they don't make friends easily and don't know how to receive love or how to be intimate. They fit the counter-dependent profile perfectly and often form co-dependent relationships with their clients in an attempt to meet their own unmet developmental needs to be liked and valued.[9]

The Training of Therapists

Most training programs for psychotherapists do not require any self-analysis or personal therapy, and this doesn't help students who bring their developmental traumas to the training. Instead, graduate students studying to become psychologists or therapists are encouraged to be detached, objective scientists who must not let their own values, beliefs, and needs interfere with their profession. Generally, this teaches prospective therapists to hide their weaknesses or insecurities and to "look good" to clients and colleagues. Looking good includes wearing special clothing (some therapists even wear white coats), diagnosing their clients (or "patients," as medically oriented therapists call the people they try to help), and using technical jargon that makes others think they are important and smart.

The Risky Business of Therapy

The therapy profession encourages both therapist and client to accept the disease model. As a result, therapy has taken on the following characteristics.

A short-term-symptom orientation to therapy. Managed health care policies promote short-term therapy treatments in order to contain costs. This orientation encourages therapists to treat people's symptoms and give medications rather than addressing the developmental sources of clients' issues in ways that help transform them. This superficial approach also discourages therapists from working more deeply on their own unresolved family of origin issues. From this perspective, short-term therapy really benefits insurance companies who subsidize therapeutic treatment and is detrimental to both clients and therapists.

A cognitive orientation to therapy. Psychoanalytic therapies (Freudian analysis and Jungian analysis), psychodynamic therapies (Adlerian therapy and transactional analysis), and cognitive therapies (reality therapy and rational emotive therapy) are all basically forms of "talk" therapy. Such therapeutic approaches often allow the therapist to remain in a detached and aloof position. Many cognitive therapies do not address the clients' feelings and the deeper relationship issues that co-dependent and counter-dependent individuals must address if they are to resolve their unfinished bonding and separation issues.

One of our clients, who had previously been in therapy with a cognitive therapist, was told by his therapist that he could not express his feelings in his therapy sessions because it might disturb the other therapists and clients in other offices in the building. This is a common ploy by therapists who are afraid that a client expressing his or her real feelings might trigger the therapist's own repressed feelings. Most psychotherapy still involves talking "about" feelings without actually experiencing them. We believe that, without actively expressing your real feelings in psychotherapy, you can learn only to better understand the problem and your feelings *about* it. Talk therapy by itself will not transform the developmental wounds that are the source of a problem.

A financial orientation to therapy. Therapists, like many medically oriented practitioners, charge what the traffic will bear. As a result, therapy costs have skyrocketed in the past twenty years, leaving most clients unable to afford long-term therapy unless they have good insurance coverage. Given this and the fact that insurance companies have limited either the dollar amounts they will pay or the number of sessions they will cover in a calendar year, most low-income clients are now effectively excluded and private therapy has become "a rich person's" privilege.

The poor are required to seek therapy in understaffed mental health centers that use minimally trained persons as therapists and fill the gaps with prescription drugs. Some therapists do offer a sliding scale or reduced rate if you don't have insurance, but you have to ask for it and then negotiate an affordable fee.

The use of pathological terminology. The practice of collecting third-party payments from insurance companies encourages therapists to look at what is "wrong" with their clients and give them diagnoses of pathology. The criteria for some diagnostic categories are vague and subjective, so that one psychotherapist may assign a certain diagnosis, while another therapist may find an entirely different "disease" in the same person. These diagnoses do affect the course of payment by insurance companies and can directly affect the course of treatment, particularly in prescribing medications.

The misuse of diagnoses. These diagnoses can easily get into clients' health records, which therapists are often required to release to employers or other health care providers. In other words, these diagnoses of apparent pathology can easily fall into the hands of people who do not understand what they mean, or who might be influenced when they determine the cost of these individuals' insurance payments. Moreover, people can be refused work promotions because of a "questionable" diagnosis in their personnel file.

For these reasons, many business and professional people prefer to pay for therapy out of their own pockets even though they have good health insurance coverage. This is especially true in the military. Any reference in a personnel record to a diagnosis of a mental disorder can be the kiss of death when it comes to promotions, and can even result in a less than honorable discharge. This leads to an overemphasis on denying emotional problems and a reliance on counter-dependent behaviors to look good.

DEVELOPMENTAL PROCESS WORK: A NEW THERAPEUTIC APPROACH

As part of the application of our Developmental Systems Theory over the past twenty years, we have created an intervention approach that we call Developmental Process Work. It's a short-term therapy approach for working with individuals, couples, and families who seek therapeutic help to overcome the effects of counter-dependent or co-dependent relationship problems. In using it with clients who have co-dependent and counter-dependent behaviors, we discovered that many of them can move quickly into more functional lives with focused, short-term therapy. This also extends to people who apply our Developmental Systems Theory in schools, churches, and businesses as Developmental Process Consultants. Our approach is based on the following basic assumptions:

There is a certain "rightness" about your symptoms. We look at the symptoms present in a person, couple, family, or organization as unskilled attempts to evolve. We help you see that whatever is trying to happen in any system is right, in some larger way, and the way you are approaching your problems is the best way you know how, given what you've learned.

Delayed development is caused by unhealed trauma. Trauma creates patterns or loops of behavior that are anchored in traumatic reenactment, and that keep you stuck in co-dependent and counter-dependent behavior.

You, the client, know more about your process than we will ever know. Our job is to follow your process in order to help you identify the sources of your co-dependent and counter-dependent behaviors. This places the power for change in your possession.

You, the client, are in charge of how fast you want to move. The therapist or consultant must adjust to your natural pace of assimilating and integrating emotionally charged material to facilitate problem-solving and change. This respects your boundaries and allows you to maintain personal power.

Your current conflicts and problems are the result of trauma and incomplete developmental processes from childhood. By understanding what processes you should have completed in childhood, you can find the source of your current conflicts and problems. The source is likely a trauma or set of traumas that occurred sometime in the first three years of your life.

Incomplete developmental processes from childhood continue to recycle in your life until they are completed. Your therapist or consultant can help you discover your patterns and then suggest ways you might meet these needs now.

It is never too late to meet your childhood developmental needs. Your therapist's or consultant's job is to help you clear traumas from your sensory system and to teach you skills that help you meet these needs in intimate relationships.

Therapy or consultation should consist of short-term written contracts. These contracts should specify that you will undertake three to six sessions for individual or couples therapy, or full-day sessions each week for three to six months when consulting with organizations, to work on specific problems. Group therapy contracts should be limited to eight to ten sessions. These contracts should be evaluated at the end of the specified number of sessions before your therapist or consultant decides to do further work with you.

We've found it's possible to teach therapeutic skills to nonprofessionals, who can then help others who don't have professional help available. Certain skills that therapists or consultants must have in order to be effective with this approach can be taught to your intimate partner, friends, family members, employees, or company policy makers to use in nontherapeutic settings. We've listed the key therapy and consultation skills in the sidebar "Using the Developmental Process Work Approach to Therapy and Consultation."

USING THE DEVELOPMENTAL PROCESS WORK APPROACH TO THERAPY AND CONSULTATION

- Therapists and consultants should be able to model energetically what they are able to do with you or an organization. They should be able to serve as a personal example of what they hope to help you become.

- Therapists and consultants should be able to listen for verbal signals and watch for nonverbal signals that reveal the presence of incomplete developmental processes, and then give specific concrete examples of what they hope you will learn to do on your own.

- Therapists and consultants must avoid leading you and taking away your personal power by giving advice or by asking questions. They must give you feedback, which tells you how well they are paying attention to your needs.

- Therapists and consultants must teach you how to recognize incomplete developmental processes that are causing dysfunction in your relationships or organization.

- Therapists and consultants must avoid interjecting solutions and trying to fix things too quickly.

- Therapists and consultants must teach you how to look for clues to identify unhealed traumas contained in your verbal and nonverbal behaviors.

- Therapists and consultants must provide you with a "toolbox" of techniques and activities that help you access personal information or information outside of your conscious awareness about incomplete developmental processes from your childhood.

- Therapists and consultants must teach you how to make effective contracts with yourself and others to meet your needs and to complete your developmental processes from the past.

We discovered that Developmental-Process-Work therapy and consultation can facilitate major changes in three to six sessions of individual or couples therapy and three to six months of work in organizations. During this short period, most of our clients learn how to recognize the developmental sources of the problems they have brought to the attention of the therapist, and they learn new skills that help them change their counter-dependent or co-dependent behaviors.

Self-directed and motivated clients who make the most progress in therapy have support available from spouses, friends, or support groups who help them integrate their therapy experiences. Longer-term therapy or developmental process consultation may be useful for people who aren't as self-directed, who have less emotional support outside of therapy, or who have severe early childhood traumas. Longer-term therapy is often necessary for those with the severe co-dependent behaviors characteristic of borderline personality disorder, or the severe counter-dependent behaviors characteristic of narcissistic personality disorder. Organizations can suffer from similar dysfunctions. In these cases, long-term consultation may be necessary to create lasting change. However, many individuals with co-dependent and counter-dependent behaviors are misdiagnosed as belonging in these more pathological categories, primarily because of the therapists' or consultants' lack of experience or their desire to prolong their contracts.

IS COUNTER-DEPENDENCY A DISEASE
OR NOT A DISEASE?

The following chart lists some of the classic symptoms of love and sex addiction (left-hand column) and possible developmental explanations for each of these behaviors (right-hand column).

Characteristics of a Love or Sex Addict	Incomplete Developmental Processes Involved
Constantly obsesses about finding sex	Seeks unconditional love and connectedness missed during childhood
Uses compulsive sex like a drug	Wants to avoid traumatic childhood feelings, such as sadness, grief, anger, or fear, that are anchored in abandonment or betrayal
Believes that sex is the only way to be intimate	Needs nonsexual touch and nurturing; may have been sexually abused as a child
Uses sex to feel validated and affirmed	Seeks the mirroring or positive affirmations he or she lacked as a child
Searches for magical qualities in others, which makes the addict feel special by association	Seeks unconditional love and acceptance missed in childhood
Uses sex to bring excitement and intensity into his or her life without having to admit to having unmet needs	Generates adrenaline to help avoid feelings and to avoid reexperiencing the traumatic memories from childhood
Is drawn to people who are not available	Is attracted to people who remind him or her of the unavailable parents
Fears abandonment and rejection in intimate relationships	Replays childhood betrayal, abandonment, and abuse and acts out the need for experiences of deep bonding
Feels empty and lonely when not in a relationship	Had poor bonding in childhood, but is afraid of appearing needy and dependent
Tries to lose himself or herself in romantic obsessions	Projects his or her need for the nurturing and unconditional love missed in childhood, particularly from the mother
Has unhealthy dependent relationships that leave him or her feeling trapped	Lacked secure bonding as a child; gives up self in hopes of gaining love and doesn't know how to be emotionally separate

Traditional methods for treating people with addictive sexual behaviors use the disease concept to reassure clients that there is nothing morally wrong with them, that they are just "sick." Patrick Carnes writes, "The illness concept helps affirm the personal worth of the addict. . . . Furthermore, realizing that one has an illness decreases the shame of being out of control."[10]

Our Developmental-Process-Work approach says that sexual-addiction behaviors are anchored in developmental trauma. Which would you rather be told: "You have an illness from which you may not recover," or "You have trauma that you can clear, one that left you with unmet needs that you can learn to meet." The latter is obviously a more empowering and hopeful vision of recovery.

As we stated earlier, in order to relieve guilt, the disease approach reassures you that you have done nothing immoral. However, the approach does reinforce feelings of shame.[11] Even though the disease approach relieves guilt, it ultimately traps you in the shame of your addictions. Our developmental approach avoids this by reframing the cause of your problems.

Because this is an imperfect world, there's a good chance that you'll encounter therapists or consultants with co-dependent or counter-dependent behaviors who haven't worked through their own unfinished business from childhood. In order to avoid a "diseasing" relationship with your therapist or consultant, we suggest taking the following steps.

- Interview at least three therapists or consultants before starting therapy or a consultation to determine which one makes you feel the most comfortable. Many therapists or consultants offer free introductory sessions.
- Use the inventory at the end of this chapter to examine therapists or consultants for "diseasing" tendencies.
- Ask your therapist or consultant what he or she has done to deal with his or her own co-dependent or counter-dependent patterns. If you meet with resistance to your questions, seek another therapist or consultant.
- Ask to set up specific written goals.
- Ask your therapist or consultant for references from former or present clients you can speak to about the results they have achieved. While most therapists or consultants will claim this is confidential information, some may have clients who have completed their therapy and who are willing to share their experiences.

- If you enter therapy or a consultation process and are not satisfied with the results you are achieving, talk directly with your therapist or consultant about your needs. If you do not get a supportive response, it's time to terminate your work with them.

HAS YOUR THERAPIST LABELED YOU AS "DISEASED"?

Many therapists or consultants are comfortable with the medical model that allows them to be in control and keeps clients diseased and diagnosed as co-dependent. The following inventory may help you identify "diseasing" tendencies in your current or prospective therapist or consultant.

SELF-QUIZ

Does My Therapist or Consultant Use the Disease Model?

DIRECTIONS: Place a number in the blank before each statement to indicate the degree to which this statement is true in your experience.

1 = Never   2 = Occasionally   3 = Frequently   4 = Almost always

Does your therapist or consultant
_____ talk too much in your sessions?
_____ need to look good and have all the right answers?
_____ ask leading questions without telling you why?
_____ seem overworked and exhausted?
_____ sit in his or her "special chair"?
_____ let sessions run overtime?
_____ take credit for your progress?
_____ refuse to acknowledge or work on his or her own co-dependency or counter-dependency issues?
_____ take phone calls during your sessions?
_____ use professional jargon and try to intimidate you by using special terms?
_____ get defensive when you ask questions or give negative feedback?
_____ give you fee reductions to make you seem special?
_____ tell you what you are doing wrong rather than how to improve?
_____ seem formal or distant in sessions?

_____ wear clothing that seems to set him or her above you?

_____ use disease-oriented diagnostic terms to describe your problem to you?

_____ act threatened if you want to interview other professionals or get a second opinion?

_____ set the goals of therapy or consultation for you?

_____ have unclear or open-ended therapy or consulting contracts that leave the length and goals of the therapy undetermined?

_____ get very upset if you have to change a scheduled session?

_____ Total score

SCORING: Add up the column of numbers to find your score. Use the following guidelines to interpret it.

20–40 The disease model has had little or no damaging effect on the therapeutic or consulting relationship. Very little evidence of the disease model is present.

41–60 The disease model has had some damaging effects on the therapeutic or consulting relationship. The therapist or consultant has some tendency to see clients as diseased.

61–80 The disease model has had many possibly damaging effects on the therapeutic or consulting relationship.

THE BOTTOM LINE

- There are empowering approaches to recovery that use an established set of effective principles and practices.
- Labeling addictions as diseases disempowers people and interferes with their recovery.
- A developmental view of addictions recognizes them as traumatic reenactments and attempts to avoid feelings anchored in uncleared developmental trauma.
- Choose your therapist or consultant carefully after first interviewing several. Ask them questions to assure that you will find safe and effective help.

5. The Counter-dependent Culture

*There are a number of signs that we in America
may be on the threshold of a period as a nation
when we shall no longer be able to
camouflage or repress our despair.*

— Rollo May

Each day seems to bring more news of the disintegrating fabric of our American way of life. We experience economic downturns, war and threats of terrorism, racial unrest, growing levels of air and water pollution, the breakdown of family structures, the loss of constitutional freedoms, and a resurgence in the repression of human rights. And we experience or read about new examples of shameless corporate greed and graft; more scandals in high-level political offices; deteriorating highways, cities, and other kinds of infrastructure; growing numbers of homeless individuals and families; a rise in the number of violent crimes; and an epidemic of people using addictions to mask their feelings about the decline in the quality of life.

The list of problems is so large that just thinking about their magnitude can be overwhelming and traumatizing. It's easy to become immobilized with fear or anxiety and to feel like a helpless, hopeless victim, for it seems as though the whole world is on the verge of collapsing. It's much easier to escape into denial through addictions than to face the truth: something is dreadfully wrong in the world.

The external world is both contributing to and reflecting back our inner states of chaos and confusion. Addressing your wounds and the addictions you've used to deny your inner chaos can make you truly live "one day at a time." Sometimes the personal process of breaking free from counter-dependent behaviors can catapult you back into a child's reality and make you feel less able to cope with the chaos in the outer world. It is the express intent of this book to provide you with an empowering framework for addressing both the internal and the external chaos in your life — one that will help you create functional relationship patterns and improve the quality of your life.

This task requires a larger context not only for understanding your addictions but also for understanding how your unresolved co-dependent and counter-dependent issues can help create problems in the world. This chapter is about that larger context.

DEVELOPMENTAL SYSTEMS THEORY:
APPLYING OUR DEVELOPMENTAL MODEL TO THE WORLD

We created the Developmental Systems Theory to map the evolution of consciousness in human systems. During our research over the past twenty years, we have applied our four-stage model to all human systems and have shown that they all go through the same four developmental stages that individuals go through. In this chapter, we apply our theory to couple relationships, families, organizations, and cultures, to the United States and other nations, and to the whole human species. This helps you see yourself and your problems in a broader perspective.

> You feel more connected to others when you realize that the whole world is working on the same developmental issues and problems that you have.

The following two tables describe the developmental processes that we have mapped out at each of the six levels of human systems.[1]

THE DEVELOPMENTAL STAGES AND ESSENTIAL DEVELOPMENTAL PROCESSES: MICROSYSTEMS

Stage of Development/ Primary Process	Essential Developmental Processes of Individual Evolution	Essential Developmental Processes of Couple Evolution	Essential Developmental Processes of Family Evolution
Co-dependency **Bonding**	• **The Mother** has good prenatal care **The child:** • experiences nonviolent birth and interventions to heal birth trauma • experiences consistent, secure bonding with parents • experiences secure bonding with immediate family • builds a secure internal working model of self/others • develops primal trust through consistent, resonant connections with parents • develops emotional resiliency skills • builds healthy emotional communication and social engagement skills with parents and others	**The couple:** • creates secure and consistent bonding experiences with each other • establishes deep primal trust in each other • develops ways to quickly repair any disruptions to couple resonance • establishes good communication and social engagement skills with each other • establishes an identity as a couple	**The family:** • creates secure bonding experiences between parents and children • establishes primal trust between family members • establishes healthy emotional communication and social engagement skills among family members • establishes an identity as a family

THE DEVELOPMENTAL STAGES AND ESSENTIAL DEVELOPMENTAL PROCESSES: MICROSYSTEMS (*continued*)

Stage of Development/ Primary Process	Essential Developmental Processes of Individual Evolution	Essential Developmental Processes of Couple Evolution	Essential Developmental Processes of Family Evolution
Counter-dependency Separation	The child: • completes psychological separation from parents • bonds with extended family • resolves internal conflicts between oneness and separateness • develops healthy narcissism • learns to trust and regulate thoughts, feelings, and behaviors in socially appropriate ways • completes the psychological birth to become an individual	Members of the partnership: • become functionally separate individuals in the relationship • identify and accept individual differences in thoughts, feelings, and behaviors in each other • resolve internal conflicts between needs of self and other • develop effective win-win ways to resolve conflicts between wants, needs, values, and beliefs	• Parents and children learn to assert their individual needs and have them supported by other family members The family: • uses fair, equitable, and nonshaming methods of limit-setting and discipline • resolves conflicts effectively between needs of parents and needs of children
Independence Mastery	The child or individual: • masters self-care • masters functional autonomy from parents • masters object constancy • masters effective social engagement skills • develops core personal values and beliefs • bonds with peers	Members of the partnership: • master self-sufficiency within the relationship • develop autonomy within the couple relationship The couple: • develops core values and beliefs as a couple • achieves object constancy as a couple	The family: • develops individual and couple autonomy within the family structure • develops core values and beliefs as a family • achieves object constancy as a family • bonds with nature as a family

	The child or individual:	Members of the partnership:	The family:
Inter-dependence Cooperation	• learns to cooperate with others • learns to negotiate to meet needs • learns to accept responsibility for personal behavior and life experiences • develops a social conscience • bonds securely with peers and other adults • bonds securely with own children • understands the influence of incomplete developmental processes on one's life and how to heal developmental traumas • bonds securely with the culture	• learn to cooperate with each other in getting important needs met in the relationship • experience the deepest human connection possible with each other • develop equality in the relationship • cooperate to help each other heal developmental traumas • cooperate to develop each member's fullest human potential	• builds consensus among family members • learns to cooperate so all important needs are met • creates rituals that sustain a spiritual dimension in the family • creates divisions of labor based on individual interests and abilities • cooperates to help each other heal developmental traumas • cooperates to develop each member's fullest potential as a human being

THE DEVELOPMENTAL STAGES AND ESSENTIAL DEVELOPMENTAL PROCESSES: MACROSYSTEMS

Stage of Development/ Primary Process	Essential Developmental Processes of an Organization	Essential Developmental Processes of a Culture or a Nation-State	Essential Developmental Processes of the Human Race
Co-dependency **Bonding**	• Creates bonding experiences for employees • Builds trust between employers and employees • Creates an organizational identity • Provides for the basic needs of employees and managers • Fosters healthy emotional communication and social engagement skills between employees and employers • Builds an organizational esprit de corps	• Creates bonding experiences that unify all subcultures around common values and practices • Builds trust between the leaders and the citizens • Creates a national identity • Establishes healthy emotional communication and social engagement skills for all citizens • Provides opportunities for all citizens to meet their basic needs • Builds a national esprit de corps	• Bonds securely with the world of nature • Creates a connection with the supernatural • Establishes an identity as a species • Develops right-brain functions within the individual

Counter-dependency *Separation*	• Supports employees as they assert their needs; takes them seriously • Identifies and promotes the unique contributions of each employee to the organization • Uses fair, equitable, and nonshaming methods of limit-setting with employees • Establishes rules and policies in equitable ways • Resolves internal conflicts between the needs of employees and the needs of employers • Understands the influence of incomplete developmental processes on work performance and provides ways to heal developmental traumas at work	• Supports all citizens as they assert their needs; takes them seriously • Guarantees freedom of expression and protects minority and cultural rights • Identifies and promotes the unique contributions of every citizen to the nation • Establishes fair, equitable, and nondiscriminating laws and national policies • Uses the rule of law to provide equal justice for all citizens • Identifies the unique strengths of cultures and the nation • Develops effective ways to resolve conflicts between the needs of cultural groups and between nations • Understands the influence of incomplete developmental processes on national health and provides ways to heal developmental traumas of all citizens	• Explores ways to become functionally separate from nature • Establishes diversity in the species • Develops left-brain functions within the individual • Creates separate nation-states • Creates religions that are based on the supernatural and separate from nature • Resolves conflicts between nations and religions

	THE DEVELOPMENTAL STAGES AND ESSENTIAL DEVELOPMENTAL PROCESSES: MACROSYSTEMS (continued)			
Stage of Development / Primary Process	Essential Developmental Processes of an Organization	Essential Developmental Processes of a Culture or a Nation-State	Essential Developmental Processes of the Human Race
Independence / **Mastery**	• Creates an organizational culture with mutually determined values and beliefs • Supports individual autonomy within the organizational structure • Gives employees responsibility for self-regulation of emotion and self-care • Fosters employees' true pride in their work • Provides specialized training and development for each employee to enhance individual contributions to the organization	• Creates a national culture that honors and protects diversity of all cultures • Creates an economic and social safety net for those in need • Guarantees the voting rights of all citizens • Gives citizens responsibility for self-regulation of emotion and self-care • Fosters true cultural and national pride among citizens	• Reunites with the world of nature as partners • Develops whole-brain thinking functions and "both/and" thinking • Creates individual cultures • Celebrates the diversity between cultures • Resolves conflicts of needs between cultures • Provides for the basic needs of all citizens • Develops systemic thinking
Inter-dependence / **Cooperation**	• Creates organizations run cooperatively by employees and employers • Utilizes team-building activities • Promotes cooperation-building between teams • Creates rituals that build and sustain employee morale • Creates divisions of labor based on individual interests and abilities • Fosters cooperation among employees to develop each person's fullest potential as a human being	• Cooperates to create three interdependent and balancing branches of government with equal power to govern • Cooperates to build consensus between cultural groups and between nations • Cooperates to create meaningful national rituals that build and sustain citizen morale • Creates equal opportunities for all citizens to develop their fullest potential	• Establishes a planetary partnership culture based on cooperation and respect for differences • Develops the global brain • Develops transsystemic thinking

Our extended consulting trips in Russia and Ukraine, and our experiences while living, studying, and working for seven months in Switzerland and then in Slovakia, helped us recognize the larger developmental picture. When we visited private homes in the former Soviet republics, we found ourselves deeply immersed in a culture that is quite different from ours. Our experiences there helped us look more deeply at our model for understanding individual development. As we did this, our perspective deepened, broadening and shifting our focus. We began to understand the world more clearly and to see the relationship between the evolution of the consciousness of an individual and the evolution of the human race as a whole.

A Systems Perspective of Counter-dependency

Seeing the relationship between the "micro" (the individual) and the "macro" (large human systems) is useful, for it helps you find your place in the universe. If you can see that common patterns of behavior replay at each interlocking subsystem level of the larger system, then you will better understand that everything operates on the same developmental principles, whether at the individual level, the couple level, the family level, the institutional level, the national level, or the international level. When you can view development in this way, your world expands and, at the same time, appears less complex and more sensible. Viewing the total development of human consciousness in this way helps remove the myopia of the moment and provides you with an expanded vision of human possibilities. Let's apply the four-stage model of development to the couple relationship.

A Relationship Perspective

When two people create an intimate relationship, there is a period of symbiosis and closeness. During this period, which parallels the co-dependent stage of individual development, bonding is the primary developmental process.

Depending on how conscious a couple is about recognizing they have an opportunity to complete gaps in their individual bonding, and depending on how willing they are to risk sharing their incomplete-bonding issues, they may or may not be able to clear away early developmental trauma so that they can meet their unmet bonding needs. At some point in the relationship, one or both members will begin to move away from intimacy. One person may decide to explore the world outside the relationship by getting involved in new activities or by developing auxiliary relationships. Or one member may become frightened or feel suffocated by the intimacy and want to flee from it by creating some physical and psychological space.

These conflicting pulls between oneness and separateness occur almost daily in most relationships, particularly those of people who lack the awareness or the skills needed to handle these conflicts. Without the awareness that the desire for some individuation is a normal developmental process, people in intimate relationships may try to individuate in destructive ways by having affairs, feeling victimized by their partners, complaining to others about their partners' shortcomings, escaping into addictions, withdrawing emotionally, or even separating or divorcing. If they want to build a sustainable relationship, couples must address the incomplete developmental process of individuation that naturally takes place during the counter-dependent stage of development.

If both parties in a relationship are aware of the feelings of fear or anxiety that accompany the normal need to individuate, and are committed to addressing them, then the individuation process becomes an opportunity for mutual growth that supports sustainability. For this to happen, both parties must understand the developmental stages and create a common, cooperative vision of reaching the stages of independence and interdependence while they work through any incomplete issues related to individuation. Doing so is almost impossible unless they understand the developmental sources of such issues and have learned good conflict resolution skills (see chapter 11 for a discussion of conflict resolution skills).

A Family Perspective

Families also replay these same developmental stages. Family bonding begins when children arrive. They begin to develop a cohesiveness parallel to the co-dependent stage of individual development. The school years, when the children gradually separate from the parents, parallel the counter-dependent stage of individual development. The college years, when the children live independently but still receive some financial support, parallel the independent stage of individual development. The empty-nest years, when children and parents can negotiate various degrees of closeness and separateness, parallel the interdependent stage of individual development.

When people are unaware that families go through these developmental processes, they often get stuck in the counter-dependent stage. Here family members may try ineffective ways of resolving the separation issues. They may play out the drama triangle, sink into victim consciousness, and expect to be rescued by another family member or someone outside the family. Parents may attempt to hold on to their children too long, causing the children to act out in rebellious ways in order to become separate.

A Religious Perspective

The history behind the settlement of the United States reveals why counter-dependent behavior is so prevalent in this country. We traced the roots of this phenomenon in the religious history of Europe. Most of the Europeans who came to this country in the beginning did so because they wanted to separate from mainstream (parental) religions and were being persecuted as religious dissenters.

Organized Christianity, which began with the Church of Rome, united Christians under the umbrella of the Roman Catholic Church. This unity, which parallels the co-dependent stage of individual development, lasted until the Protestant Reformation, when many religious dissenter groups formed the Lutheran, Anglican, Greek Orthodox, and Russian Orthodox churches.

The process of fragmentation became a generalized movement in religion as the Lutheran Church grew into Protestantism. Then, as the Protestant Reformation movement developed, other subgroups formed, such as the Methodists, Presbyterians, and Baptists. This splintering process in religion, which is one of differentiation and separation, parallels the counter-dependent stage of individual development. Many Europeans felt victimized when they were persecuted as religious dissenters and chose to reject the prevailing religious dogma. Their subsequent choice to leave their countries and emigrate in large numbers as Quakers, Pilgrims, Puritans, and Mennonites extended the separation process.

In reviewing this history, it's possible to see how European emigrants used the common and ineffective ways of separating from their homelands, which caused their personal development to stagnate. Most of the religious emigrants separated from their religions and their religions' leaders by viewing them as bad organizations and individuals. Determining that a person or group is bad or wrong in order to separate from them never works. Because these emigrants did not leave their early religions or home countries feeling "I'm okay for wanting to separate, and you're okay for staying behind," they brought their victim consciousness to this country — and it has been played out here repeatedly.

For example, the Puritans ended up persecuting their members who wanted the religious beliefs of the group to evolve, just as they or their ancestors had been persecuted in Europe. This religious persecution forced some to emigrate to other settlements, just as they or their ancestors had fled Europe. Much of U.S. expansion across the continent occurred because people kept separating from something they saw as "bad." Most wars in the world have been fought over differences between various religious groups, and they reflect the victim consciousness present in unresolved counter-dependency issues between various religious groups all over the world.

A Political Perspective

European political dissenters carried their political ideals of freedom, liberty, and justice for all to America. So strong was their need to differentiate, to break free of restrictive religious or political rules, that they relinquished their homes, vocations, and historical and family roots for a wilderness life of hardship in an unknown continent thousands of miles away. Eventually, they established a system of government that separated politics and religion in order to prevent persecution of individuals for their religious beliefs. These European immigrants initially settled the coastline east of the Appalachian Mountains, living first in separate colonies.

By the time this area had incorporated into thirteen colonies, many residents had already begun to bristle at the restrictive laws and move westward. Some who left were drawn by the promise of free fertile land or wealth from gold and silver strikes. Others just didn't like the restrictions that grew out of close contact with neighbors and wanted more space and freedom, or they sought adventure. The human urge for wealth, freedom, space, and adventure spawned a westward movement in the United States that propelled people to the Pacific coastline. When no more unsettled space remained in the West, people headed for the Alaskan frontier. As Alaska became more densely populated, Americans created spaceships and headed for the moon and outer space.

We can see how strong this drive for freedom and separation is in the United States. All wars fought on our own soil were fought over the issues of freedom and independence. A central issue of the Revolutionary War was colonists' desire to separate from the British Empire, while the Civil War was fought, in part, over the right of African American people to be free from slavery.

Americans have fought elsewhere, too, for freedom and independence and the right to be self-governing. The United States got involved in both World War I and World War II to stop the aggressive governments of Germany and Japan from threatening and occupying other countries. The United States did not enter World War II, however, until the bombing of Pearl Harbor made the loss of freedom seem personal and imminent.

The need to be separate is still particularly strong in the Appalachian and Rocky Mountains, where the "mountain man" and "Marlboro Man" archetypes are alive and well. In these mountains, people seek remote home sites without the confinements of close neighbors or restrictive zoning laws. In California, counter-dependency is evidenced by the custom of "one person, one car." In fact, many Americans consider ride sharing and public transportation to be restrictions on their personal freedom. They highly value their ability to come and go as they please. They view coordinating schedules with other people and waiting for a bus or train as a loss of their individual rights and personal freedom.

An International Perspective

The collapse of the USSR into fifteen republics is an excellent contemporary example of individuation happening at the international level. Many residents of the republics felt victimized by the suffocating domination of "Mother Russia" and expressed a desire to have their own government, defense system, economic system, culture, and language. Their move toward separation and autonomy ended a long period of nationhood, during which a totalitarian government ruled the residents of these republics in a co-dependent manner. Communism supported symbiosis, dependency, powerlessness, and helplessness, and it penalized any individual initiative. The citizens of these fifteen republics, made up of many religious and ethnic groups and speaking more than one hundred languages, had been forced to adopt a common language (Russian) and to give up their religious and ethnic histories in favor of a single political, social, economic, and cultural system known as Communism.

Mikhail Gorbachev instituted policies of glasnost (openness) and perestroika (restructuring) during the mid-1980s, which supported people's inner desire and developmental drive for differentiation, freedom, individuation, and separation. Unfortunately, these policies also made the Russian leaders into the bad guys in order to effect the separation. This made it more difficult for the new republics to create democratic governments that support the development of independence and, ultimately, interdependence. In their quest to become more Western, they adopted more counter-dependent behaviors and discounted some of their highly effective social policies, such as family leave and universal medical care.

Most of the developing nations of the world have economic, social, and political systems that encourage co-dependent behaviors in their citizens, and most of the developed nations still have systems that encourage counter-dependent behaviors. There are many economic, social, and political problems in the world today that seem to require independent and interdependent solutions. As we become better at creating independent and interdependent solutions at a personal level, we will become better at creating them at national and international levels. The foundation of the European Union is one example of an attempt at an interdependent solution.

An Evolutionary Perspective

Looking at human development from an evolutionary view helps to identify repeating patterns of behavior. Anthropologist Gregory Bateson describes this phenomenon as "the pattern that connects."[2] In biology, the phenomenon of repeating patterns was once described as "ontogeny recapitulates phylogeny," an idea first formulated by the German zoologist Ernst Haeckel in the late nineteenth century. In this concept, the development of a human fetus repeats the biological history of the whole human species as it starts from a single cell and moves through all the stages of development in animal evolution (amphibian, reptilian, mammalian). Cell biologist Bruce Lipton says that we are moving out of the reptilian stages of development and consciousness and into the mammalian stages, where nurturing, partnership, and cooperation are becoming more evident.[3]

Riane Eisler's *The Chalice and the Blade* describes a prehistoric culture that she calls the "partnership society."[4] Characteristics of this society correlate with the co-dependent stage of human development: a strong attachment to the (mother) earth, dependency on the (mother) earth, and the inability to see oneself as separate from the (mother) earth. The early peoples of this period were primarily hunters and gatherers who wandered from one place to another to find food. About 3,500 BC, the hunters and gatherers began to settle down. At this time they began to cluster in villages, where they domesticated animals and learned to grow crops. The point that many cultural historians cite as the beginning of the end of this co-dependent era is the point at which humans first put the plow into the earth. Instead of feeling victimized, they now wished to dominate.

The formation of villages and nation-states can be seen as part of the drive for humans to separate from each other and from the earth. Inside this movement is a desire to dominate the earth and make it grow food. This movement included a gradual drive to dominate women, neighboring villages, nation-states, and anything that threatened the survival of the governing group or system. In our current culture, humans use technology, war, and violence to help keep themselves separate from each other and from Mother Earth. Eisler describes this culture as a dominator society. The contemporary "I'll show you I don't need you" attitude toward the (mother) earth, and reactionary, rebellious behaviors that peril the very existence of the human species, parallel the attitude and behaviors of two-year-old children, who are in the throes of the counter-dependency stage.

The characteristics of the emerging partnership society that Eisler describes correlate with those of the independent and interdependent stages of human development. This partnership society and the independent and interdependent stages are all characterized by cooperation, egalitarian intimate relationships, connectedness, unity, and cocreation. The following chart looks at the evolutionary history of the early partnership society, the dominator society, and the emerging partnership society and shows how they parallel the stages of individual development in humans.

Being able to recognize and acknowledge the presence of an evolutionary or developmental force at work in the world removes some of the helplessness, powerlessness, and victimhood that we may feel when we see the world through the lens of counter-dependency. This larger view focuses our attention back on ourselves. To change a culture, the nation, or the world, we must change ourselves. This means confronting and breaking free of victim consciousness that keeps us stuck in counter-dependency. When enough people have successfully completed their counter-dependent stage of development, the counter-dependent culture will change. This evolutionary perspective is embedded in the saying "Think globally, act locally."

EARLY PARTNERSHIP SOCIETY	DOMINATOR SOCIETY	EMERGING PARTNERSHIP SOCIETY
• Co-dependent	• Counter-dependent	• Interdependent
• Sensory understanding of the world based on physical senses	• Mental understanding of the world based on Newtonian physics	• Spiritual understanding of the world based on quantum physics
• Tribalism	• Egoism, individualism	• Collectivism
• Humans in harmony with other humans	• Humans dominate other humans	• Humans cocreate with other humans
• God exists in nature	• God exists in heaven	• God exists inside us
• Humans are in harmony with nature	• Humans dominate nature	• Humans cocreate with nature
• Tribalism: a local focus on problems	• Nationalism: a national focus on problems	• Globalism: worldwide focus on problems
• Decentralization: nomadic tribes, hunting and gathering	• Centralization: cities, agriculture, technology, hierarchical management	• Decentralization: an ecology of diverse cultures, appropriate technology, self-organizing, community
• Superstition	• Rationalism	• Mysticism
• Earth rituals, rites, and sacred sites	• Churches and religious structures	• Cocreating with the gods
• Undifferentiated unity	• Separateness and alienation	• Connectedness; unity in diversity
• Undiscovered Self	• Denial of the Self	• Fulfillment of the Self
• Sensorimotor and preoperational thinking	• Preoperational and concrete operational thinking	• Formal operational and unitary operational thinking
• Material world rules the mind	• Matter and mind dualism	• Mind creates matter
• Education-supported survival	• Education used for socialization and controlling consciousness	• Education used for transformation and raising consciousness
		• Voluntary simplicity
		• Belief in wise use of resources and doing more with less

REDEFINING FREEDOM: A CRITICAL TASK

Even the concept of freedom has become entangled in counter-dependent behavior and co-dependent thinking. For adults with unresolved counter-dependent issues, freedom is often the freedom from external controls. This kind of thinking is common among Americans, who have a strong drive for freedom from persecution, repression, restriction, and bondage. This definition of freedom, however, keeps us stuck in victimhood with unresolved counter-dependent issues created by our perception that they are caused by something outside ourselves. This enables us to rebel against the authority figures that we perceive are victimizing us. While this definition helps us develop a false cultural sense of individualism, it also keeps us separate and isolated, creates competition, sets up opportunities for domination, emphasizes differences, and helps cause wars.

On the other hand, people with unresolved co-dependency issues also want freedom from having to take responsibility for themselves. This "freedom from freedom" perspective keeps us externally focused, so that we remain victims and can blame others when things go wrong. No one can hold a victim responsible, which allows us to use passivity, overadaptation, and enmeshment as coping mechanisms. For example, those with co-dependent behaviors might say that it's impossible to do anything about the high U.S. income taxes rates, because politicians and bureaucrats make all the decisions. This definition of freedom keeps us feeling powerless, inhibits personal autonomy, emphasizes collective conformity, creates individual stagnation, and sets up victimization and learned helplessness.

Neither of these two definitions of freedom, nor the rebellious or blaming attitudes they create, gets us what we want or need. For example, a person with unresolved co-dependency issues expects to be taken care of through extensive retirement pensions, insurance settlements, unemployment benefits, and other programs that address their dependency needs. People with co-dependent behaviors often look to the government as their primary caretaker. A person with unresolved counter-dependent issues may see the government as the main source of economic oppression because of the high taxes it levies on its citizens, rather than looking at his or her own out-of-control spending habits. Neither definition makes us ultimately responsible for taking care of our own needs or for looking at how our personal behavior is part of a larger problem.

A third and more interdependent definition of freedom comes from transforming these two externally focused worldviews. This definition of freedom requires us to understand the Self and psychological independence. We must first look inside ourselves for our power and control and then effectively use it externally by acting responsibly to meet our needs and wants. This gives us the personal freedom to develop effective social skills and act responsibly to help meet our own needs and wants and the needs and wants of others, without interfering with their freedom.

This means, for example, if we have unresolved co-dependent issues, we must learn how to take charge of meeting our own needs. There is no perfect parent out there who will look after them for us. This co-dependent attitude permeates much of the thinking in the New Age movement, in which people believe they can manifest abundance without dealing with their unresolved dependency needs from childhood. This kind of narcissistic thinking, which is characteristic of individuals who have not developed boundaries and learned the lessons of limitation, supports dominator behaviors and overconsumption on a planet with finite resources.

If you have unresolved counter-dependency issues, you must recognize that it is not something outside you ("our evil and oppressive government") that is oppressing you economically. It is more likely the extravagant and often compulsive spender within you (the *internal* source of the problem) that helps create an overspending government. When you decide to live with less and voluntarily simplify your lifestyle (internalizing the responsibility), then you no longer need to identify yourself as a victim or the government as your persecutor. This is another example of how you can change your culture by first changing yourself.

When you have internalized this third view of freedom, you'll be able to recognize that the structure of the outer world reflects your inner world. When you're able to create a healthy balance between these two worlds, you will have found true freedom.

THE COUNTER-DEPENDENCY CRISIS

At this moment in history, it is critical that we recognize the relationship between the psychological development of an individual and the psychological evolution of couples, families, groups and organizations, nation-states, and the human species. Once you can see the parallels among these systems, you can begin to understand the sources of the problems we are facing in the world. You can also see that global solutions must address both the individual and the collective issues of counter-dependency.

Let's look again at typical two-year-olds in the counter-dependent stage of development. Their parents are helping them through the process of ego-reduction, and they are learning to limit their natural narcissistic belief in their omnipotence and to limit their grandiosity, sense of entitlement, and euphoria. Two-year-olds (whether this refers to individuals or a culture) are struggling to separate from their primary caregivers, especially the mother, and to become separate, individuated people. Those who don't fully experience ego reduction and healthy separation become stuck at this stage of development. They demand more than their share of resources and divide the world into good and bad, and all or nothing. They use manipulation, pride, justification, self-centeredness, and addiction to mood-elevating drugs to help maintain control. When confronted with limits to and consequences for their bratty behavior, they have tantrums and fits of rage and want to destroy themselves and those around them, rather than grow up.

Behaviorally, two-year-olds are opposed to anything adults suggest. The underlying theme of a two-year-old's thinking appears to be: "No! I don't need you. I can do it all myself." Power struggles, rebelliousness, egocentrism, outbursts of anger, and the need to be right are typical of the two-year-old struggling to become an emotionally separate human being.

When we juxtapose the two-year-old's counter-dependent behavior patterns with patterns in the history of human evolution, we can see similarities between the two-year-old's behavior and that of contemporary cultures in developed countries. Since humans began their gradual separation process from Mother Earth between five thousand and ten thousand years ago, they have been declaring (unconsciously) to the earth: "I can grow food by myself. I will force you to produce it." This dominating declaration of separation from the Earth Mother has been amplified many times. We find contemporary farmers demanding more and more from the earth with the use of fertilizers, herbicides, insecticides, and other pesticides in an attempt to increase crop yields. U.S. farmers in particular have become a model for developing countries in their continued drive for power, domination, and individual wealth. The use-it-up, throw-it-away behavior of Western peoples is stripping the planet of its natural resources so quickly that the end of many nonrenewable resources is in sight. This has put us at the edge of a global ecological crisis that also has political, economic, social, and evolutionary implications.

It is imperative for us to realize that most of us, as a species and as individuals, are psychologically between two and three years old. We have mature bodies and appear to be adults, but often we relate, react, and behave as small children who believe that we are in control of the world. The implications of this are awesome. On this planet, we currently have enough nuclear weapons to destroy the whole planet many times over. This doesn't account for biological, chemical, or conventional weapons. Can you imagine turning this arsenal over to a two-year-old child whose inflated psyche is filled with anxieties and frustration about separation?

That we are in such a predicament at this moment is sobering. We can no longer view counter-dependency as a medical problem or as a disease. We must look at it as a developmental issue with roots in our early childhood experiences. We must resolve it at the individual level by using specific, inexpensive, and effective tools that allow both the individual and the collective culture to move quickly into independence and interdependency.

CASE EXAMPLE

The United States is an excellent case example of a counter-dependent culture. The highly egocentric behavior of its citizens focuses on material wealth as part of an addictive, consumptive lifestyle in which about 8 percent of the world's population consumes 28 percent of its resources. These cultural behaviors can keep us from having to examine our own values and beliefs and from dealing with the traumatic feelings left from our dysfunctional childhoods.

Our narcissistic need to be free from economic, religious, political, social, and interpersonal limits has been indulged to such an extreme that we in the United States, with our overconsumptive lifestyles, have become the primary cause of global environmental problems.

Our narcissistic collective need for personal comfort, individual wealth, and domination of the environment has set the whole world on a collision course between overconsumption and environmental limits. Television programs exported into developing countries are also exporting cultural expectations that make all world citizens want our consumptive lifestyle. As developing countries attempt to emulate our bad example, we can expect an even greater depletion of natural resources. Global environmental experts such as Lester Brown predict an impoverished planet for our grandchildren unless there is a dramatic reordering of our values and our priorities in order to reduce our consumption and pollution.[5]

Insulated inside our single-family dwellings, our two cars, and our daily job routines, we're able to ignore the shrinking rain forest, the growing hole in the ozone layer, the problems of homeless children and families, AIDS, and the increasing environmental pollution. In spite of the warnings of many scientists, researchers, and futurists, many people in the United States continue to live in denial about the severity of the problem.

It's difficult to reach clients who are absorbed in counter-dependent behaviors, because they have strong narcissistic defenses against self-examination and self-reflection. Intervening too quickly sometimes prevents the needed crisis from coming to a head. Effective therapy with clients requires that the therapist be patient and wait until clients are in a crisis severe enough to break down their defenses and denial and put them on the journey back to wholeness and interdependence. Only then do people (and cultures) with counter-dependent characteristics seem ready to take in new information and begin the process of change.

Unfortunately, the United States too may need a series of collective crises that confront us with our narcissism. We may have to face the loss of our homes, our families, and everything we have worked for, before we break through our denial and begin to deal with the wounds of our childhoods, the problems in our intimate relationships, the dysfunction in our families, and the crises in the world.

Treating a counter-dependent culture is obviously a more complex matter than treating individuals. It requires consultants with information about how large human systems operate and theoretical approaches for facilitating change simultaneously in multiple social and cultural systems. We call such change agents developmental process consultants; they can help identify where they are stuck developmentally and help facilitate change. The job requires broadly trained professionals who are generalists rather than specialists, and who are able to synthesize ideas, information, and tools garnered from many fields of study. It's necessary for these consultants to have done their own personal work and cleared their co-dependent and counter-dependent behavior patterns so that they can work and live at the higher level of consciousness that emerges in the interdependent stage of development. Developmental process consultants must be able to move beyond the individual therapy model so they can work with large groups of people at one time to facilitate collective therapeutic processes. They must also be able to teach by modeling — by walking the walk as they talk their talk.

Once you have developed an evolutionary view of humankind and a developmental view of your own psychological growth, and you have cleared your life of drama built on old traumas, you are on your way to becoming a developmental process consultant. Self-therapy ultimately becomes a form of global therapy.

SELF-QUIZ

The Interdependent Living Inventory

It is necessary to take notice of how we are living our lives. This inventory may help you become more aware of the choices available to you and the choices you are currently making.

DIRECTIONS: Place a number in the blank before each statement to indicate the degree to which the statement is true for you.

1 = Never   2 = Occasionally   3 = Frequently   4 = Almost always

_____ I use natural ventilation instead of air conditioning in my home.

_____ I conscientiously turn out lights when not in use.

_____ I avoid buying and using unnecessary technological gadgets.

_____ I use mass transit or a bicycle to travel whenever possible.

_____ I own a car that gets forty miles per gallon or more.

_____ I eat less meat and more vegetables and grains.

_____ I grow some of my own food.

_____ I separate and recycle newspapers, glass, aluminum, and plastic.

_____ I avoid prepackaged and processed food.

_____ I compost my leaves, grass, and kitchen wastes.

_____ I use only natural herbicides and other natural pesticides on my yard and garden.

_____ I grow drought-resistant landscape plants and avoid extensive lawn watering.

_____ I actively support organizations such as the National Audubon Society and Greenpeace that help preserve the natural ecology.

_____ I do not smoke.

_____ I vote at local, state, and national elections.

_____ I attend personal growth seminars and workshops.

_____ I am a member of a twelve-step group or a personal support group.

_____ I participate regularly in family meetings.

_____ I volunteer for or contribute to a nonprofit social service organization.

_____ I participate in citizen diplomacy activities such as home stays in other countries or having guests from other countries stay in my home.

_____ I speak at least one foreign language.

_____ I write to my state and/or national senators or representatives about my concerns.

_____ Total score

SCORING: Add up the column of numbers to find your score. Use the following guidelines to interpret it.

75–100 High degree of participation as an interdependent citizen
50–74 Moderate degree of participation as an interdependent citizen
25–49 Some participation as an interdependent citizen
0–24 Little participation as an interdependent citizen

THE BOTTOM LINE

- The stages are the same in individual development and in the development of couple relationships, families, organizations, cultures, nation-states, and the whole human species.
- This understanding can help you see your personal struggles in a new way and in a larger context.
- Seeing problems and conflicts in the world from a developmental perspective makes them easier to understand.
- As you complete your unfinished developmental processes left over from childhood, you become better able to understand larger systems and to help them complete these same developmental processes, moving us collectively toward planetary consciousness.

Part 2
PATHWAYS TO INTIMACY

6. The Elements of Breaking Free

Remember always that you have
not only the right to be an individual;
you have an obligation to be one.
You cannot make any useful contribution to life
unless you do this.
— Eleanor Roosevelt

Our developmental approach to breaking free of counter-dependent behaviors recognizes that any development process not completed at the appropriate age is carried forward to the next stage of development. Unmet needs recycle over and over again unconsciously in your relationships as trauma dramas, until they are met.

RECYCLING UNFINISHED BUSINESS

People with counter-dependent behaviors generally have problems with intimacy because they are recycling their incomplete developmental processes for secure bonding and psychological separation left over from early childhood. Because they know they're needy and recognize that something is wrong with this, they try to hide their "neediness" from others and use indirect or covert means to meet their needs. Eliminating these counter-dependent behaviors requires breaking through the protective wall of defenses and learning new skills that open the way to intimacy.

Intimacy is difficult when there are unresolved counter-dependency issues. Close relationships activate all our old traumas, our memories of engulfment, invasion, betrayal, abuse, and manipulation. In other words, all the feelings related to our unfinished business and unmet needs begin to surface when we become close and intimate in a relationship. This is the bad news. The good news is that this is the first step to healing these counter-dependency issues.

The common co-dependent/counter-dependent relationship dynamic creates predictable conflicts over intimacy. Those with unresolved co-dependency issues have an intense need for touch and physical closeness, and they may attract partners with counter-dependent issues. In contrast, those with unresolved counter-dependency issues want intimacy but stay alert for signs of engulfment and quickly erect protective boundaries.

Either way, the stage is set for intense competition and conflict, which results in little authentic intimacy. People with co-dependent issues will actually create conflict when the relationship is not intimate enough. Those with counter-dependent behaviors create conflict when the relationship is too intimate. Much of couple conflict involves a struggle to determine how much intimacy and how much separation partners can tolerate in the relationship.

THE SEARCH FOR INTIMACY

You, like many others, probably learned about intimacy vicariously by watching television and movies, by reading books, magazines, and newspapers, and by listening to popular or country music, because you didn't see much intimacy in your family while you were growing up. Since our culture is filled with distorted and dysfunctional images about authentic intimacy, there is a good chance you learned a lot of misinformation about intimacy.

You may have assumed that only *your* family wasn't very intimate. Because you didn't spend spent a lot of time with other families, you supposed that their lives were peaceful and happy, as in *The Brady Bunch*. When you were old enough to think about sexual relationships, you may have learned about sexual intimacy by watching or reading about the contrived onscreen and offscreen romances of television and film stars.

False images of intimate relationships and family life such as these may have made it difficult to reconcile yourself with the conflict, competition, and fighting present in your day-to-day experiences with family and friends. If you got stuck in black-and-white thinking, you may tend to split your experiences in close relationships

> We need a new definition of intimacy that includes both the good times and the not-so-good times.

into all good or all bad. When your relationship is going well, you may see it as all good ("We'll love each other this way forever"). When there is conflict in the relationship, especially the kind of conflict that brings up childhood issues or intense feelings, then your relationship may look all bad ("It's time to get a divorce"). Neither view is realistic in close relationships.

A NEW DEFINITION OF INTIMACY

If you look more closely at what is trying to happen in a relationship between partners with co-dependent behaviors and counter-dependent behaviors, you'll notice that the partners are often competing to meet their conflicting needs for closeness and separateness. This combination is ideal for activating each person's unmet developmental needs. The person with a co-dependent need for intimacy activates the other person's counter-dependent need for protection from invasion or abuse.

On the other hand, the person with a counter-dependent need for space and safety can activate his or her partner's co-dependent fear of abandonment. Unless the partners understand what is really trying to happen in their relationship, they may head for the divorce court. Partners in a sustainable relationship redefine intimacy and place it in a developmental context that includes healing their incomplete developmental processes.

When we do relationship therapy with parents and children, employees and employers, couples, or siblings, we work together as co-therapists. This provides two outside perspectives on what is happening and prevents the usual feelings of "two-against-one" from developing in pairs of clients. Our first objective as therapists is to identify the incomplete developmental processes from childhood still present in the relationship, as well as each person's unmet needs. Once we do this, we can reframe the clients' issues and help them see how they are using indirect ways to try to meet these needs in the relationship.

The next objective is to help them see the wounded inner child in each other and to develop empathy for the pain this child has experienced. When they are able to do that, a couple is often ready to move to a third step: making an agreement to cooperate and help each other transform the wounds of his or her inner child by contracting for corrective reparenting from each other.

Since we developed this approach in our own personal relationship, we sometimes share our own experiences with our clients. We've taught many of our clients how to reframe their conflicts and helped them develop new ways of healing wounds related to either not enough intimacy or too much of the wrong kind of intimacy. Our approach helps couples develop a kind of intimacy so rich and so deep that we describe it as "touching souls." In the "Troubleshooting" sidebar, we list the essential elements needed to bring more intimacy into your relationships.

TROUBLESHOOTING

What It Takes to Experience More Intimacy in Your Relationship

- Cooperate with your partner to heal your developmental trauma drama through reparenting contracts.
- Tell the truth about who you really are and what your needs really are.
- Share power and find soul-evolving solutions to all conflicts.
- Create abundance by being willing to share your life with your partner on many levels: mental, emotional, spiritual, and physical.
- Negotiate with your partner to meet your needs for closeness and separateness and to create opportunities for becoming interdependent.
- Integrate: see your partner as a complete and separate person with some traits you like and some traits you don't like.
- Be assertive: be willing to ask for what you want 100 percent of the time.

When you're able to expand your definition of intimacy to include these elements, every relationship experience has the potential for intimacy. Your relationship becomes a dance that moves you and your partner from one opportunity for intimacy to another. These are the essential ingredients of an interdependent partnership relationship. We discuss these essential ingredients more fully in chapter 13.

CHANGING YOUR COUNTER-DEPENDENT BEHAVIORS

If you are just beginning your work on your counter-dependent and co-dependent issues, you may wonder, "Where do I begin?" If so, please refer to the Awareness Activity at the end of chapter 2, and the "Step-by-Step Program for Changing Your Counter-dependent Behaviors" at the end of chapter 3. They give you concrete steps to take and show you where you can begin, along with an overview of your longer-term work. You can begin to imagine how to change your counter-dependent behaviors by using a variety of resources. Some of the steps can be done on your own, some work more effectively in therapy, and others work better when you're in a committed relationship or a support group. You'll need to create your own plan for changing your counter-dependent behaviors.

RESOURCES FOR CHANGING YOUR COUNTER-DEPENDENT BEHAVIORS

Working Alone

For someone just beginning the breaking-free process, it may be easier to work alone. Reading books, attending workshops and seminars, and taking time off from work and relationships to do some reflecting and soul-searching are excellent ways to begin working on your issues. Working alone allows a person with counter-dependent behaviors to feel safe from any invasion or prying. In this safe zone, it may be easier for your shadowy side to emerge — the side that may be insecure, vulnerable, wounded, and afraid.

Completing the writing exercises in this book is another excellent way to work alone. You might also keep a journal, write and repeat daily affirmations, and use exercise, such as walking, hiking, running, or bicycling, as an opportunity for reflecting on your feelings, thoughts, and behaviors. While working alone, you can also address the mental aspect of transformation, which helps you to develop an understanding of how the layers of your onion are connected and to see that they reveal early developmental traumas.

Removing the mask of the False Self is an important part of working alone. Here you can look at how your tough "I don't need anybody" stance, which served you so well earlier in your life, may have become a prison that keeps you from the warmth and intimacy you now crave. When you understand what your real needs are, you may be ready to risk changing your behavior.

Working in Support Groups

A person experiencing counter-dependent symptoms who decides to enter a help program may assume he or she is the only person going through such problems. However, outside support is available in either group therapy or twelve-step support groups, both of which can offer excellent opportunities to shed this belief. When people with counter-dependent behavior patterns participate in a group, often the first thing they learn is how similar people are when they remove their masks. Support groups allow people to share their common struggles and can provide a variety of opportunities to clear your counter-dependency issues.

Support groups can also be risky places for people with counter-dependent issues, as they require individuals to let down their defenses in front of other people. Those who take this risk, however, usually discover a source of love and support they've never known before. Thousands of alcoholics and people with other addictions have had such experiences when they attended their first Alcoholics Anonymous or other twelve-step meeting.

Working in Therapy

People with counter-dependency issues often are therapy-phobic, because therapy requires sharing personal issues with a stranger. Life has to get really bad before they finally seek help. Those with counter-dependency issues usually enter therapy feeling scared and vulnerable. Because safety is critical for them, it's important that they find a therapist they can trust. We discussed how to do this in chapter 4. You may want to reread that section before looking for a therapist. Beginning with cognitive therapy may be best for those with counter-dependency issues, as it helps to build the trust necessary for looking at deeper and more emotional issues.

Working in Conscious, Committed, Cooperative Relationships

This type of work requires people with counter-dependency patterns to make a leap of faith. They may feel scared initially because they must become vulnerable and risk being hurt again. For relationships to support change, partners must take the steps listed in the sidebar "Dos and Don'ts of Partnership Relationships."

DOS AND DON'TS OF PARTNERSHIP RELATIONSHIPS

- Do agree to work cooperatively on your relationship issues for six months in order to allow enough time for results.
- Do create together a set of goals to accomplish during this time.
- Do agree to make some changes in yourself or your behavior, if necessary.
- Do commit to learning new communication skills that will help you make this relationship work.
- Do set aside enough time each week to work on your relationship. This is important: if you don't do it, it won't happen.
- Do periodically evaluate how you are doing, and make corrections if necessary.
- Do be truthful with your partner about who you are and what your needs are.
- Do agree to resolve conflicts without using power plays, threats, or manipulation.
- Don't expect it to happen without some planning.
- Don't expect it to work smoothly at first. Be patient and learn how to work on your relationship together.
- Don't try to do too much all at once. Set manageable goals.
- Don't have one foot out the door. Do close the exits by agreeing to stay in the relationship during a contracted period of time and not running away if there is conflict.

Because co-dependent and counter-dependent patterns are caused by relationship dysfunctions, the best place to heal these dysfunctions is in a relationship. You can create many forms of committed, conscious, cooperative relationships where you can begin to work on this healing process, such as those between friends, business partners, or parents and children, or as a couple.

People with counter-dependent patterns need to learn how to be vulnerable and take risks. Rather than remaining guarded about their problems or needs, they must learn to ask for help from others, be less self-centered, and develop empathy for others. Working in a partnership relationship is a great opportunity to teach each other how to develop and sustain intimacy.

SKILLS FOR CREATING INTIMATE RELATIONSHIPS

The development of intimacy requires that people with counter-dependent behaviors learn important communication skills. Recovering the capacity to be intimate is a different process for each person. Learning to be intimate can take considerable time and effort, because it often requires a shift from self-centeredness to other-centeredness. Other steps, such as learning to safely release old or repressed feelings, can require intensive work, considering the strong need for safety and security among counter-dependent individuals. Here are the six essential skills that we teach our clients and students who have problems with their counter-dependent behaviors. We explore each of these skills in depth in separate chapters.

Empathy Training

Empathy is the ability to experience the world the way another person does and to be interested in how he or she thinks, lives, and feels. Empathy is the desire to know others from a place of compassion and caring. This is a big change for a person with counter-dependent issues, who may have learned to gather information about people only as part of his or her need to judge, control, dominate, and defend.

Before people with counter-dependency issues can develop empathy, they must understand why they haven't yet learned this skill. Certain conditions in their families-of-origin made it difficult or unsafe to be empathetic. The key tasks in learning empathy are to release control, give up domination, and break through self-denial.

Boundary Setting

Letting down boundaries is an important part of the process of change for people with counter-dependency issues. As children, they likely experienced violations of their physical, mental, emotional, and spiritual selves, forcing them to erect defensive walls. The biggest issue for people with counter-dependency issues is having too many boundaries or walls. Their need for safety while growing up required them to establish these boundaries to protect them from assault. As a result, they learned to tune out what others have to say. People with counter-dependent patterns often develop thick layers of muscle or fat, which provide a kind of body armor and discourage intimate touch. They may also try to stay in control of situations by telling other people what to feel or not to feel.

The second boundary issue for people with counter-dependency issues involves crossing the boundaries of others. Their aggressive "I'll get them before they get me" tactic is really a disguised defense mechanism that works well in the business world but fails miserably in intimate relationships. Aggressive behavior in intimate relationships helps create conflict and perpetuates the gender battles. The challenge is to develop sufficient protection without being overly armored and to avoid violating the boundaries of others.

Skills in Reclaiming Projections

When people see negative traits in other people, but don't recognize these same traits in themselves, they are projecting. For people with counter-dependent issues, projection is a serious problem, because often they are unaware of their unmet co-dependency needs. They can see the same needs quite clearly in other people and often make harsh judgments about these "needy" people. A typical counter-dependent game is "Courtroom," in which everyone is on trial. In this interpersonal game, the counter-dependent player takes others "to court," tries them, and convicts them for being imperfect, because no one can meet their needs. This game is an excellent defense against intimacy because it focuses attention on what is wrong with others and keeps the person with counter-dependency issues looking good — and from looking inward. It also helps this person stay separate, one up on others, in control, and feeling safe.

Corrective Parenting Skills

People in committed, conscious relationships can create contracts to help each other meet their unmet needs and provide a vital foundation for creating intimacy. Relating at this deep level, where old wounds, pain, abuse, abandonment, and the scars of growing up in a dysfunctional family are shared, can create connections as intimate as sexual sharing. By creating cooperative contracts that enable them to finally meet their unmet needs, people can transform a relationship from one of pain and conflict into one of intimacy and nurturing.

Conflict Resolution Skills

Intimacy requires people to be skilled in resolving conflicts between needs and wants, and between values and beliefs. Some conflicts involving deep wounds can recycle and become intractable. In order to resolve this variety of conflict, it's important that the partners learn skills for working on all three kinds. Our book *Conflict Resolution: The Partnership Way* is an excellent resource.

Sexual Communication Skills

The bedroom is another place where true intimacy is difficult for people with counter-dependency issues, for here their partners are likely to demand an emotionally intimate and honest relationship. This can push people with counter-dependency issues behind their wall of defenses. Because they didn't learn to nurture or be nurtured, it becomes difficult for them to venture beyond the mechanics of lovemaking and into the deeper levels of intimate sharing. As a result, they find ways to avoid sexual intimacy by keeping very busy, by having multiple sexual partners, or by convincing their partners that they are unattractive or sexually deficient in some way.

Once on the path to freedom and wholeness, people find that there seems to be no returning to the old ways. In moments of despair, discouragement, and depression, it is sometimes tempting to give up. In these moments, a form of spiritual courage deep inside people's souls often pushes them forward, encouraging them to adopt healthier thinking, feeling, and behaving.

CASE EXAMPLE

Linda came to Colorado for two weeks of intensive therapy with us after fifteen years of many other forms of therapy. She had attended a workshop we'd given in her home area several months earlier, and in that workshop Linda had had a breakthrough experience that encouraged her to do further work with us.

Linda's case turned out to be one of the most bizarre we have worked with. The oldest child of very wealthy parents, she grew up in an environment that, from the outside, appeared normal, even ideal. Her parents, however, were two of the most abusive people we have heard of. As a result, Linda had developed many counter-dependent behaviors. Her mother fit the co-dependent behavior prototype perfectly: powerless, highly passive, and totally dominated by her tyrant husband. He had the classic counter-dependent symptoms: he was egotistic, judgmental, perfectionistic, and highly demanding. Linda compared her childhood with these parents to growing up in a concentration camp.

In the beginning of her treatment, we devoted several hours to helping her reconstruct the pieces of her trauma drama. We examined the dynamics of her parents' relationship; her role in keeping the relationship between the two of them in some form of homeostasis; the unconscious psychic agreements she had with each of them; the values, beliefs, assumptions, and expectations she had used to structure her life experiences; the recurring patterns in her list of betrayals; and the original developmental trauma that had scripted her life.

Because of the extreme abuse she had experienced throughout her childhood, we knew that her core developmental trauma must have been severe. We explored with her the circumstances of her birth. She knew that her mother had been drugged and unconscious, and that at one point in the birth process there were difficulties that put Linda's life in peril. The attending physician, who managed to pull her out with forceps, caught her by her right arm as she was delivered. She also believed that the physician held her upside down and spanked her bottom to get her breathing. With this information, we were able to begin piecing together with Linda the elements of her life trauma drama.

We could see how Linda's birth became a metaphor for her life. Her mother continued to play the passive, unconscious role she had played during Linda's birth by "blanking out" whenever Linda was being harmed. Her father, an attorney, took up the role of the abusive physician. Together the parents re-created Linda's birth trauma. Linda always experienced her childhood as though her life were constantly in danger.

In the privacy of their upper-class home, they subjected Linda to sophisticated psychological and spiritual torture using the "Courtroom" game. Linda was kept under constant surveillance like a prisoner. Any time she violated the smallest rule (and there were many), she was brought before her parents. Here they described to Linda the nature and severity of her transgression in terms that left her feeling like a criminal. Her father, who played the prosecutor, presented the case against her. He would often call Linda's mother as a witness to testify against her. She was taken before the judge (again her father), where she was always found guilty. Then she would receive her "sentence." When she was small it was often a spanking, but as she grew older it was mostly humiliation, shame, degradation, discounting, and name-calling.

In one instance at the age of three, she got scared in the middle of the night and went into her parents' bedroom and awakened her father. He was so angry with her that he marched her down the hall to the bathroom, made her stand in front of the open toilet, pulled down her underpants, and then spanked her bare bottom. The force of the angry march down the hall while she was half asleep, the sight and smell of the open toilet, and the humiliation of having to stand half-naked while her father spanked her so terrorized her that the incident left a permanent scar in Linda's psyche.

The trauma of Linda's birth and other similar early childhood developmental traumas created the theme for her life: "I'm constantly on trial for my life." This theme was woven through various relationships and job situations, and it even appeared in an experience with a well-known doctor when she conferred with him about psychiatric treatment. Over the years, Linda had accumulated a large file full of old letters, journal writings, newspaper clippings, and other materials that she used to document the terror of her childhood. Thinking that we were going to judge her, she used this file as a resource to support her "case for the defense." When she would get scared during her therapy work with us, she would pull out clippings or various pieces of information she had saved to help her prove her innocence to us — and to herself — over and over again.

The point when she was able to clearly see the core developmental trauma and the overlaying experiences of her life was enlightening for Linda. A flash of comprehension seemed to move through her as she understood for the first time the whole picture of her life. This seemed to shock her into a state of clarity.

As we discussed the aspects of Linda's developmental trauma drama, Janae suggested that she might have become bonded to her drama, attaching to it as she might a doll or blanket as children often do when they experience a deficiency in early parenting. This suggestion startled Linda, and we could see her shift internally as she reflected on this possibility. Janae suggested that this might have been a survival mechanism for her while she was small, because there was nothing else that was safe for her to bond with. In the present, she now had people with whom it was safe to bond, and she could begin to meet her needs. We explored with her the old reality of "I'm constantly on trial for my life" to see how much of it was still true. She admitted that she was no longer a child and was no longer living anywhere close to her parents, and that in reality her life was no longer in danger.

Just speaking this truth released some of the tension in her body as we sat together. Then we led her step-by-step through the "Completion Process with Your Parents" exercise, designed to help clients understand and complete any unfinished business with their parents. (See the skill-building exercise at the end of chapter 10.)

By the time the two-week period of therapy was over, we could see a dramatic change in Linda's appearance and behavior. She appeared lighter, softer, and gentler. She radiated an incredible loving energy. She also spoke gently and acted more centered. The angry, agitated woman she had brought to therapy two weeks earlier had been transformed.

After Linda's return home, she kept us posted with progress reports that were a continual affirmation of her life change. In one letter three months later, Linda wrote, "My healing has held up. My body is very peaceful. I have reduced my sleeping needs from eight to five hours and wake up feeling rested. All this healing is a gift, a blessing, and a miracle." In other exuberant letters, she described the joy she was finding in burning and throwing out the many boxes and stacks of "defense materials" that she had collected over such a long period. The process of letting go of her developmental trauma drama has been a joyful and healing one for Linda. We've received periodic letters over the years from her, and she is continuing to make excellent progress.

AWARENESS ACTIVITY: HOW TO IDENTIFY YOUR INCOMPLETE DEVELOPMENTAL PROCESSES

The following chart can be helpful in identifying any incomplete developmental processes and unmet needs. Read through the list of developmental processes and needs and place a check mark next to those you believe may be incomplete or unmet in you. Next, check the adulthood indicators of incomplete processes to see if you identify with any of them. Then check the corrective activities to see what you can do to complete these processes now.

ELEMENTS OF BREAKING FREE
FROM CO- AND COUNTER-DEPENDENCY

Essential Developmental Processes and Needs during Bonding (Co-dependency Stage, 0–6 months)	*Indicators of Incomplete Developmental Processes*	*Corrective Activities for Completing Developmental Processes*
Being in charge of your birth process as much as possible.	Fear of trying new things; passivity, letting others lead.	Take assertiveness training to learn how to take charge without guilt.
Being born into a comfortable environment with soft lights, soft music, with adults dressed in ordinary attire (not white uniforms).	Frequent attacks of anxiety and fear. Frequent upper respiratory problems (bronchitis, asthma, shallow breathing, pneumonia).	Learn breathing techniques such as rebirthing. Reenact your birth in a safe, comfortable setting using special, connected breathing techniques.
Being able to nurse right after birth.	Compulsive overeating or overdrinking. Compulsive buying or hoarding.	Ask a trusted friend to hold you and feed you from a baby bottle. Ask a trusted friend to hold, rock, and sing to you.
Having maximum skin-to-skin contact with both parents for the first twenty-four to thirty-six hours after birth.	Trouble relaxing, chronic body tension. Feelings of being deprived of nourishment. Compulsive eating, drinking, sex.	Get a regular or infant massage. Ask to be held and rocked.
Bonding securely with mother, father, and other family members.	Feelings of insecurity and fearfulness. Difficulty in trusting others. Avoidance of touch.	Ask to be held and comforted when you feel sad or scared. Ask for hugs and physical, nonsexual nurturing. Develop self-nurturing skills.
Having immediate and extended family available at your birth to bond with.	Feelings of being disconnected or isolated from others, being a loner. Problems with trusting that others will be there for you.	Reenact your birth, and have other people play family members. Find a therapy group where you can work on trust issues. Do trust exercises with a partner, such as falling backward and having him or her catch you.

Essential Developmental Processes and Needs during Bonding (Co-dependency Stage, 0–6 months)	*Indicators of Incomplete Developmental Processes*	*Corrective Activities for Completing Developmental Processes*
Being received lovingly, and being assured of immediate care, so that the adrenal stress reaction is not activated.	Difficulty relaxing, chronic body tension. Addiction to activity or stimulations.	Nurture yourself with warm baths or other comforting activities. Learn meditation and relaxation tools.
Having your True Self mirrored back by parents and other adults.	Low self-esteem, undervaluing of self. Lack of awareness of your needs.	Make a list of things you wanted to hear from your parents, and have someone say these things to you. Look at yourself in a full-length mirror and affirm positive things about your body, your abilities, and who you are in your essence.
Developing effective ways to let others know your needs.	Inability to ask for what you want or need. Not knowing what you need.	Ask for comfort and support when you are identifying and expressing deep feelings.
Having your needs respected and taken seriously by primary caregivers.	Denial of needs; poor diet, lack of personal care. Feeling like a victim or using self-discounting language.	Learn to identify your needs and ask directly for help when needed. Develop good self-care habits.
Being touched and stroked in loving, nonsexual ways.	Avoidance of touch and intimacy. Feeling deprived of nourishment. Compulsive eating or drinking.	Develop self-nurturing skills. Get regular or infant massages. Sleep nude and let your body experience the softness and texture of the sheets.

ELEMENTS OF BREAKING FREE
FROM CO- AND COUNTER-DEPENDENCY (*continued*)

Essential Developmental Processes during Separation (Counter-dependency Stage, 7–36 months)	Adult Indicators of Incomplete Developmental Processes	Corrective Activities for Completing Developmental Processes
Having your emerging True Self mirrored by your primary caregivers.	Feeling others don't love you.	Ask for positive, unconditional mirroring from others. Find a teddy bear or doll to represent your inner child. Rock, hold, and sing to your inner child, using your bear or doll.
Having caregivers who enjoy playing with you.	Feeling unloved or unwanted. Feeling abandoned or engulfed by others.	Join a therapy group and bring up these issues. Learn to ask for reassurance when having feelings of abandonment.
Receiving support and encouragement for safely exploring your world.	Being easily bored. Needing others to stimulate your interest in life. Having difficulty relaxing. Having chronic anxiety.	Try new things in increments to build your confidence in exploring. Set goals, and make plans to achieve them. Develop a vision for what you want in life.
Discovering how the world around you works, by trusting your senses.	Rejecting or avoiding help from others even when you need it. Striving for perfection. Having difficulty in admitting mistakes. Being unable to trust your senses or intuition.	Join groups who do things that you enjoy for support in exploring the world. Spend time listening to birds and smelling nature. Walk or hike in nature and watch the seasons changes.

ELEMENTS OF BREAKING FREE
FROM CO- AND COUNTER-DEPENDENCY (*continued*)

Essential Developmental Processes during Separation (Counter-dependency Stage, 7–36 months)	Indicators of Incomplete Developmental Processes	Corrective Activities for Completing Developmental Processes
Having your feelings supported and accepted by significant others.	Denying problems or discounting the importance of problems. Having an excessive need to look good.	Ask for positive, unconditional mirroring from others. Join a support or therapy group where you can express your pain about not being seen, and where people will be able to see you.
Receiving twice as many yeses as nos.	Being rebellious and fearing being controlled by others. Being self-centered. Having low tolerance for frustration.	Learn empathy skills. Learn how to distinguish between your needs for nurturing and for sex. Integrate your power and your information-gathering and relationship skills.
Receiving emotional support from your parents for expressing all your feelings.	Having difficulty being emotionally and physically close. Being intolerant of others' mistakes.	Ask for support for doing new things. Receive help and feedback without resistance. Find safe ways to express repressed emotions.
Learning to ask directly for what you want and need.	Having an excessive need to be right or to have the final word. Expecting others to read your mind.	Consciously commit yourself to a relationship, beginning perhaps with a therapist or therapy group. Learn partnership conflict-resolution skills. Identify and learn to love your shadow parts. Take charge of getting what you want without guilt. Be willing to ask for what you want 100 percent of the time.

THE BOTTOM LINE

- For most of us, our families and the culture at large were poor models for intimate relationships.
- True intimacy includes conflict and requires effective tools for resolving it.
- A set of essential communication skills exists that will help you change your counter-dependent behaviors.
- Engaging in a committed relationship is one of the most effective ways to break free of your counter-dependent behaviors and meet your previously unmet developmental needs.

7. Empathy
A Path to Intimacy

The impact of someone's failure to listen[,]...
the absence of response[,] has painful,
numbing consequences.
— Clark Moustakis

Empathy comes from the German word *einfuhlung*, which means "feeling into." It is the ability to understand another as deeply as you understand yourself. The more you understand yourself, and the more empathetic and compassionate you are with yourself, the more you'll be able to feel empathy for others. This was one of the great lessons in our own relationship. We processed and cleared much developmental trauma together, which opened our hearts to ourselves and to each other in ways we wouldn't have imagined possible. And, while our healing process exposed a lot of old pain, it also opened our hearts, which has been a great gift in our committed relationship.

WHAT IS EMPATHY?

Someone who is empathetic can crawl into the skin of others and experience the world the way they do. Empathy develops naturally when parents are able to attune to their baby's energy and to synchronize with his or her emotional states. This kind of deep emotional connection creates a resonance between parent and child in which they experience oneness. In this deep state of interconnectedness, babies have their first experience of empathy.

Unfortunately, many people do not experience empathy in their relationship with their parents and, when they become parents, do not know how to be empathetic with their children. If you, like us, did not have empathetic parents, you can learn it in a more formal way. In this chapter, we discuss some of the skills you can use to become more empathetic.

Empathy involves listening to another so well that you can repeat back what he or she said in such a way that this person feels seen, understood, respected, and supported. It doesn't necessarily mean you agree with what the person said, but indicates that you understand it. There are several components to empathetic listening, outlined in the following list:

1. Listen carefully to what the other person is saying.
2. Avoid thinking of how you'll reply while he or she is talking.
3. Tune in to the other person's feelings while also staying separate from them.
4. Face each other and occasionally look each other in the eye while you're talking.
5. Reflect back what you heard the other person saying, and identify the feelings you think this person experienced while talking.
6. Paraphrase, rather than "parroting" back word for word what you heard.
7. Ask the person if you accurately reflected what he or she said and felt.
8. Use language similar to his or hers to help the other person feel heard, accepted, and understood.

Humanistic psychologist Carl Rogers says that empathy is the most effective skill for "improving a person's relationships and communications with others."[1] You need to use both verbal and nonverbal listening skills in communicating empathetically. These include attending, following, and reflecting.[2] Later in the chapter, we discuss additional skill-building exercises for each of these skill areas.

WHAT ARE FEELINGS FOR?

People often confuse and misuse feelings when they communicate. They say, "I feel that you are trying to control me," when they mean "I think" instead of "I feel." Or they may say, "You made me mad," when they mean, "I chose to get mad." (No one can make another person feel anything.) Also, people often think that they must justify their feelings, give reasons for them, or wait until they find something that justifies expressing a feeling. For example, say a person tells a friend not to call after 10:30 pm, and the friend calls at 10:35 pm. That person may choose to really let him have it.

What most people don't know is that each of our feelings has an important function. There are six primary feelings, and each has a separate distinct function, as outlined in the following chart.[3]

BASIC FEELINGS AND THEIR FUNCTIONS	
Feeling	*Corrective Activities for Completing Developmental Processes*
Anger	Your natural response to not getting your wants or needs met. You may also feel scared to ask directly for something that will meet your needs and may get angry instead, hoping to get what you want without asking directly.
Fear	Your natural response to perceived physical or emotional danger. You may believe you can't think and feel at the same time and, therefore, may not think to notice whether there is actual danger. You may also use fear to cover your anger.
Sadness	Your natural response to the loss of a person, object, or relationship (real or fantasized). Sadness is an important part of giving up something you were attached to. You may also have some anger connected with the loss.
Shame	Your natural response to crossing some personal or social limit. Healthy shame helps us monitor our behavior in public situations and also helps form our ethical code.
Excitement	Your natural anticipation of something good that you expect to happen. Fear and excitement are often closely related. Some people never got permission as children to show excitement.
Happiness or Joy	Your natural satisfaction at getting what you want or need or at doing something effectively. Some people don't know it's okay to be happy. They may be addicted to struggle.

WHY PEOPLE WITH COUNTER-DEPENDENCY ISSUES DIDN'T LEARN EMPATHY

If you went exploring during the counter-dependent stage of development and got scared or hurt, you needed to be comforted and nurtured. If you were made fun of or rebuffed in some way, this developmental trauma caused you to build protective defenses against being hurt again. Perhaps you wanted to prove to your parents that you were strong and didn't need anyone. Repeated experiences like these convince children they should avoid telling others when they feel scared, insecure, sad, or confused. The message they internalize is, "Take care of yourself and don't trust anyone." The classic counter-dependent deodorant commercial shows a football coach saying to men, "Never let them see you sweat." Counter-dependency behaviors involve creating defenses that make sure no one knows your real feelings and uses them against you.

People with counter-dependency issues who weren't protected as children often become hypervigilant, watching everyone and every situation to determine if they are going to be hurt or ridiculed. This takes an inordinate amount of energy, and little energy remains for getting to know people, beyond seeing them as potential threats to one's well-being.

Some children are unable to separate from their parents. Their mothers may have used them to help fill their own childhood bonding needs. Perhaps you were told that your own needs were not as important as your mother's. If so, you may have relinquished your personal needs. Some parents try to create a perfect child to show the world that they are perfect parents. You may have been warned not to show your feelings because having feelings is a sign that you're less than perfect. Perhaps you were also rewarded for doing things well, but it led to pressure to keep doing things to please your perfectionistic parents. You may have been told that you can do anything as long as you "look good" and do what your parents say. Protecting the image of the perfect family or of the perfect parents may have been more important to your parents then meeting your emotional needs.

As a result, you may have developed counter-dependent traits that allow you to be capable (although you may constantly worry about failure), but you may not feel very lovable. You may realize that you were used as an object to satisfy your parents' desires and dreams — the price tag for getting your parents' approval and recognition. You may have a lot of repressed rage and sadness about not being loved for who you really are and, at the same time, have defenses that help you avoid feeling these feelings. In reaction to the loss of the

True Self, those with counter-dependency issues often inflate the False Self in an attempt to look like the real thing. Inside, they feel fragmented and afraid to risk the emotional closeness of an intimate relationship that could bring up old feelings. They literally have no time and energy to focus on another person, and if people with counter-dependent behaviors were to attempt intimate relationships, they might fear serious consequences, such as abandonment or rejection. Many people with counter-dependency patterns are addicted to perfection or at least to "looking" perfect. This may have been the only way they could get any recognition or approval from perfectionistic parents.

SELF-DEFEATING CORE BELIEFS RELATED TO COUNTER-DEPENDENCY

Developmental trauma leaves its mark on people at very deep levels. Children believe there is something intrinsically wrong with them when adults are not emotionally present and able to meet their needs. The scars they carry particularly influence their thinking and beliefs as adults. The "Troubleshooting" sidebar lists some common beliefs found in people struggling with counter-dependency issues.

TROUBLESHOOTING
Common Self-defeating Beliefs

- If I pay much attention to the other person, I'll lose myself.
- If I listen to what others say, I'll get talked out of my own beliefs and views.
- If I get close to someone, he or she will see how unlovable I am and reject me.
- If I listen to other people's feelings, this may stir up my own.
- If people get to know me, they'll see how weak I am and lose respect for me.
- If I open up to someone, they'll abandon me and I may die.
- If I cry, I'll never be able to stop.
- If I get angry, I might kill someone.
- If I express my pain, it will be unending and I might go crazy or die.
- If I cannot handle my pain of rejection, I don't know what will happen to me.
- If I'm not in control, I won't get what I want.
- If I'm not in control, people will take advantage of me and control me.

THE FEMININE FORM OF SURRENDER

Surrender involves letting go, and it has two forms: The masculine form is about taking charge of one's life without feeling guilty. The feminine form is about releasing judgments in order to receive information, love, and care from another person without resistance. Generally, women are more skilled in the feminine form and not the masculine, while men may know the masculine form but have an undeveloped feminine side. It's important for both men and women to develop each of these two forms of surrender in order to have an intimate relationship.

People with counter-dependency issues have difficulty receiving without resistance, so they are often not very empathetic. Frequently, they judge what they hear before even thinking about it. They resist taking in anything others say that appears to be critical or threatening. This reflects their built-in protection system. So, people struggling with patterns of counter-dependency must learn to let go enough to hear what others say without resisting it. If you get quick responses or negative responses from someone, you know your words have been evaluated but probably not considered very carefully. We discuss the masculine form of surrender in more detail in chapter 12.

Letting go of the tendency to make quick judgments is an important skill for creating and sustaining intimate relationships. The following case example illustrates this vital point.

CASE EXAMPLE

This firsthand account illustrates how Dawson, one of our clients, transformed himself. We asked him to tell his own story of how he uncovered and subsequently changed many of his counter-dependent behavior patterns.

"When I first learned about developmental needs people should get met in early childhood, I was quite dismayed. In the course of my birth and early childhood experiences, I received few or none of those things that are now recognized as essential for healthy, successful development.

"I was born via C-section. There was little apparent bonding with anyone in my family. My mother has told me of her feelings. She perceived me as an ugly baby and didn't particularly like to hold me or care for me. Obviously I wasn't nursed, and in fact, I was schedule-fed according to the infant-rearing practices in vogue in 1940. According to my mother, my father questioned his paternity and showed little interest in me.

"My half sister, ten years older than myself, showed some interest. However, her background of physical and sexual abuse precluded my being able to have a healthy and truly nourishing relationship with her. My memories of infancy, recalled in regression, showed me that, in what I think was a desperate attempt to get my needs met, I created repeated crises of pneumonia. Frequently, I had to be rushed to the hospital and put in an oxygen tent. This was regarded as a bother and inconvenience by my parents, and my mother has told me that she considered just letting me die on more than one occasion.

"I did bond to a considerable degree with our family dog. She became so protective of me that my mother decided to get rid of her when I was about four. At that time, I reconciled myself to a life of loneliness and isolation.

"My father left for World War II when I was three. I then became an object of competition, between my mother and sister, for the male energy in the household. The abuse I experienced from them left me with a deep mistrust of women. These experiences of abuse also became the foundation for patterns of sexualizing love, physical touch, and nurturing, and for bonding with female sexual perpetrators. After my father's departure for the war, my mother took a lover. After the war, my parents attempted unsuccessfully to reconcile their differences, and their marriage finally ended in divorce.

"The dynamics in my family turned betrayal and failure into my model for intimate relationships. My sister and mother fought bitterly. My sister, who was a bright and gifted person, left home at sixteen. I lost track of her soon thereafter. At this point, neither my mother nor I know her whereabouts, life, or circumstances.

"At the age of seven I was sent off to a boys' prep school. My mother and I corresponded irregularly, and my father visited every couple of weeks or so. My sense of life as an isolated and lonely experience deepened. One of the older boys 'befriended' me. Subsequently, he took me out into the woods near the school and raped me. He also threatened me with death if I ever told anyone. I was already experienced as a keeper of family secrets. I kept that secret, even from myself, for forty-three years.

"My next recollection after the rape was being in the school infirmary and my body covered with boils. I could keep a secret, but I couldn't contain my rage. I felt betrayed by my father, whom I thought should have been there to protect me. I felt betrayed by my 'friend' and began a pattern of mistrust of male friendship and found myself bonding with male sexual per-petrators. At the age of eight I felt alone, insecure, and unworthy, and con-cluded that there must be something inherently wrong with me. I had become a shame-based person.

"I managed to hide my shame well enough to graduate from college and later go on to become a successful businessman. I still had difficulty in my relationships with men, however, where my employers, colleagues, and cus-tomers appeared as male sexual perpetrators. My 'success' came from my will-ingness and proclivity to put myself in a 'one down' position. Since I had no formal business training, I often placed myself in the role of student or learner and cultivated business relationships quite successfully from that place. I also became skilled at faking strength and power and was able to negotiate busi-ness contracts for the benefit of my employers. Inside, I felt insecure and pow-erless concerning my own position in the company. Much of my time, I felt intimidated by many of the men I met in a business context. Eventually, I had to leave the corporate world when I was asked to make business decisions that were in conflict with my own values and sense of integrity.

"I twice married and divorced women who were very aware of my deep levels of pain. I believe that we were drawn together because of our similar histories of abuse. Although there was a great deal of healing in both relation-ships, we lacked the skills and guidance to take it any further than we did.

"The patterns of betrayal, neglect, mistrust, fear of intimacy, abuse, sab-otage, failure, and denial, however, played out again and again in my life. Eventually I left the corporate world and took refuge in nature. My con-nection to nature has been a consistent thread throughout my life. I also began cultivating a spiritual life through the practice of yoga and medita-tion. These activities helped ease somewhat the sense of isolation and detach-ment I experienced in my human relationships. My inherent longing and drive to meet my unmet developmental needs, coupled with my mistrust and fear of intimacy, produced a constant cycling between the extremes of co-dependent and counter-dependent behavior patterns. I became a master at the dance of intimacy. I could use intimacy to support my dysfunction and, at the same time, as a key to healing. The grief, frustration, and lack of fulfillment I experienced in the co-dependent part of the relationship dance are well known to me, as is the illusion of healing that comes when I flip into the counter-dependent phase.

"For reasons about which I am not exactly clear, perhaps through a kind of grace, I have held the vision of myself as a healed and happy person, as well as a member of a healed and functional family, extended family, community, and society in which I would be a participating cocreator and partner. The pursuit of this vision has guided me on an extraordinary adventure of life, in which I have known the depths of sorrow and despair and the pain of failure, frustration, and disappointment. It has also provided me with a depth of compassion and understanding that now supports me in helping others heal their childhood wounds.

"I have been a spiritual seeker and finder much of my life and, in recent years, a man of prayer. My work with spirit guides and teachers of Native American descent has taught me more about my connectedness to all beings and things of this world and to the world of spirit. My Native American practices have also shown me the value and power of ceremony and prayer in my life.

"Through my training in Native American traditions, I became aware of my bondedness to Mother Earth. I have spent many hours out on the land being nurtured and comforted by Her. She became the one mother I could depend on for solace and healing. She has been my primary source of parenting for many years.

"Only recently did I risk bonding again to humans. I knew that my only pattern for bonding in relationships was to bond with sexual perpetrators and create abusive relationships. I had, however, never found people who were safe enough or who really understood the nature of my childhood wounds with whom I could work to change this pattern.

"The isolation from other humans and my loneliness finally grew too great for me to bear. I knew from the conflict and pain in my life that the unresolved issues from my childhood were sabotaging my adulthood. After I met Barry and Janae, read their book on co-dependency, and saw their therapeutic approach, I decided to enter therapy with them. My first session was bonding work with Janae. For about forty-five minutes she held me while I cried, releasing the years of suffering from abuse, abandonment, neglect, and rejection. It was the first time in my life that I felt safe enough to let down my protective walls, at a deeper level than I had previously been able to do, and really allow someone to see my pain. It was also the first time that

I allowed myself to be comforted by another human. Always before I had retreated inside myself or gone out on the land to my Earth Mother.

"In subsequent sessions with both Barry and Janae, I did corrective parenting work with them. I asked to be held, mirrored, sung to, and appreciated for who I am. Having two safe, loving, available people to provide my missing developmental needs healed a deep place inside me. For the first time in my life, I experienced in my body the feeling of being loved by someone who was not a sexual perpetrator. I now knew the feeling of two kinds of relationships: safe and loving and unsafe and abusive. Because I can now tell the difference between healthy and unhealthy relating, I have choice. If the relationship feels safe and healthy, I know that I can stay. If it feels like part of the unsafe and unhealthy pattern from my past, I know that I need to leave quickly.

"Breaking through patterns based on a history such as mine has opened up a whole new world for me at the age of fifty. At this point in my life, I have come to believe that I chose my family of origin and do not now see myself in any way as a 'victim of circumstances.' I am grateful for the opportunity to be alive to clear what I believe are my karmic patterns. I know that my parents did the best they could, given their own histories and conditioning."

SKILL-BUILDING ACTIVITIES:
LEARNING TO BE EMPATHETIC

Verbal and nonverbal behaviors are important parts of learning the skill of empathy. These behaviors include opening to empathy, empathetic listening, following, and reflective listening.

Opening to Empathy

- Remove any physical barriers, such as desks or tables, between you.
- Minimize environmental distractions and noises.
- Find a comfortable distance between yourself and the other person.
- Maintain an open position, with arms and legs uncrossed.
- Face the other person squarely and maintain good eye contact.
- Lean slightly toward the other person while listening.
- Look away if the other person shows signs of discomfort.

- Try to mirror the body movements of the other person as much as possible.
- Avoid distracting motions and gestures.

Empathetic Listening

People use verbs that are visual, auditory, kinesthetic (related to movement), or proprioceptive (related to feeling). Notice which kind of verbs they use most often, and respond using the same kind of sensory verbs so that they'll feel better understood. For example, if I say, "I *saw* the whole problem *clearly*" (visual), you might reply with, "So you were able to *see the big picture?*" If you were to reply, "I *hear* that you have a better *feel* for the problem now," I wouldn't feel understood. It helps to stay focused on what the other person is saying, rather than to use the situation to get into your own agenda. (For example, don't veer off-topic: "That reminds me . . .")

Following

This is another type of listening skill. Here are some of the most common conversational aids, which will encourage meaningful conversation:

- *Door openers* help get someone started. For example, tell the other person: "I'm interested in what you think about that" or "Do you want to talk about how you're feeling? I'll listen."
- *Minimal encouragement* keeps things going. Say things like: "Tell me more" or "Really?" or "And?" Or just say, "Mm-hmm," which says, "Keep talking."
- *Open-ended questions* help the person keep talking. It's more effective to say, "What's going on?" Don't say, "Are you sad?" This doesn't give the speaker much room to expand on the message.
- *Attentive silences* allow the speaker to reflect on what he or she has said. These may be uncomfortable at first, but if you use them often, they become a natural part of communicating.

Reflective Listening

- *Paraphrasing* is a concise response that captures the essence of the content of what was said *but* uses your own words. Use your own words so that you don't sound like a parrot.

- *Reflective responses* involve paraphrasing to capture the feeling tone or feelings that were spoken. For example, a friend might say, "I'm not sure what to do. Every time I think I'm going to get the job, someone else is picked." Your reflective response might be: "You sound really frustrated and discouraged."
- *Reflecting meanings* combine both feelings and content. Using the above example, a response that combines both content and feeling might be: "You really seem discouraged and sad about this job hunting process, and you probably just want to give up sometimes." The main message should be: "You seem to feel_____ because_____." Do always make your response tentative so the person can agree if it fits and can correct you if it doesn't. This helps bring more clarity.
- *Summary reflections* are useful when you've covered a lot of ideas, feelings, and topics or have come to the end of a conversation. A summary reflection is a brief restatement of the main ideas or feelings expressed during a longer conversation. It verifies that you are still "with" the person, and it may help the speaker clarify the main themes of the conversation. You might say things like: "Let me see if I'm still following this. You said _____ and _____. Is that right?" Or you might say, "It seems to me as I listen to all this that your main concern is _____."

Reflective Listening Exercise

See how well you can identify the feelings in the following practice statements. After reading each one, write one or two words describing the feelings in them. Disregard the context. When you're finished, compare your answers with ours (listed after the end of the exercise) and decide which ones best reflect the unwritten feelings.

The Person Says	The Feeling Is
1. "I'd like to go on a vacation this summer, but I don't know if I can afford it."	

The Person Says	The Feeling Is
2. "She thinks she's so smart. Just because she got a promotion. Big deal!"	
3. "Why do things always turn out this way for me? I never seem to get what I want."	
4. "I'm so stupid. I don't know what I would have done if you hadn't helped me."	
5. "This is the best relationship I've ever had, and I sure don't want to lose it."	
6. "Gee, I'm not having any fun today. I can't think of anything I want to do."	
7. "Look, I just bought myself a new dress. What do you think?"	
8. "No one wants to be my friend. I don't have much to offer."	

Reflective Meaning Exercise

Reread each of the statements in the "Reflective Listening Exercise," and write out a reflective response to the speaker that captures the essence of the feeling and the meaning.

Answers to Reflective Listening Exercise:

(1) fear, (2) anger, (3) sadness, (4) shame or happiness, (5) happiness or fear, (6) fear, or maybe anger, (7) excitement, (8) fear

THE BOTTOM LINE

- Your defenses that prevent people from getting close to you are there for a good reason.
- It's important to identify what may have caused you to build these defenses. (You can't really fix something until you know what's broken.)
- Once you know the how and why of your defenses, you can learn new skills to help you create and sustain more intimacy in your relationships.
- Learning how to be more empathetic will also help you create more intimacy in your relationships.

8. Boundary Setting

Remember, no one can make you feel inferior
without your consent.

— Eleanor Roosevelt

Boundaries provide a structure to prevent people from crossing into each other's space. Like neighborhood fences, they help identify what is "yours" and what is "mine." As Robert Frost once wrote, "Good fences make good neighbors." Appropriate boundaries allow you to be separate physically, mentally, emotionally, and spiritually and to create safety in relationships. People learn how to create boundaries by being with people who have boundaries. Families with very clear boundaries help children learn the mine/not mine distinction quickly. When there are fuzzy or inconsistent boundaries, it's very difficult to develop distinct ones.

Once you decide you want clear boundaries, you will likely experience more conflict, because you'll find yourself informing people when they cross them. Now this can sound like a bad thing, but it really isn't. When you let someone know where your personal "fence" is, this person will become more aware of his or her own. Your kind but clear manner of informing this person that he or she has inadvertently crossed your personal boundary will be instructional. You may be one of the first people this person has encountered who recognizes the importance of boundaries and understands how to create them. If you frame your boundary work as a "learning" experience, for yourself and others, then there's no need for shame about not having boundaries and having to learn about them.

Physical boundaries help us feel in charge of our own bodies. These boundaries protect us against invasions such as abuse, sexual aggression, and people coming too close physically. When people lack boundaries, they learn to armor their bodies against potential violations of their space by adopting protective postures or growing more muscles or even fat. Emotional boundaries allow you to have feelings and to express them, and to know the difference between your feelings and the feelings of others. Mental boundaries permit you to have thoughts and perceptions that you know are different from the thoughts and perceptions of others. Spiritual boundaries help you know the part of yourself that seeks transcendence or a connection with some Power higher than yourself.

BOUNDARIES: A COUNTER-DEPENDENT PERSPECTIVE

People with counter-dependent behaviors often struggle with creating appropriate boundaries. Their need for protection while growing up was so strong that they had to create *walls* instead. However, they often protect themselves by crossing the boundaries of others after learning to adopt an "I'll get them before they get me" attitude. This is the opposite of what is experienced by people with co-dependency behaviors, who lack boundaries and get invaded by others. They often have to learn how to draw appropriate boundaries around themselves.

BOUNDARY WORK IN THERAPY

We find that working in individual therapy with clients who have counter-dependent issues usually takes longer than working with those with co-dependent behaviors, because counter-dependent individuals are often less in touch with their feelings. When clients with counter-dependency issues begin therapy, we start by supporting their need to maintain rigid boundaries. This approach, which looks at what is right about their behavior, is important for two reasons. First, it supports their need to look good and reduces the anxiety they typically have, when entering psychotherapy, that they will be judged or found lacking in some way. Second, it helps develop safety in the client-therapist relationship so that they can slowly remove the mask of the inflated False Self. Gradually, they feel safe enough to reveal their wounded inner child. Reframing the problem is especially important for people with counter-dependency issues, because, like most clients, they expect the therapist to take the "critical parent" role and tell them what they are doing wrong and how bad they are.

We've found that clients with counter-dependency issues initially need this support, rather than confrontation and criticism, because it helps create the kind of safe environment they needed during childhood and never got. In a safe and supportive environment, they can explore the circumstances that originally created their need for rigid boundaries. A safe environment also helps validate people with unmet counter-dependency needs who experienced abuse and violation during their childhoods. This "naming" of the abuse is an important step in helping them identify their experience correctly, particularly if they cut themselves off from their wounded inner child.

In therapy, it's also important to help people with unmet counter-dependency needs recognize that their decision to erect walls very early in life was done out of necessity. They lost their ability to create boundaries when they were violated so early and so often. Just speaking this fact causes many clients to visibly relax some of the tension in their bodies and soften layers of armoring. We go very slowly, encouraging them to keep their walls up until they feel safe. We acknowledge their history of violation and do all we can to avoid playing the perpetrator role in their lives.

This supportive approach often creates a new experience for these clients, which allows them to feel safe to freely explore what and how to change. As children, people with narcissistic wounds stemming from the counter-dependent stage of development were always in a reactive state, ready at any moment to respond to a potential threat of physical or emotional harm or invasion. Going slowly, building trust, creating safety, and establishing rapport as an ally, rather than as an authority, are essential in the development of a successful therapeutic relationship with clients who suffer from wounds during the counter-dependent stage of development.

As a client, you can help yourself break free by working on some of these ideas in your therapy. It's highly appropriate for you to cocreate your therapy treatment plan by choosing a therapist who supports your goals. Your relationship with your therapist can become one of several relationships where you work in committed, conscious, and cooperative ways to meet your counter-dependent or co-dependent needs.

CREATING APPROPRIATE BOUNDARIES

People with unmet counter-dependent needs are often hypervigilant, watching for the next incident of invasion or abuse. In their hypervigilant state, they often misidentify what they believe are the first signs of a possible attack or invasion and make a countermove to short-circuit their opponent. This protective reaction and "I'll get you before you get me" behavior makes them frequent violators of other people's boundaries and makes them appear aggressive. If aggression is a problem for you, you may be carrying anger from your past that needs to be released.

RELEASING ANGER

- Release the stored and repressed feelings about your early childhood violations and/or abandonments. This will reduce your fear of accidentally exposing them.
- Release your anger in therapy or a safe relationship, rather than while you are alone.
- Learn to discriminate between real and imagined threats.
- Use perception checks to sort out what is real and what is imagined (see chapter 9).
- Remember that no one makes you feel angry.
- Take responsibility for creating your feelings.
- Monitor your impulse to protect yourself by crossing the boundaries of others.
- Learn defensive martial arts techniques to protect yourself, without harming your attacker, when you're being physically attacked.
- Remember that revenge escalates and leads to further violence.
- Ask your loved ones to help you stop invading or attacking others, as they may be aware of your invasions before you are.
- Make amends as soon as possible when you become aware that you have crossed someone's boundaries.
- Demonstrate your willingness to address problems peacefully.

KINDS OF BOUNDARIES

If you want to create and sustain intimate relationships, you need healthy boundaries in four areas: physical, emotional, mental, and spiritual. Let's look at how each kind pertains to counter-dependency issues.

Physical Boundaries

Physical boundaries allow you to have dominion over your body and over your possessions. They determine how physically close others can come to you. Physical boundaries allow you to say how and when you want to be touched and who you want to touch you.

People with counter-dependency issues often had their physical boundaries continually violated through some form of abuse. They might have been spanked, hit, beaten, slapped, ridiculed, or shamed to intimidate and control them. Their parents may have even invaded them in the guise of love and affection by teasing, touching, tickling, kissing, and roughhousing with them without giving them a choice.

Children typically learn two kinds of responses as the result of such invasive experiences. The first is to avoid all physical touch. They do not allow people to get very close to them and they avoid getting too close to other people. As adults, they usually don't enjoy snuggling, cuddling, and other kinds of nurturing activities unless it's associated with sexual foreplay.

The second type of response is to cross the boundaries of others. This allows them to maintain their offensive, one-up position, which serves them in two ways. Crossing boundaries, especially in an abusive manner similar to what they experienced as children, allows them to unconsciously pass on their own pain. This transmission of child abuse and pain to others is called the "vicious cycle of cruelty."[1] People with unfinished counter-dependent issues learn that it's not safe to express their true feelings to their abusers. Instead, they express their anger to someone they perceive as weaker. The second way that invading others serves people with unmet counter-dependency needs is by helping them repress old feelings and avoid facing their neediness.

Healing emotional wounds caused by physical abuse, and learning to create healthy boundaries, begins by paying attention to your body and the bodies of those around you. Notice how your body responds when you anticipate a violation coming. Do you recoil, stiffen, or withdraw? Do you hold your breath? As soon as you notice this kind of cue, you can pause for a moment and examine what real choices you have.

Old choices might include making an escalated attack to overpower your opponent quickly, or throwing up a wall of defense based on fear and anger, or running away. These are primitive responses wired into us as part of the adrenal stress response, to fight, flee, or freeze. New choices might include using assertive "I" statements that protect you and also allow you to stay in a relationship with the other person. For example, say: "When you borrow my car without asking, I feel angry and violated. What I want from you is for you to ask permission before you use or borrow any of my belongings. Are you willing to do that?" or "When you touch my body..."

Emotional Boundaries

Emotional boundaries involve how we relate to others at the level of feelings. Having healthy emotional boundaries allows us to differentiate between what we feel and what others feel.

People with counter-dependency issues often deny their own childhood feelings and the feelings of others as a way of protecting themselves from reexperiencing them. Here are some common ways that people violate others' emotional boundaries:

- *Discounting* involves devaluing or minimizing someone's thoughts, feelings, or behavior.
- *Refocusing* involves shifting the attention from one person to another in order to avoid taking responsibility for something.
- *Manipulating* involves using indirect communications, such as those of the drama triangle to try to get what you want.
- *Diverting* shifts the focus of attention away from feelings when they begin to emerge. It's like passing the emotional hot potato on to someone else as quickly as possible.

Examples of discounting and refocusing statements are: "Oh, you're not angry. You're just a little upset." "You get upset too easily when things don't go your way." "You should do something about your short fuse." "Why are you making such a big deal out of this? I was only kidding." Emotional manipulations like these are painful to encounter. Such defenses keep others off balance, making it difficult for them to stay with their feelings and maintain their own focus.

Healing the wounds of an emotional violation requires releasing the old, unresolved issues and repressed feelings from your childhood. This is best done while working with a therapist or with your partner in a committed relationship. Once these old feelings are released — in a safe, supportive environment — it's easier to stop the vicious cycle of abuse associated with the violation of emotional boundaries. Changing these destructive counter-dependent behaviors also requires an understanding of the function of your feelings so you can use them appropriately.

Mental Boundaries

Mental boundaries involve how we view the world. They allow us to know what we value, believe, think, want, and need so we can separate our perceptions and experiences from those of others.

A common mental-boundary violation related to unmet counter-dependent needs is defining other people's reality. Those with counter-dependent behaviors often assume that they know more about the world, particularly that of their children, spouse, and subordinates, without ever asking them. Another common mental-boundary violation is to interrupt people who are talking and prevent them from completing their thoughts. Punishing, ridiculing, and overruling the opinions of others are also common mental-boundary violations.

Defining another person's ideas as crazy or stupid is a common way that people with counter-dependency issues violate people's mental boundaries. Paraphrasing a statement by Carl Rogers, we can say that, if we accept as a basic fact of our human lives that we all live in separate realities; if we can see those differing realities as the most promising resource in the history of the world for learning about each other; and if we can live together while seeking to learn from one another without fear; then a new age could be dawning.[2]

Denial is another common form of mental violation. People with counter-dependency issues deny not only their own problems but also other people's perceptions as a way of maintaining control and domination. Healing the wounds caused by violations of your mental boundaries during childhood requires developing a stronger sense of object constancy: the ability to know that you're worthwhile even when others attack your thoughts or ideas or when you make a mistake.

Developing object constancy and healing old wounds requires creating a safe space inside yourself where you can explore your own ideas, beliefs, perceptions, and experiences. Here you can begin to construct your own way of looking at who you really are and how the world operates outside your family of origin. Keeping a journal is an excellent way to do this, as it helps you come to terms with your needs to be perfect and look good and to have others recognize your accomplishments. When you're writing in your journal, you're in a relationship only with yourself.

Another important way to develop effective boundaries is to make and keep effective agreements. People with counter-dependent behaviors often have trouble with both parts of agreements. First, they often make agreements they can't keep, because they want to look good. Then they don't keep agreements, because they don't want to be controlled. When they break an agreement, they often try to blame it on others or on circumstances beyond their control and refuse to take responsibility for breaking the agreement.

Spiritual Boundaries

Spiritual boundaries allow you to experience higher, more transcendent aspects of yourself. They allow you to feel the oneness and unconditional love of a higher power or greater force in the universe. Spiritual boundaries also help you to develop spiritual object constancy and to love yourself unconditionally even when you feel imperfect. When children are violated spiritually, they often blame themselves for their abuse or neglect, fall out of love with themselves, and then disconnect from their spiritual selves. Spiritual violation is often experienced as terror.

Terror is a combination of shame and fear that involves highly controlled behavior, demands perfectionism, and contains a threat of death. Statements such as "God will punish you!" and "You're going to burn in hell for that!" are common forms of spiritual terrorizing that many people with counter-dependency issues experienced in childhood. As part of the perpetuation of the vicious cycle of cruelty, they may use these same spiritual weapons on others, especially their own children. Children then learn to view God and their parents as violent, unpredictable, and punitive. In this way, people with unmet counter-dependent needs can see God as an ally only when they're attempting to control others.

Another form of spiritual violation commonly used by people with counter-dependency issues is "playing God." They put themselves on a pedestal and refuse to reveal their humanness. This stance imposes one person's reality on others without negotiation, and it violates the spiritual boundaries of those who approach with love and kindness or ask for comfort.

Transforming spiritual violations usually takes longer than any of the other kinds of boundary violations, because they traumatize people's souls. Reaching into a damaged person's soul requires a lot of skill, patience, and unconditional love. Transforming the wounds caused by spiritual violations must be done gently and with compassion. This may involve hours of listening and becoming attuned to others in an ongoing state of unconditional positive regard while they reveal their wounds. Good spiritual counseling can even encourage clients to forgive those who transgressed against them. When the wound is finally healed, there is room for an influx or flow of love from the Divine. In twelve-step programs, this is sometimes described as a "spiritual awakening."

CASE EXAMPLE

Jeff had many of the classic counter-dependent behaviors. He was bright and self-confident but had real difficulty with intimate situations and stayed as far away from feelings as he could. He walled off his feelings and created boundaries to avoid close intimate situations where he feared he could get hurt. In therapy, we had explored the reasons behind his fears of intimacy, looking for events in his childhood in which his boundaries had been violated. He recently had remembered an incident of childhood sexual abuse. Sexual abuse is one of the most damaging kinds of boundary violations, for it crosses through all the levels: physical, mental, emotional, and spiritual. It leaves the victim permanently scarred, often with feelings of having been terrorized.

Jeff's brother, who was eight years older, had sodomized him when he was six. This experience was traumatic for Jeff. When he told his parents about the abuse, however, he was blamed for the incident. Neither parent supported him in his feelings of shock and hurt. His mother actually spanked him and shamed him horribly as punishment. His father withdrew from disciplining him but said nothing in his defense.

In the session he had with us, he spoke of two issues related to this incident that he wanted to work on: his anger at his brother and the lack of support from his parents. He said, "I really need to get angry at my brother, but I can't. It's still so difficult for me to get angry." (This told us that getting angry would be an important part of Jeff's work.)

Janae asked, "Do you have a mental picture of yourself getting angry at your brother?" Jeff thought for a moment and then shook his head, "No, I don't." (This indicated to us that Jeff was not yet ready to confront his perpetrator. Had he been ready, he would have had some image of it. So we shifted.)

Barry said, "Maybe you need to deal with your lack of support from your parents before you can address the issues you have with your brother." As Barry said this, Jeff leaned sideways and rested his chin on his hand. (This self-supporting signal indicated that Barry should explore working on the support issue with his parents.)

Barry asked him if he would like to work on the support issue with his parents. He thought about it for a moment and then indicated that he wanted to role-play the scene where he told his mother and father about the abuse. He asked us to take the roles of his parents, and we agreed to do that. Then Barry asked Jeff what he wanted to get out of this particular instance of role-playing. Jeff said he wanted to replay the scene with a new ending: he wanted support for his feelings from both of his parents, and for them to protect him from his brother.

Barry asked Jeff what he wanted him to do as his father. He said, "I want you to tell my brother off and then protect me from my mom's anger and shaming." At that point Barry turned to an imaginary brother and told him, "You leave Jeff alone! You have no right to do this to him! Get away from him this instant, and don't you ever do this to him again!" (By now Jeff had moved behind Barry and huddled up small, as if hiding from his brother. He looked and sounded like a scared seven-year-old.)

Then Barry turned to Jeff and asked him how he was doing. He said, "I'm scared, Dad. Will you hold me?" As Barry held him, he told Jeff how sorry he was that he hadn't protected him when Jeff needed his father. Barry also assured him that he would not let his brother hurt him again.

When Barry asked Jeff what he needed from him to help him deal with his mother, he said, "Will you go with me to talk to her about how she hurts me when she criticizes and shames me?" Barry said he would do that.

The two of them moved toward Janae, who was playing his mother. Jeff began to talk to her about her hurtful remarks and how they affected him. As he talked, he began moving slowly behind Barry until he was completely hidden from his mother. Barry turned to look at Jeff and said, "You seem to be hiding behind me. Are you scared?"

Looking relieved that Barry had come to his aid, Jeff said, "Will you talk to her for me?" (Jeff needed modeling on how to be appropriately angry with his mother, so that he could deal with his brother later.)

Barry told Jeff's mother (Janae), "If you ever spank him like that again, I will turn you in for child abuse. What you did to Jeff was abusive, and it has to stop." At this point, Jeff reported that he was afraid that his mother might go away, and that he would lose her. So then Barry added, "This boy needs a mother and a father. If you don't know how to raise him, ask me."

Jeff then started to talk to his mother from his sheltered position behind Barry. He told her how he felt when the incident happened, and asked her to support his feelings and not criticize him. She was able to respond to his request, and he began to relax and move out from behind Barry. (At this point, Barry knew that Jeff was integrating an internal protector and didn't need him to play that part any longer.)

We asked Jeff if he had gotten what he wanted from the session, and he said yes. He now knew what appropriate anger looked like, and he had finally gotten the protection he had always wanted from his parents. (These were important missing developmental pieces for Jeff that he needed in order to defend himself in future situations where he formerly would have felt victimized.)

SKILL-BUILDING ACTIVITY:
BOUNDARY-BUILDING EXERCISE

In this exercise you'll learn how to create appropriate boundaries rather than walls. You'll also be able to experience what it feels like to be both the invader and the one being invaded and determine which role you feel most comfortable in. Toward the end of the exercise, you'll learn how to raise and lower your boundaries, which will allow you protection when you need it and intimacy when you want it. It's important as you do this exercise to remain fully aware of what's happening in your body at all times.

DIRECTIONS: This exercise is best done on a floor with a pile carpet or other surface where you can make an imprint on the surface with your finger. You need a partner for this exercise, and each of you needs to take turns, following the set of instructions given below. Choose a partner and sit on the floor across from each other. Decide who's going to begin acting the part of the invaded person, and who will play the one who invades. The person being invaded will complete the exercise first. Your partner will play the invader. At the end of this exercise, you'll exchange roles so that each gets to experience both roles. You'll find directions for each role in the exercise.

Step 1. No Boundaries

This part of the exercise is designed to let you really feel what it's like not to have protective boundaries. Partners sit across from each other about three feet apart. Your partner should start making some sort of aggressive or threatening nonverbal move toward you.

He or she should move toward you slowly, with awareness. Notice how it feels to have someone approach you without warning. What feelings emerge? What reaction do you notice in your body? What thoughts come into your mind?

Step 2. Boundaries, No Protection

In this part of the exercise, you'll learn what it feels like to have a boundary. Knowing what it feels like heightens your awareness in building boundaries. This time you'll know where the boundary is between yourself and your partner, and you'll notice what you experience when someone crosses your boundary without permission.

1. PARTNER 1: Draw an imaginary circle around yourself while sitting on the floor. Use your finger to trace the circle in the carpet, if possible, or use

string, magazines, pillows, or whatever you have handy to form the circle. Feel what it's like to have the circle (boundary) around you.

PARTNER 2: Feel what it's like to be outside this circle and not have a boundary like your partner has.

2. PARTNER 1: When you have your boundary (real or imaginary) created, tell your partner outside the boundary to begin playing the invader.

PARTNER 2: Using one hand, gently cross your partner's boundary. Each partner should pay attention to how it feels to play the particular role (invader or invadee). Ask yourself if you like the role you are playing.

Step 3. Creating Boundaries with Protection

This part of the exercise is for developing an awareness of what an appropriate boundary looks and feels like.

PARTNER 1: Using the boundary created around you as a base, now create an imaginary egg-shaped sphere that completely surrounds you. As you mentally set the sphere in place, notice how it feels to have this imaginary protection around you. Next, charge your egg with your own energy by breathing it full of breath through quick bursts of breathing, by radiating out energy from your whole body, or by imagining it full of some color, sound, or other kind of comforting support.

PARTNER 2: Notice what it feels like when your partner begins to isolate himself or herself from you in this protective egg. Do you notice any emotions rising in you? Do you have any other kind of response?

Step 4. Protecting Your Physical Boundaries

In this part of the exercise, you'll learn how to protect yourself against physical boundary violations.

PARTNER 1: When you have your egg full of protective energy, ask your partner to attempt to physically invade your space by slowly moving one hand toward your egg. As the hand comes toward you, you can protect yourself in two ways. First, use the energy in your egg to make it impenetrable by your partner. Second, if the hand gets inside your egg, make a countering move with your hand to block your partner's hand. Use only enough force to stop the encroachment and to assert your strength. If you undermatch the oncoming energy, you set yourself up to be victimized. If you overmatch the oncoming energy, you set yourself up as an aggressor.

PARTNER 2: Invade your partner in a way that feels appropriate for him or her. If you're working with a timid partner, use less forcefulness. If you're working with a stronger partner, then you can use more force.

Step 5. Protecting Your Mental Boundaries

This part of the exercise focuses on mental rather than physical boundaries and involves letting other people define your reality by telling you what you think or by giving you negative messages that cause you to doubt yourself and your abilities.

PARTNER 1: Think of something that people say to you that causes you to lose confidence in your ability to think. You'll share this information with your partner, who will use it in the exercise in an attempt to violate your mental boundaries. Perhaps it's some kind of message that says you're stupid, dumb, or crazy. Now share this message with your partner while you are standing or sitting outside your boundary. Then return to the safety of your egg, making sure it's full of energy or whatever kind of protection you have filled it with. Your partner is going to repeat the message you just shared with him or her while you stay in the safety of your egg. When you have your egg ready, indicate to your partner that you're ready to begin.

PARTNER 2: Speak the disturbing message that your partner shared with you. You can repeat it with different inflections, and then begin to add variations of your own that you intuitively sense will fit with the original message.

PARTNER 1: Continue to keep the shell of your egg impenetrable. Use the protective devices you have created (color, sound, energy) to repel your partner's attempts to cross your mental boundaries. You can close your eyes, look away from your partner, or sing a song to yourself if you need to. When you're able to do this successfully, you can tell your partner to stop. If your partner's words begin to penetrate your shell, ask him or her to stop while you recharge your egg. Continue with the exercise until you know you can protect yourself against mental violations without difficulty.

Step 6. Protecting Your Emotional Boundaries

This part of the exercise focuses on emotional boundaries and involves letting other people define your reality by telling you what you feel or by giving you negative messages that cause you to doubt your own feelings.

PARTNER 1: Remember the kinds of things people do or say to you that cause you to give up, modify, or hide your real feelings. These could be seductive messages, such as "Please rescue me, I'm helpless," or "You're so important; we really need you to do this job," which appeals to your need to be important. Now share this message with your partner while you're standing or sitting outside your boundary. Then return to the safety of your egg, filling it again with protection. When your egg is ready, give your partner the signal to begin the invasion.

PARTNER 2: Speak the message your partner shared with you. Use body language and voice inflections that amplify the emotional part of the message. For example, if your partner's message had a victim tone in it, look and sound like a real victim.

PARTNER 1: Continue to keep your egg impenetrable as your partner gives you your message. Give yourself comforting messages if you need to, saying things like: "My feelings are mine, and they are okay." When you can successfully resist your partner's message, tell him or her to stop. If you have difficulty at any point, stop the invasion and recharge your egg. Continue until you can protect yourself against violations of your emotional boundaries.

Step 7. Protecting Your Spiritual Boundaries

This part of the exercise focuses on your spiritual boundaries. It involves letting other people define your spiritual reality by telling you what you experience in it or by giving you negative messages that cause you to doubt your ability to connect with the world of spirit.

PARTNER 1: Think of the kinds of things that people have done that violated your spiritual boundaries. These could be terrorizing statements that invoke the wrath of God. They could also be things that attack you at the very core of your being through shame, humiliation, or judgment, things that make you want to die. Now share one of them with your partner, and return to the safety of your egg. When you've filled it with protection, tell your partner you're ready to begin.

PARTNER 2: Repeat back the message your partner shared with you in a way that resembles a Divine pronouncement. Look and sound like an authoritative God or parent.

PARTNER 1: Hold your own strength, resisting your partner's attack and abuse. If you need to pray or ask God or some other higher power for support, you can do that. When you can successfully resist your partner's message, tell him or her to stop. Stop the process any time you have difficulty resisting, and recharge your egg. Continue until you can protect yourself against violations of your spiritual boundaries.

At this point, it's time for partners to switch places. Partner 1 should remove the imprint drawn on the surface of the carpet or floor before moving on to repeat the exercise with his or her partner. When both partners have learned how to protect themselves from physical, mental, emotional, and spiritual violations and can actually feel the protection that the egg-shaped sphere provides, it's time to move on to the next part of the exercise.

Step 8. Moving in the World with Protection and Boundaries

In this part of the exercise you'll learn how to take your egg with you as you move about in the world. Both partners should make sure they have their eggs positioned around them. If you were the first Partner 1, take the time to firmly reestablish your protective egg. When both partners have their eggs in place, they should stand up, each imagining his or her egg as a hoop with handles. Picking up your egg-hoop, begin to move around the room. Notice how you react as you encounter your partner and as he or she comes close to your egg. Do you have an impulse to make your egg stronger and invade your partner? Or do you find yourself giving up your boundary? As you move around the room, try to keep your boundary intact. Stay out of your partner's egg, and keep yourself totally separate.

Step 9. Raising and Lowering Your Boundaries

This is a very important step for people with counter-dependent issues, who have little experience in allowing other people inside their boundaries. It's important to go slowly and experiment with this step.

As you walk around the room with your partner, notice when you feel safe and when you feel unsafe. When you can identify people whose energy feels safe, try opening and closing your egg as you come close to one of these people. To envision how you might let others inside your egg, you can imagine having a sliding door in your egg's shell, or a window blind with a pull string, or little lens-type holes that open and close. Become aware of what it feels like to actually be in charge of deciding who enters your space and how far they can enter. It's the ability to open or close the shell of your protective egg that really allows you to be in the world safely and still be intimate. For many people with unmet counter-dependent needs, this kind of exercise will provide the first experience of both safety and intimacy.

Step 10. Touching and Maintaining Boundaries

This can be the most difficult part of the exercise, for it requires you to actually let someone completely penetrate your egg while you still maintain your boundaries. This exercise also requires that you learn to give off nonverbal signals congruent with your desire or lack of desire to be touched. And it requires that you learn to read the nonverbal signals of other people that indicate their desire or lack of desire to be touched. This kind of knowledge is valuable for the person with counter-dependent issues who never had an opportunity to develop these skills.

As you walk around the room, nonverbally let your partner know whether or not you want him or her to touch you. Use your face and body to give off clear signals about your position on being touched. Also, notice when your partner invites you to touch him or her. Learn to read the nonverbal signals that indicate how much and where to touch. Approach your partner slowly and cautiously, so that you can stop quickly if you reach the limit.

Step 11. Discussion and Interpretation

Now discuss with your partner what you learned by doing these boundary exercises. Talk about ways you can use this information in your life — how you might use what you learned to create healthy boundaries for yourself in your relationships.

THE BOTTOM LINE

- People with unmet counter-dependency needs often had their boundaries violated when they were children, and they built walls to protect themselves from further harm.
- In order to protect themselves, people with unmet counter-dependent needs often cross the boundaries of others.
- Healthy boundaries are an important part of sustainable intimate relationships.
- It's never too late to learn how to create physical, mental, emotional, and spiritual boundaries.

9. Me and My Shadow
Reclaiming Projections

When a man points a finger at someone else,
he should remember that four of his fingers are
pointing at himself.
— Louis Nizer

In the clever little ditty "Me and My Shadow," the singer-dancer is in a relationship with his shadow as he recounts how they stroll together down the avenue. People with unmet counter-dependent needs, however, are *not* in a relationship with their shadows and may not even know they have a shadow. In psychology, the "shadow" usually refers to unwanted aspects of ourselves that we are unaware of, that we try to ignore, or that we can see only in other people. Reassigning your own shadow to other people and judging them negatively because of it is known as "projecting."

WHAT ARE PROJECTIONS?

Projection is a defense that people with unhealed developmental traumas use to avoid or hide aspects of themselves that they learned as children were unacceptable.

Counter-dependent people tend to be more aware of others' flaws and insufficiencies than they are of their own unmet needs and flaws. Counter-dependent individuals use projections to protect themselves from encountering the reality of their own unmet needs. If they are in a relationship with someone who has co-dependent behaviors, they see this person as the sick or needy one in the relationship. This one-up position allows the person with counter-dependent behaviors to project his or her own shadow and look like the "good," or "healthy," partner.

HOW AND WHY WE DEVELOP A SHADOW

Your shadow consists of all those aspects of yourself that you hide from others and from yourself. These are usually aspects that your parents, teachers, or society told you were wrong, deviant, bad, unruly, or uncivilized. Your parents may have told you things like: "Don't be so active; sit still," "Don't play with your food," "Sit up straight," "Don't play with yourself; that's bad and dirty," and "Good girls don't get angry" or "Big boys don't cry." So you learned to hide all the unacceptable feelings, thoughts, and behaviors associated with these shadow parts by putting them in a "bag."

Hiding these natural aspects of your True Self and pleasing others at a young age allowed you to survive. As you grew up, you had to drag this bag of unwanted or unappreciated traits behind you. By the time most people are nineteen or twenty, they have split off their most vital parts and stored them in this bag, including their creativity, their passions, their sexuality, their ability to have deep feelings, their energy, their spontaneity, their hungers, their enthusiasms, their dreams, and whatever else was deemed frivolous, unattractive, or otherwise unacceptable by others.

What's left? Only behaviors, thoughts, and feelings that peers, parents, teachers, and other adults find acceptable and nonthreatening, which is usually not much of your authentic self. People with counter-dependency issues usually become overidentified with their False Self. This keeps them trying to look acceptable enough, or nonthreatening enough, to others, all in the hopes of meeting their unmet developmental needs. They hope that if they conform enough they'll get the respect, love, and recognition they've always wanted. Of course, this doesn't work. Instead, they find themselves on a treadmill, doing as much as possible to look good to others but feeling empty inside.

One of the core beliefs of people with unmet counter-dependency needs is that they are not enough. They are not lovable enough, not handsome enough, not good enough sons, fathers, daughters, or mothers, and so on. They hope no one will notice they aren't good enough, and they fear that others will somehow discover this. This belief often drives their behavior and everything they say and do.

Most people keep the real self, or True Self, from accidentally popping out of the bag by focusing on unacceptable things that *others* are saying and doing. Here projection is a useful defense. Interestingly, when you project a quality of your own onto others, it's like giving it away, and it becomes difficult to reclaim if you ever want it back. For example, a man projects his ability to express feelings onto his wife, and lets her feel all the feelings in the relationship. Then when one of his children has a problem expressing feelings, he finds himself dependent on his wife and unable to help his child. It's difficult to reclaim these split-off parts, but this is exactly what people with counter-dependency issues must learn to do.

THE SHADOW AS YOUR INNER CHILD

The awful closet full of monsters, or the bag you've been dragging behind you since childhood, contains the juiciest parts of your True Self. Many times when people with counter-dependency issues realize how disconnected they are from their inner child, they weep over the loss. It's necessary to mourn the lost years with your True Self, or your inner child, so that you can begin the often scary and sometimes painful process of reclaiming the parts of you that you gave up in order to be accepted by others.

> Your shadow is none other than *your own inner child.*

Breaking free of counter-dependency requires facing your weaknesses, insecurities, fears, and shadow parts and then learning to love each one of them as you would love a hurt and rejected child. In therapy, we sometimes suggest that clients buy themselves a doll, teddy bear, or stuffed animal to represent their inner child or other split-off parts. By hugging this doll, bear, or stuffed animal and saying loving things to it, they learn to love these lost parts. One of our clients, a businessman who travels a lot, bought a travel bag to carry his teddy bear on his trips. Others strap their bear or doll into the passenger seat of their car and carry on a conversation with their inner child while traveling to and from work.

THE ROLE OF SHAME IN CREATING PROJECTIONS

The most effective tool for making others split off parts of themselves is toxic shame. The message of toxic shame is: "There is something wrong or unacceptable about you." Your parent might have said, "Shame on you for talking back to your mother: you're an insolent brat!" Or "Shame on you for playing with your genitals: you have a filthy mind."

Guilt and shame are two different emotions. Guilt implies that you did something bad or wrong and you must stop it. It carries with it certain conditional negative messages, such as "You have *done* something bad." Shame implies that you are bad or flawed at a soul level. It carries with it certain unconditional negative messages, such as "You *are* something bad, and there is nothing you can ever do about it." Although there are elements of having done something bad in the shame example above, the underlying messages are: "You are bad" and "There's something wrong with you." John Bradshaw writes, "I had one of those life-jolting discoveries that significantly changed everything. I named the core demon in my life. I named it 'toxic shame.'" He adds, "Toxic shame is unbearable and always necessitates a cover-up, a False Self. Since one feels his True Self is defective and flawed, one needs a False Self that is not defective and flawed. Once one becomes a False Self, one ceases to exist psychologically."[1]

Bradshaw lists the following characteristics of toxic shame:

1. It becomes a core identity that leaves you feeling flawed and defective, and that you are powerless to change.
2. It causes you to hide your inner feelings and thoughts from others, and it means you must guard against letting other people see these inner thoughts and feelings.
3. It causes people to constantly guard against exposing these qualities to themselves.
4. It is experienced as an inner torment or a sickness of the soul.
5. It produces shame about shame, so you are ashamed to have toxic shame and won't admit shame.

In order to hide your shame, you may try to shame others. It's like a knee-jerk reaction; you are shamed in some way, and you quickly get the monkey off your back by shaming someone else. This dynamic is at the heart of projection.

TROUBLESHOOTING

How to Spot Projections

- Remember an incident in which you experienced a sudden rush of feelings in your body, where you felt the blood rushing through your veins, your heart started beating faster, and you froze or wanted to fight or run away. These are symptoms of an adrenal stress response that your body automatically had because you felt unsafe. If you went into a "fight" response, you may have been projecting.

- Remember an incident in which your reaction was far greater than what was called for, and you made a mountain out of a molehill. Your reaction indicates that your feelings may have been coming from some previous incident. Ask yourself, "Am I actually unsafe in the present situation?" If the answer is no, then ask yourself, "When have I felt this way before?"

  This helps you recognize that you are regressed back to an earlier time in your life where you felt unsafe. Ask yourself, "What about that earlier situation is still unfinished and causes me to react and feel unsafe now?"

- Remember a conflict in which you were totally focused on what the other person said or did. Overfocusing is a form of projection that helps you avoid feelings and/or looking at your part in causing the conflict. Notice what you felt in this conflict, and ask yourself, "When have I felt this way before?" Also notice if you're using emotionally loaded or provocative words like "always" or "never" to describe the situation. If you are, then this too may be an attempt to avoid intense feelings from an earlier incident.

Bradshaw also discusses three ways that people learn shame. The first way involves identifying with shame-filled role models, usually parents, who pass on their internal shame by shaming their children. The second way is through the trauma of abandonment, in which you may have been abused, neglected, or forced to abandon your own needs and take care of your parents. This means you learned to distrust your needs, feelings, and natural instincts. You may feel ashamed for even having needs, feelings, or instincts. The third way you may develop toxic shame, according to Bradshaw, is by experiencing profound betrayal and a violation of primal trust when you were shamed as a child. There was no time to grieve this loss and no support available to help you grieve.

This points to one major difference between a developmental trauma and an "owie." When something unexpected happened to you as a child, like falling down and skinning your knee, it may only have been an "owie" if someone was there to comfort you and support you emotionally. If no one was there to support you, you experienced abandonment, and then even a small event like this became a developmental trauma. This original pain or instance of hurt feelings needs to be identified, expressed, and supported before the effects of the toxic shame can be released.

You can see that toxic shame helps explain why people who have counter-dependency issues split off aspects of themselves. Until they identify the core shaming experiences that created their original pain (developmental traumas in their trauma drama) and get help in expressing this pain, they won't break free of the shame and it will continue to color their intimate relationships.

SKILL-BUILDING EXERCISE:
USING PERCEPTION CHECKS TO SEPARATE REALITIES

An important communication skill that people with counter-dependency issues need to learn is the "perception check." When you find yourself feeling blamed or projecting blame onto others, it's important to check your perceptions. For example, in the therapy session we describe later in the chapter as a case example, one client, Jane, said to her partner, Art, "I don't think you really want this relationship to work. You just want to blame all our problems on me like my mother did and then leave [like my father did]." I (Barry) asked her if she would label that as her "perception" of Art, and I suggested she ask him if any of what she said was true "for him." Jane hesitated, but finally said, "Art, is any of what I said true?" Art replied, "No, Jane, I really want this relationship to work, and I'm not going to blame it all on you and then leave."

It was important to acknowledge that Jane's perception contained a grain of truth. So I asked Art to tell me what, if anything, *was* true about Jane's fears. Art thought for a minute, and then said, "Jane, I was at the end of my rope and feeling hopeless about things when I threatened to leave you last week. What I really wanted was a time-out from the struggle. I can see now how this could make you feel afraid and believe that I actually meant it." I asked Jane if there was anything she wanted from Art and, if there was, to ask him directly for it. She replied, "Art, when you threaten to leave me, I get really scared. Will you agree to not make threats like that anymore unless you really want to leave?" Art answered, "Yes, I'm willing to make that agreement."

Almost all projections can be handled in this manner, if both people are willing to help each other. It's also helpful to remember that the person who is not projecting may recognize the presence of projection before the other person does. To help the person who is projecting, the other person might say, "It looks and feels as though you might have a projection operating here. Are you willing to take a look at what you're saying or doing to see if there's a projection involved?" Or one person can simply ask the other if he or she is willing to do a perception check.

HOW TO RECLAIM PROJECTIONS

After most people have spent the first twenty, or even thirty, years putting things into their shame bag, then comes the task of the next twenty or thirty years: realizing what they have done and trying to reclaim these split-off parts. With proper support for our True Selves from the beginning of our lives, we would never hide parts of ourselves and, therefore, would not have to use projections.

Robert Bly writes about a five-stage process of working with projections.[2] The first four stages involve trying to make projections work for us. He says that in stage 1 we try as hard as we can to keep the projections intact. In stage 2, we realize that our projections don't really work. For example, our spouse sometimes is loving toward us and wants to get close. What can we do in such situations when it's difficult to see him or her as bad or uncaring? He says this dilemma is frightening for people with counter-dependency issues because it brings up old fears and insecurities. They may try to provoke or manipulate their partners back into their False Selves. The solution that many couples choose at this stage is to have children and project their shadow parts onto them. Children can't fight back and are always doing things they shouldn't be doing, so they make great targets for projections.

In stage 3, according to Bly, things break down so badly that people must use moral rightness to justify their actions. Parents may claim that what they do to their children is "for their own good" when they punish them severely. The message is, "Don't question my authority; I am right." If the family is religious, they may even pull in God: "God will punish you if you don't behave or listen to me."

In stage 4, people with counter-dependent patterns may let down their guard enough to see what they're doing. They may recognize that they've diminished themselves through the projection process, which leads them to take inventory of their lives and decide to change them. At this stage, they may also start therapy or join a support group and begin piecing things together.

In stage 5, according to Bly, the task is to "eat" your shadow. This means facing everything you've pushed away from yourself and projected onto others. You have to chew up, swallow, and digest all that you've been afraid of. By reintegrating these split-off parts, you can begin to express deeper feelings, feel more passionate about life, become more spontaneous, and become more healthful and spiritual. According to Bly, people who have eaten their shadows tend to "be" more than "do" and show more grief than anger. They often have more energy, need less sleep, and are wiser and more discerning in their decisions.

The following case example shows how projections operate for people with counter-dependency issues in relationships. It also shows some of the tools you may need in order to begin reclaiming your shadow.

CASE EXAMPLE

Art and Jane, who were having serious relationship conflicts, came to me (Barry) to start couples therapy. We negotiated a three-session contract to see if we could work together effectively and to determine whether they were getting what they wanted. During the first session or two, I focused on helping them find the source of their conflict. Together we tried to iden-tify the unfinished business that each of them had brought into the rela-tionship.

I thought they had gained a lot of insight, so at the beginning of the third session I was pleased to hear Jane announce, "I've been thinking about our last session, and I now realize what the biggest problem in our relation-ship is." I asked, "What is it, Jane?" To this she replied, "It's him," as she pointed her finger at her husband, and then launched into a nonstop sham-ing litany of all the things he had done or not done to her that had ruined the relationship. This was obviously an attack in which she tried to project blame for everything that was wrong with the relationship on him.

Apparently, I had moved too fast for Jane, and she had become really scared that she would be blamed for all their relationship problems, just as she had been blamed for all her parents' relationship problems. I was able to recognize Jane's terror and immediately knew that she had been triggered back to a childhood memory. It wasn't "Jane the angry bitch" talking, but "Jane the scared child" who was yelling at her husband. I let her know I saw her frightened child: "You look really scared Jane. Just close your eyes and sink into that feeling." She did this, and she began to sob. Between sobs, she told a story of something that had happened one night when she was six: her father, who was drunk, crawled into bed with her and sexually molested her. The next day she told her mother, who immediately ordered her father out of the house, and they divorced.

Later on, Jane's mother periodically blamed Jane for breaking up her parents' marriage. Jane's mother never remarried, and she lived out the rest of her life as an angry, miserable victim. Jane believed that her parents' divorce actually was her fault, and she took all the blame for her mother's unhappiness. Whenever she got into a conflict with her husband, Art, she became afraid that he would leave, as her father had.

This illustrates how projections get set up and reveals that, frequently behind these projections, such as Jane's, there's a shamed little child. Projec-tions are often difficult to sort out in a relationship because there's usually a grain of truth to the accusation. In Jane's case, she actually believed that Art did *all* those things she accused him of doing, because he really had done a *few* of them.

HOW TO EAT YOUR SHADOW ONE BITE AT A TIME

- Do some bodywork to loosen up those tight and constricted places in your body that you have used to armor yourself. Regular massages, deep tissue work such as Rolfing, Lomi work, Trager work, or myotherapy may be a good adjunct to your psychological work.
- Develop your creative and artistic talents. Try dance and movement classes, clay work, drawing, or playing a drum or another musical instrument to retrieve your lost resources.
- Make a list of the projections you have used and whom you have projected things onto.
- Go to these people and tell them you are taking back your projections. Ask them to return the projections you put on them. Some people may resist this, particularly if you have been projecting "light" parts of yourself, such as your creativity and spontaneity.
- Do things to awaken your sense of smell, taste, touch, sight, and hearing to help you feel more alive.
- Do freewriting. Write whatever comes into your mind for about ten minutes. Continue writing without pausing so that you can record everything. This can open up creative doors in your mind.
- Buy a doll, teddy bear, or other stuffed animal to represent aspects of yourself that you thought were not acceptable. Learn to love and care for this object as you learn to love and care for those aspects of yourself.
- When you meet someone new, look for things that you have in common. This may help you feel more open and connected to other people.
- Use perception checks when you are aware of having unusually strong reactions to what someone else is doing or saying. Say, "I'm having a reaction to something you said, and I want to check it out. Did you mean...?"
- Buy or make masks to represent your internal demons, witches, or ugly giants. Wear the mask and try acting out this part. Try writing out a dialogue with this part, asking it what it represents and what it has to teach you. This can be fun, and you can learn more about these hidden parts.

SKILL-BUILDING EXERCISE:
FACILITATING BLAME

Blame is one of the most destructive forces in relationships, and one of the most common ways that projections are used in relationships is to blame others. The following exercise can be done alone, or with a partner if you are involved in mutual blaming. If you do this alone, it can be strictly a writing process. You can use a pillow or empty chair to represent the other person if you want a dialogue with that person. If you're working with a partner, you can each write a "blame sheet" and then each read the other's, or you can speak these blaming statements directly to each other. If you are working with a partner, you may want to take turns doing each step so that you are working in parallel.

Step 1. Blame It All on Them.

In a conflict where you think the other person is to blame, you may want to look for secret blaming you may be hiding. Write out all the things you are blaming the other person for. Blame him or her 100 percent for what happened. Get it all on paper, or speak it all to your partner. Your partner's job is to make sure you have not taken *any blame* for what happened. If you are doing this alone, read and evaluate your written blame sheet, and correct it if you actually accepted *any* of the blame. Notice how this feels for you. It usually feels good to blame everything that happened on someone else.

Step 2. Blame It All on Yourself.

This time you need to look at yourself and blame everything that happened on yourself. Again, write or speak this out completely. If you have a partner, his or her job is to make sure that in this step *you* accept *all* the blame. Again, notice the feelings you have in accepting all the blame. Compare these feelings to those in Step 1.

Step 3. Whose Responsibility Was It?

Responsibility is different from blame: it means "ability to respond." This time look at what happened from a new perspective, asking yourself, "How much ability to respond did I originally have in this situation?" "How much more experience and information do I now have in this situation?" "How can I use my ability now in similar situations?" Write or speak your answer to this question, and communicate it to your partner, if appropriate.

Step 4. What Have I Learned?

Ask yourself, "What could I have done differently if I had used my ability to respond more effectively?" Write or speak your answer to this question and communicate it to your partner, if appropriate.

THE BOTTOM LINE

- Projection is a major defense that blocks intimacy and reduces the sustainability of a relationship.
- Projections are present in most conflicts and in wars.
- Being able to do a perception check is an important skill in creating and sustaining intimate relationships.
- Your shadow is made up of parts of your inner child that others refused to accept or recognize.
- Reclaiming vital parts of yourself that have been split off can be fun and rewarding.

10. Self-parenting
Healing Your Inner Child

You grow up the day you have your first real laugh at yourself.
— Ethel Barrymore

We haven't yet found anyone who had all of his or her developmental needs met before reaching adulthood. No one's parents were perfect. They had their own unmet developmental needs, which colored their parenting, and they unwittingly passed misinformation on to you. They probably knew very little about the developmental needs of children and, from this ignorance and lack of knowledge, traumatized you by committing "sins of omission and commission." (Recall the awareness activity on this topic at the end of chapter 2.)

In order to fill in the gaps, correct any misinformation you received, and locate and heal any developmental traumas, you can finish growing up by parenting yourself. The only other path available, which a lot of people choose, is to blame your parents, teachers, or other adults in your life for screwing up and causing your problems. But taking this path will keep you stuck in childhood. A place to start with the process of self-parenting as an adult is to reconnect with your inner child.

CONNECTING WITH YOUR INNER CHILD

Many people with counter-dependency issues grow up cut off from their inner child. Either they put aside many of the qualities of their inner child to protect themselves from parental shame and abuse, or, because of parental neglect, they never experienced having these qualities. As adults, unfortunately, people often treat their inner child the exact same way they were parented as children. At some point, you must stop shaming your inner child with abusive messages like the ones you heard growing up. This is a form of self-hatred. Using the examples in the sidebar "Shaming Messages Your Inner Child May Have Received," create your own list of messages you use to shame and abuse your inner child.

SHAMING MESSAGES YOUR INNER CHILD
MAY HAVE RECEIVED

- "Stay out of my way."
- "I don't need you in my life."
- "Don't embarrass me."
- "Don't make any demands or have any needs."
- "I don't have time for you."
- "I don't like you."
- "I don't like your feelings."
- "I hate you."
- "You must be crazy."
- "You can't do anything right."
- "You are so stupid!"
- "You'll never amount to anything."
- "Why would anyone love you?"
- "Who do you think you are anyway — the Queen of Sheba?"

If you remember receiving messages like these, notice how many of them you still say to yourself. These messages present areas of healing where you can reclaim your True Self. Self-parenting is a really important part of healing your wounded inner child.

HEALING YOUR INNER CHILD

After you have established solid contact with your inner child, try to remember as much as you can about the circumstances in your childhood that caused you to split off parts of your True Self. The awareness exercises in the first part of this book may help you begin to piece things together.

Taking charge of this healing process is very important, because it helps you break free from victimhood and co-dependency. You cannot wait for someone else to do it for you. Our hopeful message is that, despite all the wounds your inner child suffered as a result of abuse or neglect, you can heal these wounds as an adult. You can learn ways to meet your unmet developmental needs and heal your traumatized inner child. For the most part, it's not a question of unlearning something. It's really an opportunity to learn something new for the first time — something that you did not get a chance to learn as a child.

John Bradshaw, in his book *Homecoming: Reclaiming and Championing Your Inner Child*, offers ten nurturing rules, adapted in the sidebar, "Your Inner Child's Bill of Rights" (see next page), to use when you parent your inner child.[1] These are sort of a bill of rights for healing your inner child. They are birthrights you may have been forced to give up as a child, and that you can now reclaim as part of healing your inner child.

WORKING WITH YOUR FEELINGS

The most essential part of healing your inner child is remembering and expressing repressed feelings, because, when they remaining repressed, they anchor old patterns of thinking and behaving that keep you from moving forward. Children are often punished for expressing angry or sad feelings, and they witness others being punished for expressing these feelings. In addition, many of our core feelings of fear of abandonment, grief, rage, and shame may have been too overwhelming to express as a child, even with supportive parents. So it is likely that you have grown up without feeling or expressing many of your deepest emotions from your childhood.

As we discussed in chapter 7, many people were not given accurate information about the function of their feelings by their parents, teachers, and other adults. Skills that should have been learned in kindergarten may not have been learned at all, and this may continue to act as a barrier to intimacy in adult relationships. An important part of your adult self-parenting is to learn to use your feelings to create more intimacy.

YOUR INNER CHILD'S BILL OF RIGHTS

1. You have the right to feel all of your feelings. There is no such thing as a "bad" feeling. You can learn effective ways to use your feelings to get your needs met.
2. You have the right to want whatever you want. You can actively seek what you want by asking for it directly.
3. You have the right to what you see and hear. You have the final say about what you see and hear.
4. You have the right to have fun and play whenever you want to. You can decide when, where, and with whom you want to play.
5. You have the right to tell the truth as you see it. You can listen to how others see things and still decide what is true for you.
6. You have the right to set your own limits or boundaries. This helps you feel safe and secure.
7. You have the right to your own thoughts, feelings, behaviors, and body. You do not have to take responsibility for anything that is not yours.
8. You have the right to make mistakes. There really is no such thing as a "bad" mistake. Mistakes are good because they help us learn.
9. You have the right to privacy and a responsibility to respect the privacy of others. Do not consciously violate the privacy of others.
10. You have the right to have problems and conflicts. You don't have to be perfect to be loved.

An almost universal childhood feeling is abandonment, which is particularly strong if parents and others did not support or mirror a child's inner feelings. The illusion that most young children have is that their parents know how to reflect back their inner feelings. When parents don't do this, children experience the abandonment of their inner self. After numerous such episodes, children just abandon their own inner self. Children who do not become emotionally competent often depend on the opinions of others to define who they really are. In short, as adults they remain cut off from their inner child.

Another common form of abandonment is physical abandonment. Young children under the age of two cannot tolerate prolonged absences by their mother and others with whom they are bonded. For example, if parents go on a weeklong vacation and leave a child under one year of age with a sitter or relative, the child may experience abandonment. If a mother goes to the hospital to have another child, this can be a double abandonment (physical and emotional), because when she returns, all her attention may be on the new baby. For this reason, we recommend spacing children at least three years apart. By then, they'll be more self-sufficient and ready for independence.

It is important for parents, even when leaving small children for a short period of time, to look into their eyes and tell them that the parents are leaving and when they will return. Even if children don't understand time concepts, they will understand the tone of the message. One of our clients with a severe eating disorder told us that, when she was two years old, her grandmother distracted her by feeding her cookies in the kitchen while her parents sneaked out the front door and left for a two-week vacation. This client now suffers from intense abandonment fears in her relationships and cannot eat when these fears appear.

Psychotherapist James Masterson says that underneath the depression that typically accompanies abandonment experiences are overwhelming feelings of panic, terror, rage, shame, grief, despair, and emptiness.[2] Repressing these memories keeps these overwhelming feelings out of our awareness. The problem is that, while the feelings associated with these memories were overwhelming when they happened to the child, they no longer are to the adult. Most adults, however, behave as if they were still one or two years old and avoid experiencing these core feelings. No adult has ever died from experiencing core feelings, no matter how overwhelming they might seem. Many adults, however, have repressed their feelings and died from illnesses caused by repressing them.

Depressed people who come into therapy are usually not in touch with these deep core feelings. It usually takes time to build enough trust that clients will risk sharing the deep feelings beneath their depression. More and more medical research has confirmed what many mental health people have known for a long time: that most degenerative diseases, such as cancer, heart disease, arthritis, and strokes, may be caused by repressed emotions. These emotions get stored energetically in the body and place chronic stress on all the internal organs, until something breaks down and causes a degenerative disease.

Alice Miller writes about the importance of grieving the loss of your True Self and the loss of your innocence in childhood.[3] It's true that you can never return to childhood. It is gone forever. But as an adult, it is possible to feel those important feelings and then move forward to complete developmental processes from your childhood. There probably isn't an adult alive today who doesn't have some unfinished childhood business.

Most people try to work around this unfinished business by finding ways to compensate for their deficits. For example, those who have problems with emotions might develop relationships with people who are very expressive and social. By repressing the memory of your unmet developmental needs, however, you miss opportunities to meet these needs as an adult. Perhaps your unmet developmental needs have motivated you to develop certain aspects of yourself that you wouldn't have developed otherwise. Nevertheless, this unfinished business still remains, and it holds you back in some way. You no longer have to tolerate this handicap. You can repair the trauma and free yourself to live a happier life in sustained, intimate relationships.

THE LAYERS OF FEELINGS

The following illustration shows the layers of feelings that people create. The outer layers serve as layers of defense against experiencing the core feelings. Notice that both positive and negative feelings are part of the core, so gaining access to these core feelings can lead to more joy, love, ecstasy, and bliss.

The process of uncovering and expressing your core feelings can best be done in group therapy, because groups seems to provide the safety and support that people need in order to break through their fear of experiencing these feelings. Witnessing other group members doing deep emotional work often triggers emotional responses that you can't hold back any longer. Self-help or twelve-step support groups are not usually structured to handle deep emotional work, but they can provide useful cognitive support before and after emotional work is done.

A final word of caution about processing memories related to abandonment. Rage, which is one of the core feelings, is a common response to abandonment. When a person expresses rage, it can look like a tantrum by a two-year-old. Because people are releasing primal feelings, they can hurt

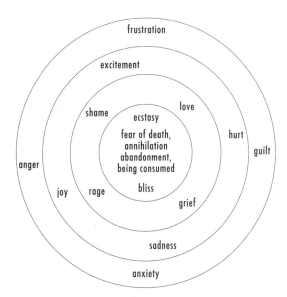

themselves or others. Rage needs to be expressed in a safe environment, and group members can help individuals safely release rage by holding their arms, legs, and heads so their bodies can move freely and fully express the rage without hurting themselves. In order to release rage, you will need to work with a therapist who has been trained in facilitating rage work.

Rage work, if done correctly, can be accomplished quickly and with highly beneficial results. If you are a therapist working with a client, before undertaking rage work make sure that the person does not have any medical problems that would be exacerbated by it, such as heart disease or high blood pressure. Another effective, though less violent, form of rage work is to have the person squeeze and twist a towel. (This is particularly good for clients who feel like choking those who abused them.)

An additional effective way we have found to help people express intense anger is to have them beat on a mattress or a vinyl beanbag chair with a tennis racket. As the tennis racquet strikes the vinyl, it makes a loud cracking sound that many people find particularly satisfying. We always emphasize that they are not hitting the person they are angry at, but are just expressing feelings. It can be helpful to place a pillow nearby to represent a person whom clients would like to have witness the anger they are expressing over their parents' sins of omission and commission.

SELF-PARENTING SKILLS

Learning self-parenting skills means taking charge of healing your inner child and actively championing that child. This requires letting go of the illusion that, if you become perfect enough, clever enough, or obedient enough, your parents or other parent substitutes will provide you with what you need. The only way you're going to heal your inner child is by asking directly for what you want from those who have what you need and by providing the rest yourself. Let's look at four sets of corrective parenting skills that can help you do this.

Identifying Your Incomplete Developmental Processes

Each developmental stage has specific needs that must be met in order to complete that stage's developmental processes. It's important to know what these processes are and which of yours were not completed. In the chart in chapter 1 (pages 32–35), we've listed the essential processes for each developmental stage. Once you identify which ones you still need to complete, you are ready to begin your self-parenting work.

Using Developmental Permissions

These are the positive supportive messages you needed to hear as a child. If you didn't get this type of message, and/or you got negative messages, then you still need to hear these positive messages from others and to learn how to give them to yourself. These include "I'm glad you were born," "You belong here," "I love you just the way you are," "You are lovable and capable," "You can ask for what you want and need," "You can trust your inner knowing," "You can think for yourself," and "I will not abandon you." You can also go back to chapter 2 and check the two lists you made in the awareness activity "The Sins of Omission and Commission" to see if they include any developmental permissions that you didn't get and wanted to hear.

Making Parenting Contracts

Once you've identified which developmental permissions you still need to hear, find someone who is willing to say these messages to you and make a contract with him or her. If you wanted to hear them from your mother, you may want to select a female to say them to you. If you wanted to hear them from your father, select a male to say them to you. Be aware of any resistance you might still have to taking in positive messages. You've learned to live without supportive messages and may have convinced yourself that you really don't need to hear them. It's important to ask for them to be repeated until you break through any resistance you might have to letting them in. If you find you aren't comfortable hearing them, just acknowledge your resistance and wait for another time. You may need to process some of your anger and resentment in order to let in positive support.

> True love grows out of a union where each other's best interests are as important as one's own.

You can create parenting contracts with your friends, your spouse, your sister or brother, or other loved ones who are interested in helping you with this deep healing work. Pick only people you feel safe with and who are committed to supporting your growth. When a couple agrees to cooperate and support each other in meeting their unmet developmental needs, they develop many rich opportunities for a new depth of love and nonsexual intimacy.

Truly loving people are able to live from their True Selves, brokenness and all, and to support and encourage others' efforts to become whole. Establishing a parenting contract is one way a couple may support each other. The section that follows, "How to Make a Parenting Contract with a Trusted Person," presents a sample conversation that might occur between two people making such a contract.

HOW TO MAKE A PARENTING CONTRACT
WITH A TRUSTED PERSON

MARY: John, when you raise your voice in the middle of an argument with me, I feel scared like I did when I was a little girl. I was never able to respond to my father when I was little. I know now what I would have liked to have said to him when he did that to me. Would you be willing to play my father for about ten minutes and help me finish this with my father?

JOHN: I don't want to be your father. I want to be your husband.

MARY: I know you aren't my father, but when you do certain things you remind me of my father. I want to take care of this unfinished business, so that I no longer see his face instead of yours when we get in an argument.

JOHN: Oh, well, if that's the case, sure, I can play the role of your father for a few minutes.

MARY (now talking to her father): When I was small and I did things you didn't like, you would yell at me, and I got scared of you. You were so much bigger than I was that I felt powerless to tell you how I felt. I want to tell you now. Will you listen to me and not yell at me?

JOHN (as Mary's father): Yes, I will listen to you, and I won't yell at you.

MARY (now sobbing quietly): I really wanted you to talk to me and play with me, but it seemed like you were always too busy, and that the only attention I got was when you yelled at me. I wondered what I had done to make you hate me so. You were so hateful to me. I still need you to tell me that you love me. And I need you to hold me and tell me the things that you like about me. Will you do that?

JOHN: Yes, I do love you, Mary, and I would like to hold you and comfort you. (now holding and rocking Mary) You are a wonderful little girl. You are smart and so full of life and joy. You are very lovable, and I'm glad you're my daughter. I'm very sorry I didn't tell you these things when you were a child. I had my priorities backwards then, and I was always too busy for my children. I regret that deeply. Is there anything else that you want me to tell you as your dad?

MARY: No, that is all I can think of now. Thank you, John, for playing my dad and telling me those things. It really helped. I could feel myself relaxing in your arms as you said those things. I think it will really help me to stop seeing you as my father and to see you more as John.

Parenting contracts are usually short-term agreements like the one above, and are designed to help each person meet unmet developmental needs in a clear, conscious way. Contracting works best with people who feel bonded to each other, but contracts can be used in a variety of settings with different people in your life. Everyone who comes into your life could be someone you contract with to complete developmental processes. Be sure to find people who are really safe and who will not take advantage of your vulnerability. It's absolutely necessary for the other person to agree not to use the situation to act out any sexual feelings. It is not appropriate for this person to be sexual with you, particularly if you have regressed to feeling like a small child.

Self-Nurturing Skills

One of the most difficult things to do if you have incomplete developmental processes is to nurture yourself. You may need help in learning how to care for yourself and your inner child. As noted earlier, adults with incomplete developmental processes may find it helpful to work with a doll, teddy bear, or stuffed animal to practice self-nurturing. It's very hard for many adults to carry a stuffed animal or a doll around, and they may feel embarrassed and self-conscious at first. But those who push through their fears and embarrassment report that this really helps nurture their inner child.

Making a contract to do one thing every day to nurture your inner child can help the integration process. Many adults attempting to comfort themselves turn to substitutes such as alcohol, drugs, sex, material things, and food. These don't work well and often have addictive side effects. See the "Troubleshooting" sidebar (page 210) for more productive activities that you can use instead. You can decide for yourself which ones are best for your inner child.

CASE EXAMPLE

We first met Julie in one of our workshops at a time when she was seeking more meaning in her life. She had a new home, a new car, two young children, and a graduate degree, and was living "the good life." After ten years of the same job and the same husband, she had realized that something was missing. The hollowness of her day-to-day experiences had forced her to look at her life. When she came to therapy initially, it was to do private work with me (Janae). She had targeted her marriage as the source of most of her unhappiness. Dissatisfaction in her relationship with Doug had been building, and she was at a point where she was considering having an affair. Her initial issue in therapy was exploring whether she should leave Doug.

Our first task was to look at what was really happening in Julie's life, especially between her and Doug. We began to review her childhood and young adulthood in an effort to connect the present to her past. As we did this, some interesting things emerged. First, Julie was a twin. She had two brothers, one of which was her fraternal twin. She had almost died at birth because neither her parents nor the delivering physician had expected twins. In fact, the doctor had begun to suture her mother after her brother was born, before anyone realized there was a second baby. By the time she was delivered, she had begun to breathe the amniotic fluid and was in danger of suffocating.

Because of her small size and her respiratory problems, she was kept in an incubator at the hospital for almost a month before she was taken home. Her brother, who was larger, went home after a few days. Julie and I examined this early history together and looked at what she would have needed for her birth to have been ideal. The gap between the actual and the ideal became a framework for her therapy work.

She made several calls to her parents and talked to them about the

TROUBLESHOOTING

How to Nurture Your Inner Child

- Get a regular massage.
- Soak in a hot tub, or soak in a bathtub with bubble bath or bath oils.
- Take time during your day to be alone and reflect on your inner child.
- Take regular walks in nature.
- Take a regular nap each day.
- Meditate quietly in a special place or room of your own.
- Listen to beautiful music.
- Have a friend hold you or give you a back rub.
- Write in a journal about your inner-child healing experiences.
- Write regular letters to your inner child describing the things you like about him or her.
- Sit or stand in front of a mirror and learn to love all your body parts.
- Say loving things to your inner child.
- Write developmental permissions and dictate them into a tape recorder. Play them back to yourself on the way to and from work or before you go to bed at night.
- Talk to your inner child every day, using your doll, teddy bear, or stuffed animal to represent your inner child.
- Sing to your inner child. Make up songs that affirm your inner child.
- Take your child to the circus or the park to play.

circumstances of her birth and the period following her birth to see if there were any other details that would be helpful. She also talked with her twin brother to see what she could learn. Conversations with both parts of her family helped her remember things about her birth. Julie decided she wanted to do a session of cotherapy with Barry where she could use Developmental Process Work to relive her birth. She thought this would help her remember some of her feelings associated with birth and would enable her to learn more about what wasn't finished. She asked Doug to come with her to act out the role of her twin brother in this session, while we agreed to be her parents and to facilitate the session.

The evening that we (Janae and Barry) did the session, Julie arrived with a scenario that she wanted to use as the script for reliving her birth. She asked Doug to curl up with her on the floor and directed us to get our large blanket and cover them up as though they were inside the womb. Julie and Doug began a dialogue as baby brother and sister as they waited inside their mother to be born.

Julie indicated that throughout most of her life she had felt as though her brother, Tim, had abandoned her. He had come out of the womb first, had gone home first, and had joined the male world. She had never felt close to him as a result. She identified Tim as a bad person and the cause of a lot of her problems. Julie believed that, if he hadn't abandoned her, she would not have had so many problems in life.

During her regression back in the "womb," however, Julie discovered a different perspective about their relationship. She remembered that she had been afraid to be born first, that it had seemed too scary for her to leave Tim. Because of her fright at separating from Tim, she persuaded him to be born first. It was at that point that her plan had backfired, and she had ended up being trapped in the womb. This birth trauma required her to be hospitalized in an incubator for a month, separated from both her mother and Tim.

We suspected that Julie had never been able to express her feelings of fear and abandonment related to her traumatic birth. We asked her if she would like to relive her original birth and see what feelings might come. She agreed to do that. She and Doug re-created a prebirth dialogue. ("I'm scared to go out without you, Tim. Will you go first? I'll come right behind you.") Tim (Doug) slipped quickly out of the "womb" and left Julie there alone. We quickly covered her with the blanket and simulated the doctor suturing up her mother.

In a moment, Julie was in a panic as she remembered her near suffocation. We quickly uncovered her and held her, while repeating to her the things she told us she had wanted from her parents and hadn't gotten. This provided her with some essential developmental permissions and also re-parenting. After she had been sufficiently comforted and was calmed down, she looked at us and said, "Now I want to do it right." Then she looked at Doug and asked, "Will you do this again with me?" He took a deep breath and smiled at her and said, "Sure." At this point, Julie took charge of creating a corrective parenting experience for herself.

Back into the womb they went. They went through another prebirth dialogue, this time with Julie insisting that she go first. After a few moments, Julie slipped out through an opening in the blanket. Janae caught her and held her quietly. Then Julie called to Tim to come out. Barry caught him as he emerged. The four of us sat quietly together for a time, as we played Julie's parents and spoke welcoming messages to her and Tim.

Near the end of the session, we discussed with Julie what she saw as the connection between her relationship with Tim and her relationship with Doug. She thought for a moment, and then gasped loudly, sitting upright, "I have been trying to get Doug to abandon me the same way Tim did. My attraction to other men and the temptation to have an affair were things I knew Doug would never tolerate. If he found out, he would leave me for sure. I see now how I was trying to get Doug to be Tim."

We helped Julie look at how her birth trauma had created a life drama. She could recall feeling abandoned all her life by men: first her twin brother, followed by her older brother, her father, and several boyfriends. Now she was trying to get Doug to play the abandoning male in her drama.

We also looked for other things that might be unfinished about her birth. She remembered the awful loneliness of being in the hospital incubator for that month. Julie made a corrective-parenting contract with Janae to come in for another session to work on her feelings of loneliness.

In that next session, Janae and Julie re-created the incubator with sofa cushions and a blanket, with Julie inside it. For a long period she lay quietly. I (Janae) thought there were unexpressed feelings from this incident, so I decided to re-create the original scene by leaving the room for a while. I left and closed the door loudly enough that Julie would know I was gone. I could still see and hear her through the glass in the door and could monitor the situation closely. In a minute or two Julie began sobbing. The sobbing grew louder and louder, until I knew from her crying that she was reaching core feelings.

At that moment, I reentered the room, pulled back the blanket on her "incubator," and encircled her with my arms. She reached around my neck and clung tightly to me. I held her this way for fifteen or twenty minutes, until she calmed down. She began to share with me how the terror of her time in the incubator had returned, how she had felt so powerless to get anyone to come to her, and how she had feared that, since no one would come, she would die. At that point, I saw that the incubator incident was already a replay of her original trauma, and that her life drama had begun.

The unfinished piece of healing in this part of her birth process required replaying the scene and providing the missing corrective parenting. I asked Julie if she would like to go back to the incubator period again and get what she missed the first time. She said she thought she was ready to do that. She curled up on the floor, and I rebuilt the incubator around her. After a few moments of quiet, I asked her what she would like to have had when she was that tiny baby, if she could have asked for it. She said the scariest part was being alone and missing her mother. What she wanted this time was for me to be her mother and come and get in the incubator with her.

I made the incubator a little larger, got down on the floor, and wiggled my way under the blanket with her. By this time she was beginning to feel the emotional exhaustion of the session's experience. She curled up beside me in a little ball, let out a long sigh, and fell asleep. For several minutes we lay together in our peaceful hideaway. Eventually, she moved her body out of its constricted position, and her eyes fluttered open. Smiling happily when she saw me still there, she stretched and sat up. I also sat up. I saw that Julie was shifting out of her regressed state and returning to her normal state of awareness, signaling that this part of the work was complete.

For a few minutes we sat talking about the session, discussing what else might yet be incomplete. She said she tended to make her life feel lonely and barren like her incubator, so we discussed the kinds of self-nurturing activities she could do to help relieve these feelings. She came up with several, which she contracted to do on a regular basis. She shared how helpful it was for her to see that she could change her childhood belief that "life is an incubator" by creating supportive new experiences for herself.

Julie found other missing pieces in her life drama and made separate therapy contracts to work on them. Over the course of several months, she moved out of her old patterns. She saw that the "something is missing" belief she'd had at the beginning of therapy had shifted to "something is unfinished."

Once Doug and Julie saw that Julie was primarily attracted to Doug because she expected him to play the role of Tim in her life drama, they reexamined their relationship. They began to see how incompatible they really were in many aspects. Julie, for instance, was emotionally a newborn child. She saw that she had developmental gaps in her childhood, and that she had never really been autonomous. She had always been under the care and supervision of someone who played a parent role with her. She had never really been an adolescent or learned how to relate appropriately with boys. She had never dated anyone but Doug, and she felt she needed more experience in the world of male-female relationships.

She was honest with Doug and said that he was married to an emotional child, and that she needed to grow up more before they could have a truly adult relationship. She wanted to separate and try living alone for a while. Eventually, they decided to divorce. They brought their children to therapy for one session. Jeff, their three-year-old, had trouble verbalizing his feelings. He did work at releasing his frustrations nonverbally, however, as he methodically broke a whole box of sixty-four crayons into little pieces.

When we all saw how cathartic the experience was for him, we began cheering him on. He eventually got up on his feet and jumped up and down on the crayon pieces. We all were overjoyed that Jeff could really express his feelings. Doug and Julie agreed to a cooperative parenting contract that would meet Julie's need for some alone time and also support their children's need for continuity in parenting.

Doug and Julie honored each other — who they really were and what they really needed — by the loving and gentle way they separated, and by using their experience as one of growth. We found it incredibly moving to be part of such a loving experience. We acknowledged their loving attitude toward each other and the way they were able to create a new pattern for couples to separate and not make each other into bad guys.

SKILL-BUILDING EXERCISE:
COMPLETION PROCESS WITH YOUR PARENTS

Do this exercise with a trusted partner or therapist who will guide you through the process and support and witness your experience. This exercise can take up to two hours with each parent, depending on how much previous work you've done with your parents. It lets you play both your part and your parents' part. You may find it possible to do this with your real parents, if they are willing. In that case, we recommend doing the exercise in therapy, where you'll have skilled support if the process becomes difficult or breaks down because of the intense feelings that emerge.

1. Decide which parent you will first address in the completion process. Invite your image of this parent (or parent figure) to sit down in front of you in order to go through a process in which he or she will speak his or her truth, and will listen to and validate your truth.

2. Tell this parent about any unresolved feelings (for example, pain, grief, shame, resentment) that you have in relation to him or her.

    a. Tell this parent what he or she did or didn't do that hurt you. (Use your two lists from "The Sins of Omission and Commission" activity at the end of chapter 2 to do this.)

    b. Tell this parent how you felt when he or she did or didn't do these things (physically discharge any feelings, if necessary).

    c. Tell this parent how each of these things affected your life.

    d. Tell this parent what unhealthy telepathic agreements you are aware that you made with him or her. (For example, "I'll do this for you, if you'll do this for me.") Tell him or her why this was unhealthy for you. Note: These agreements are never spoken of directly, but both parties know what the agreements are.

3. Tell this parent the new healthy agreement you want, and ask him or her to agree. (For example, "What I want from you now is . . . Are you willing to agree to that?")

4. Change seats, assume the role of your parent and answer this question.

5. The therapist or partner checks for completion of this part of the process. Was the unhealthy agreement stated clearly? Were the feelings expressed? Was the new healthy agreement stated clearly?

THE BOTTOM LINE

- Continuing to parent yourself as an adult is necessary to fill in the gaps left in your development, so that you can become a fully functioning person.
- Less then one-tenth of 1 percent of the world's adult population has successfully completed the developmental processes of the co-dependent and counter-dependent stages of development during childhood. What are *you* waiting for?
- One of your biggest challenges may be breaking free of your patterns of self-hatred. Watch how you talk to yourself, and see if your self-talk is loving and affirming or hateful.
- By doing the completion process with each parent, you'll clear away most of the barriers to creating and sustaining an intimate and loving relationship.

11. Conflict and Intimacy

The meeting of two personalities is like the contact of two chemical substances: if there is any reaction, both are transformed.
— Carl Jung

Most people have never seen a conflict resolved in a way that helps them heal developmental trauma *and* become closer. This is unfortunate, because it's impossible to move out of dysfunctional patterns of behavior without skills in resolving conflicts. As we saw in chapter 3, the relationship interactions in the trauma drama and in the drama triangle are fraught with possibilities for conflict. Conflict can also signal that you are involved in a psychological game (see *Games People Play* by Eric Berne).[1] In this chapter, we present some effective spiritual tools for working with conflicts that can help bring you closer to those you love.

LIMITING BELIEFS ABOUT CONFLICT

When a conflict erupts in a class or group that we are teaching, many participants are ready to crawl under the nearest table or run out the door. This lack of experience in seeing and believing that conflicts can be resolved without people getting hurt emotionally, physically, mentally, or spiritually creates a whole set of negative beliefs and feelings about conflict. Here are some of the most common limiting and negative beliefs that people have about conflict:

- Conflict is bad.
- Conflict is scary.
- Conflict is dangerous.
- Conflict is destructive.
- Conflict means someone loses.
- Conflict means someone will get hurt.
- Conflict is difficult to control.
- Conflict escalates and gets out of hand.
- Conflict should be avoided at all costs.

People with co-dependent and counter-dependent issues approach conflict differently. Those with co-dependent patterns usually approach it more passively: they enter a conflict expecting to end up in the victim role. The best they can hope for is to make people feel sorry for them so they can get their needs met.

People with counter-dependent patterns approach a conflict more aggressively and usually end up in the persecutor role. By staying in this role, they can hide their needs for closeness and intimacy and feel safe by keeping people away. They want to avoid being seen as wrong or as responsible for the conflict, because this might indicate they have faults. This would crack their narcissistic defenses and make them more vulnerable to criticism or shame. But for both types, the most common way of approaching conflict is to avoid it at all costs.

HOW PEOPLE WITH CO-DEPENDENT PATTERNS
HANDLE CONFLICT

Conflict is one of the most difficult things for people with co-dependency issues, because it almost always triggers traumatic memories for them. They find themselves snapping back to the memory of a childhood conflict in which they were traumatized, one that made them feel small, powerless, and afraid. Negative experiences involving conflict motivate them to avoid it, which creates dilemmas in their relationships. They have to choose between avoiding a conflict and meeting their needs. If they avoid the conflict and stay passive, then they may also avoid their childhood feelings. If they try to meet their needs and, in doing so, encounter a conflict, they may get hurt. This kind of dilemma encourages them to use manipulation or other indirect methods of meeting their needs, such as by playing victim. In this way, they try to circumvent the conflict they so fear.

What doesn't work in this approach is that it supports game-playing, the drama triangle, and other kinds of power plays, and it creates more undercurrents in relationships — all of which increase the likelihood that even more conflict will occur. The biggest drawback to avoidance is that it ultimately keeps people separate and prevents real intimacy.

HOW PEOPLE WITH COUNTER-DEPENDENCY ISSUES HANDLE CONFLICT

All the things that make conflict a negative experience for people with co-dependent patterns are actually positives for people with counter-dependent patterns, because they are interested in *using* conflict to avoid intimacy in the first place. Conflict is a valuable defense mechanism for them, because they can use it to create distance and safety when they feel threatened. Playing manipulative control games that keep relationships in an uproar allows these folks to maintain a safe distance and avoid bumping into their feelings.

In a typical co-dependent/counter-dependent relationship, for example, conflict serves as a regulating mechanism. When there is too much intimacy, the person with counter-dependency issues may begin to feel old feelings of suffocation. By moving into the persecutor role, he or she can quickly generate a heated conflict and create separation between the partners. This promptly diffuses the feelings of suffocation and reinstates a feeling of safety. If there is too much space in the relationship, and the partner with co-dependent patterns begins to feel old feelings of abandonment, he or she can go quickly into victim mode and create a conflict designed to pull the other person back into contact. This will help diffuse the feelings of abandonment and reassure the person with unmet co-dependent needs that he or she will not be abandoned, at least not as long as the conflict continues.

While conflict serves as a valuable tool in modulating the amount of closeness and separation in dysfunctional relationships, it also prevents lasting intimacy and keeps both people from addressing their unmet needs for bonding and separation that are left over from childhood. For this reason, a growing number of people who want intimacy are no longer able to live with unresolved conflict.

NEW CHOICES, NEW OPPORTUNITIES

Eventually people — particularly those with counter-dependent patterns — understand that their closed, defensive responses in a conflict situation ultimately cause them to feel isolated, lonely, and alienated. When this gets painful enough, they may decide to make new choices. According to Jordan and Margaret Paul, another choice is to follow what they call the path of learning.[2] This path focuses on two kinds of learning: learning about the other person and learning about yourself. Both kinds require empathy, which we discussed in chapter 7. Only compassion and care for your own wounded inner child and the wounded inner child in others can help you to use conflict situations to learn more about yourself and other people.

Becoming aware of your own wounds and the wounds of others removes a major barrier on the road to intimacy. Once this barrier is down and you look at the road ahead, you'll see that you are in uncharted territory and need a road map to find your way. This road map has several parts.

A Road Map and a Vehicle for Recovering Intimacy

Begin by reframing the idea of conflict. Rather than seeing the path full of unknown beasts that can hurt you, look at the path as one full of unknown challenges and opportunities to learn and grow together.

Next, you need a sturdy vehicle to get you past the ruts and wrong turns — one that can survive the marshy wetlands and the unpaved trails of the high places. Your vehicle needs gears that allow you to reverse or change direction if needed, and it has to come with a warranty. In other words, it has to be a vehicle you can depend on. With a vehicle like this, you'll find you can close the exits and commit to staying in the relationship while you're in the process of recovering intimacy.

Finally, it's necessary to develop a vision of partnership conflict-resolution that keeps you headed toward closeness. This means your vehicle needs a compass or homing device to help you navigate the road to intimacy. With this kind of support, you can navigate the perils of conflict as you head toward deeper and deeper intimacy.

THE PARTNERSHIP WAY:
A ROAD MAP AND A VEHICLE

After spending six months living in Switzerland in 1986, we began looking for a road map for resolving conflicts. We had gone there to study with a Jungian analyst named Arnold Mindell. During our studies there, we began to develop the first piece of our map, which showed us how our inner conflicts are mirrored in outer conflicts.

On April 26, 1986, the nuclear reactor at Chernobyl had exploded, and we had been irradiated while walking the streets of Zurich. We were unaware of the danger then, as were most all the people in the countries neighboring the Soviet Union. The delay in notifying countries in the path of the nuclear fallout was primarily a result of the isolationist policies of the Soviet Union at the time. That was an important lesson for us, for we could see the inherent dangers when neighbors do not speak to each other at the global level.

Around this same time, American planes had bombed Libya and tried to kill General Mu'ammar al-Gadhafi. As temporary expatriates, we learned quickly that many Europeans did not appreciate American aggression against one of their volatile neighbors. This helped us see the effects of the United States' self-serving action and its lack of concern for the welfare of its European neighbors. Both of these experiences brought home the need for effective tools and maps for resolving conflict. We decided we wanted to become part of the solution to global conflict, which would require us to take personal action.

After our return to Colorado, we established a nonprofit organization, the Colorado Institute for Conflict Resolution and Creative Leadership (now the Carolina Institute for Conflict Resolution and Creative Leadership). Since 1986, we have organized two international conferences on conflict resolution; offered numerous workshops, seminars, and classes; and field-tested our own model for working with conflict with many different groups. During this period, we looked at what was working and not working in the field of conflict resolution, and what was missing. From this research, we developed our own approach, which we call the Partnership Way.[3] Some of the assumptions of this approach to conflict resolution are listed below:

- Conflict is an opportunity for growth and intimacy. Many people avoid conflict because they fail to see the opportunities present in conflict situations. Resolving conflicts effectively brings people closer together and helps them work more cooperatively.
- A comprehensive approach to resolving conflicts is needed to help people deal with many different kinds of conflict.
- Each person involved in a conflict has an important role to play in the resolution of the conflict. Individual initiative is encouraged.
- When people are given explicit, practical, and easily understood tools, they can learn to resolve conflicts quickly and effectively.
- The sources of all major conflicts in relationships between adults can be found in their unmet developmental needs or unhealed developmental traumas.

The Partnership Way is structured as a linear map that you can follow when you encounter conflict. The map will show you how to take different "roads," or options, depending on the kind of conflict you are having. Each option has a specific exercise that you can use to guide you through the conflict. Use the five partnership exercises offered here (from our book *Conflict Resolution: The Partnership Way*) to practice the skills needed to use this approach successfully in your relationships.

SKILL-BUILDING EXERCISE:
THE PARTNERSHIP WAY OF RESOLVING CONFLICTS

Partnership Exercise 1

Preparing for a Conflict Resolution Session

DIRECTIONS: Using a current conflict, fill in the blanks below to help you get a better understanding of how to manage a conflict.

STEP 1. Focus on the Inner Experience of the Conflict
a. I know that I am in conflict because_____. (Do you find that your mind goes blank; or you experience a tight stomach, sweaty palms, dizziness, and/or rapid breathing; or you have some other physical symptom?)

b. I feel this conflict in my body in my_____. (List
the place where you most feel the conflict, such as stomach, chest,
shoulders, or other area.)

STEP 2. Center Yourself
Now take a deep breath and breathe into the area of your body where you
feel tension. As you breathe into this area, visualize the tension lessening.
When the tension has released, move your attention to your belly by placing your hand about two inches below your navel. Breathe into your belly
area while you also imagine your energy going downward toward your
feet, firmly anchoring them in the earth. Let yourself feel the flow of
energy between the Earth's core and your whole body. Notice how your
body feels when you breathe and visualize using your energy in this way, so
that you can train yourself to quickly become centered when you experience
a conflict.

STEP 3. Identify the Feelings Involved in the Conflict
a. When I think of this conflict, I feel _____.
(Identify the feeling.)
b. When I identify this feeling, it tells me_____.
(Identify the function of this feeling.)

STEP 4. Identify Your Typical Behaviors in Conflict Situations
The way that I typically deal with these feelings and body symptoms is

_____

_____.

(Describe your usual response in a conflict situation.)

STEP 5. Diagnose the Conflict
How does this conflict affect me? _____.
(If you feel the conflict is having a tangible effect on you, this means
you're experiencing a conflict between your needs and wants. If you feel the
conflict is having no tangible effect on you, this means you're experiencing
a conflict between your values and beliefs.)

STEP 6. Decide How to Approach the Conflict

Option 1. Deal directly with the person(s) with whom you're in conflict.

- Use exercise 1 to get yourself ready to approach the conflict.
- Use exercise 2 if the conflict concerns wants and needs.
- Use exercise 3 if the conflict concerns values and beliefs.
- Use exercise 4 if the conflict is not resolved using exercises 2 or 3.

Option 2. Deflect the conflict by stepping aside and deciding not to engage in it. The person you are in conflict with may be too powerful, may be over-reacting or acting aggressively, or may be someone you feel unsafe to work with on conflicts.

- Use exercise 4 to determine what in you attracts this kind of person to you.

Option 3. Deepen your awareness. You can work alone on the conflict when the other person is unwilling or unable to work on it with you.

- Use exercise 4 to deepen your awareness about your part of the conflict.

Option 4. Discover the sources of your conflict by looking at your unfinished business in past relationships. Work with a partner who will help you get to the sources of the conflict.

- Use exercises 4 and 5 as guides.

STEP 7. Establish Ground Rules for Dealing with the Conflict

a. Agree on a time frame for the conflict resolution session.

b. Let each person state his or her perceptions of the conflict. Come to an agreement on what the conflict is before trying to resolve it.

c. Let each person share a desired outcome by answering the question "How would you like to have this conflict resolved?"

d. Take turns presenting the problem according to the instructions on exercises 2, 3, 4, or 5.

e. Avoid complaining; ask directly for what you want from the other person or people involved. If someone is complaining to you, ask that person what he or she wants from you.

f. If there are obvious projections present, deal with those first. Have each person directly address the person with whom he or she had the original conflict (usually parents); your partner can play the role of this person with your help. Then deal with present-time elements of the conflict, if any are left over.

g. Agree to try out any agreements you make for a specified time to see if they work.

h. Learn to accept relapses. The old behaviors that cause the conflict may not change immediately. If this happens, ask the person who has a relapse what he or she wants or needs to do in order to successfully change his or her behavior.

i. Also agree to get together again at the earliest possible time if the agreement needs to be modified.

Partnership Exercise 2

Intimacy-Building Activity: An Eight-Step Method for Resolving Conflicts of Wants and Needs

DIRECTIONS: The person who feels the conflict more should initiate this process. In some cases, only one person in the conflict knows this method, so he or she should go first and direct the process. It's best if both people involved in the conflict have a copy of these steps to follow.

STEP 1. Describe objectively your perception of the problem or behavior. ("I noticed that you didn't clean up your dishes after you ate last night.")

STEP 2. Share the way you feel about the person or problem. ("I felt angry with you when I saw them in the sink.")

STEP 3. Describe the tangible effects or results of the problem or issue on you and/or your relationship. ("When I have to clean up your dishes, which is extra work for me, I don't want to be close to you.")

STEP 4. State clearly what it is you want from the other person. ("What I want is to be able to feel close to you. In order for me to feel good about being close to you, I need for you to keep your agreement to clean up your dishes after you eat.")

STEP 5. Ask the person clearly for what you want. ("Would you be willing to do that?")

STEP 6. Use reflective listening. Pause for a perception check after you listen to the other person's feedback or perceptions about the conflict. Do not allow yourself to get bogged down at this step in defending, blaming, escalating, or complaining. ("When I get angry at you about these things, you look like you are upset with me. Is that true?")

STEP 7. Negotiate if there are differences between what you want and what the other person is willing to give or do. ("I sometimes don't have time to clean up everything before I leave for work. Would it be all right if I just stack them in the sink until I get home, and then do them?")

STEP 8. If you are unable to negotiate the differences (usually because it's a conflict involving beliefs or values), agree to disagree or use exercise 3. ("I see that we just don't agree on this issue, and I can accept our disagreement. Will you also agree to disagree?" or "Will you agree to explore our differences using exercise 3?")

Partnership Exercise 3

Intimacy Building Exercise: A Seven-Step Method
for Resolving Conflicts over Values and Beliefs

DIRECTIONS: Find a time when both you and your partner are feeling rested and present and have an hour or more when you won't be disturbed. It can also be helpful if you spend a few moments sitting together quietly before beginning the exercise. This will help you focus on your partner and help you be emotionally present.

STEP 1. Take turns listening to each other's views of the conflict, using reflective listening. Be sure to identify the feelings as well as the content. ("It seems to you that I am trying to control you, and you also seem a little angry and scared to me. Do I understand accurately what you are saying and feeling?") This is the most important step in the process. Do not go on to step 2 until there is complete agreement that the other person understood what was said.

STEP 2. Take turns finding the sources of your conflict over your values or beliefs. ("What experiences have you had in your life where you felt people were trying to control you?") Again, listen and reflect back the feelings and content to each other before going on to the next step. It's very important to connect, to get past the personal experiences that led to the formation of the values or beliefs.

STEP 3. Take turns finding the sources of your feelings. ("What other times in your life have you felt this way?") Focus on any feelings that were part of the past personal experiences, and be sure to reflect back what you hear from the other.

STEP 4. Determine any shifts in awareness. ("Based on your exploration of the sources of your beliefs and your feelings, do you have any new perceptions of your values or beliefs?") Take turns restating any new perceptions to make sure you understand them before moving to the next step.

STEP 5. Now determine areas of agreement and disagreement. ("I think we now agree that what we identified as control was really a desire for more relationship. Because of our past history of having people trying to control us, we are prone to being indirect with each other. This could be a problem for us.") Again reflect back what you have heard, and make sure it's understood before moving to the next step.

STEP 6. Make plans to handle any areas of disagreement. ("I think if either of us is feeling controlled by the other in any way, that person should bring the issue directly to the other one, and we can talk about it again.") Get a verbal agreement on how you are going to handle any remaining aspects of the conflict in the future.

STEP 7. See if this conflict brings up strong feelings and reactions. If it does, you'll need to consult exercise 4 to help locate the source of these strong feelings and reactions.

Partnership Exercise 4

Intimacy Building Exercise: Identify the Sources of Your Conflict

DIRECTIONS: It's important when looking for the sources of a conflict to remember that you are never upset for the reasons you think you are. If the conflict brings up strong feelings, this is always a signal to look deeper for the source of the conflict. Listed below are some of the common sources of conflict, along with questions you can ask yourself to help you identify the source of a conflict. Once you identify the source of a current conflict, you can begin to look at what is unfinished in some past relationship. When you identify what's unfinished, you can complete the old issue by contracting with someone to work through it with you. You may be able to do this with the person with whom you are actually in conflict, or you can contract to do this with a friend, a partner, or a therapist.

a. Family Patterns Source. Ask yourself these questions:
   - "Does this person remind me of anyone from my family of origin?"
   - "Have I experienced this or similar conflicts in the past?"
   - "What is the unfinished business from my family that I'm attempting to complete with this person?"
   - "What kinds of people or behaviors tend to produce recurring conflicts for me that are related to things that happened to me in my family of origin?"
   - "What feelings can't I express in this conflict? How does this inability relate to what happened to me in my family of origin?"

b. Co-dependency Source. Ask yourself these questions:
   - "Does this conflict bring up my fears of abandonment or a fear of not getting my needs met?"
   - "Am I having trouble trusting this person? Who does he or she remind me of?"
   - "Am I acting like a victim in this conflict?"
   - "Am I clinging to or trying to control this person by playing manipulative games?"
   - "Do I have trouble asking for what I want from this person?"

c. Counter-dependency Source. Ask yourself these questions:
    •   "Does this conflict bring up my fears of invasion or abuse?"
    •   "Am I pushing this person away to avoid dealing with my fear of intimacy?"
    •   "Am I acting like a persecutor in this conflict?"
    •   "Am I making the other person into the bad guy so I can feel justified in going away?"
    •   "Am I talking about my conflict with a third party and creating secrets?"
    •   "Am I taking sides in this conflict rather than supporting the other person's feelings?"

d. Other Sources. Ask yourself these questions:
    •   "What is it about this person that reminds me of some part of myself that I don't like?"
    •   "How does this relationship conflict reflect an internal conflict of my own?"
    •   "How is this conflict related to a universal or global issue?"

Partnership Exercise 5

Resolving Intractable Conflicts at Their Sources

DIRECTIONS: After you have identified the developmental source of your conflict, the incomplete developmental task(s), and the unmet developmental needs, make a contract with your partner to role-play with you a scene that will help you complete these elements.

STEP 1. Create a scene from your past, and ask your partner to play the role of the person with whom you had the original unresolved conflict. Ask your partner to participate by saying something like, "Would you be willing to play my father and listen while I express the anger I felt toward him when he divorced my mother and left our family?"

STEP 2. Identify the element or elements that are unfinished or unresolved. In order to inform your partner about what you are needing, you can set the stage by saying something like, "I never got to express my anger at my father and to hear him acknowledge and accept my feelings."

STEP 3. Make a verbal contract with your partner, asking him or her specifically for what you want. You may say, "Will you play the role of my functional father and accept my feelings of anger and tell me that you heard them? After I have expressed my anger, I want you to tell me that I have a right to be angry, and that you still love me and won't abandon me. Will you do that?"

STEP 4. Complete the contract. Sit across from your partner to do this. After you have expressed your anger at your father, your partner might reply, "You have a perfect right to be angry at me. What I did changed your life and made life difficult for you. I'm glad you had the courage to tell me how you feel. I still love you, and I will not abandon you."

STEP 5. Allow yourself to feel the full impact of this role-playing. The impact may be dramatic or subtle, so allow enough time to fully feel the changes in awareness that might occur. You might report, "I am feeling much lighter and freer. My jaw seems looser, and I notice I'm feeling a little sad. I must be grieving the loss of my dad's presence in our family for the first time since he left. My anger must have blocked me from feeling the sadness."

STEP 6. Ask for any needed additional support. If you need support or feedback from your partner after taking this risk, ask for it by saying, "Will you hold me or comfort me while I experience my sadness and grief?" If you do want to be held, it's important to clarify whether it's your father or your partner who is doing the holding. If you need to be held by your father, then you must ask your partner to again play the role of your father. It's important to always keep the roles and relationships clear and separate.

STEP 7. Allow your partner to leave the role. Use a direct statement to acknowledge that your partner has completed the role-playing so that you and this person can reenter the present time and situation. Say to your partner, "I feel complete now after our role-playing. We can resume our present relationship." Thank your partner for helping you resolve your unresolved conflict with your father from your past.

STEP 8. Return to any current conflict that activated the conflict from your past. After resolving the conflict from your past, return to the current conflict to see what's left to be resolved there, using one of the other exercises if necessary. Often there is nothing left to resolve in the current conflict, or it's easy to resolve it once the old issues evoked by the current conflict are removed.

We advise you to use these exercises when any conflict comes up. When we teach this model in our workshops and classes, we have people follow these exercises step-by-step to work through a conflict. Using this model as a road map, you'll find navigating your way through conflicts can be a joyful ride that allows you to see life in new ways and feel closer to and more intimate with your companions during conflict.

CASE EXAMPLE

Ed and Lynette came as a couple to one of our conflict resolution classes. Their marriage was a second marriage for both, and they were committed to making this relationship work. Each had two children from a previous marriage. Ed's two children were older and had spent more time with their mother in another state than with their father. Lynette's children were high school age, and both lived with them. When we asked for volunteers in the class to work in front of the group on a personal conflict, they came forward.

Before beginning to work on their conflict, we asked them to describe the usual way they tried to resolve conflicts. Their process would break down when Ed would get very rational and logical at a time when Lynette was trying to share her feelings with him. The more she struggled to share her feelings, the more rational Ed would get. When the tension in this struggle reached a certain level of discomfort for her, Lynette would begin to pull away emotionally. She would become uncommunicative or even walk out of the room.

Ed would become agitated and would keep asking her questions or follow her if she left the room. They were both unhappy that so many of their attempts to resolve their conflicts ended in frustration and even more anger. Part of what they wanted was to learn how to have a good fight and get through it. We agreed that we could help them develop new ways of resolving conflicts as part of the particular issue they had.

Their current conflict involved whether Ed's twenty-year-old daughter,

Amy, and her two-year-old child could come from out of state and move in with them temporarily. After a stormy adolescence and an unplanned pregnancy, Amy had gone on welfare and was now struggling to finish community college. Ed was having a difficult time watching his daughter and granddaughter live without much emotional or financial support. He felt sad that neither of his children had been able to live in the warm and caring home that he and Lynette had created together. He still yearned to make up for some of the losses they had experienced as a result of the divorce between him and Amy's mother.

Lynette clearly stated her resistance to Amy's proposed move, "I feel overwhelmed at the thought of Amy moving home. She shuts me out, and I feel like an outsider. I'm scared something might happen to Ed and me."

Barry asked, "What are you scared might happen between you and Ed?" "Well," Lynette replied, "Amy could come and monopolize Ed's attention, and he wouldn't have time for me. He might even choose between her and me, and we could end up getting a divorce."

Janae asked Ed if he was aware of how Lynette felt. He said, "Yeah, I've heard all this before. I just get angry that I've done so much for her kids, and now she refuses to help one of mine. It doesn't seem fair."

At this point Lynette put her head down on her knees, curled one foot over the top of the other, and got very quiet. Ed watched her closely. The lowered head and the curled foot indicated that Lynette was probably moving into an inner-child feeling state. This was a signal that Ed was in that moment a player in her drama, and that she was working on unfinished business from the past.

Janae commented, "Lynette, I notice that your feet are all curled up. Who is it that is curling up her toes?"

Lynette, looking shy and innocent, said, "My little girl. She's thinking about how Ed might leave her. He sounds so angry that I won't do what he wants me to. I'm really scared."

"Who in your past left you?" asked Janae. "What happened when you were a little girl that makes you afraid that Ed will leave you?"

"My dad died," said Lynette sadly. "I get afraid Ed will go away too." At this point, we began to look for the unexpressed feelings from some trauma in her drama.

"Ed," said Barry, "I'm going to ask you to move over to the far side of the room for a minute. Would you do that as an experiment?"

"Sure," said Ed.

Barry turned to Lynette and said, "I want you to look up for a moment and see that Ed has gone. He has left you and he might not be back. How do you feel when you think about that?"

Lynette broke out sobbing, "It's my dad. He left me, and I wasn't done. I miss him so *much*."

Ed began to speak to Lynette from his place on the other side of the room, so we motioned for him to come join us again.

Janae turned to Ed and asked, "Did you know that Lynette still missed her father so much?"

By now Ed was becoming emotionally moved by Lynette's pain and grief and started moving close to her, "No, not in the way that I know it now. Lynette, I know that you were still little when he died, and that you didn't get to say good-bye to him."

"I didn't get enough hugs or spend enough time with him," she said. "Even before he died, I wanted to play and do things together, but he was never there because of his drinking." Then she looked up at Ed with teary eyes, and said, "You gave me the chance to get that feeling of being close and safe. I'm afraid if Amy comes that you will give her all your love, and there won't be any left for me. You'll go away just like my dad did, and I won't see you again."

Barry added, "So you've been seeing Ed as your father each time you get in this conflict. Is that true, Lynette?"

"I guess so. I didn't know it, though. I just thought I was afraid we would get a divorce."

Barry asked Lynette, "If you could talk to your dad right now, Lynette, what would you say?"

"I'd tell him what I missed growing up."

Barry came back with the key question, "Lynette, would you like Ed to play your father and do that right now?"

"Yes, if he would. Will you, Ed?"

"I sure will," Ed said, smiling.

Ed came close to Lynette, wrapping himself around her to hold her like a little child. Lynette, looking and sounding about seven years old, began telling Ed all the things she had wanted to say to her dad when she was a little girl. Ed held his arm around her and rocked her back and forth as she talked, speaking softly to her as he answered her back. After a few moments, Lynette stopped speaking and sat quietly as Ed held her.

After a short break, Ed, Lynette, and the class returned to review what had happened. Lynette was able to identify how much bonding and closeness she had missed with her father. She could see how much of that need she was unconsciously bringing into her relationship with Ed. Lynette was also now aware of the way she had projected her father onto Ed when he began sounding logical and rational. For her, Ed's unresponsiveness to her feelings was like abandonment. She could see that she had pulled away in the midst of their conflicts to protect herself from feeling the old pain of her father's abandonment.

Lynette asked Ed if he would contract with her to help fill her unmet need for her father to hold or nurture her, for time to play, and for time to talk. He said that he would really like to do that.

We asked Lynette and Ed if they had gotten what they wanted from their work with us. They looked at each other and glowed for a moment and then looked at us. They didn't have to say another word. It was obvious to everyone that they had broken through an important barrier to intimacy. They told us later that they experienced a dramatic increase in intimacy in their relationship following that session. They have continued to resolve their conflicts by helping each other identify the unmet developmental needs that surface during their conflicts, and are committed to helping each other meet these needs.

This form of conflict resolution has helped us see that most of the intractable conflicts in relationships are the result of unresolved conflicts from the past. The conflicts often involve some sort of trauma, and this trauma persists because some aspect of it was left unfinished: something wasn't said or done. Or something was said or done that an individual didn't understand or was hurt by, and no one present even noticed how this individual was feeling.

We often talk about the difference between a trauma and an "owie." When you're hurt either physically or emotionally and there is someone present who understands and comforts you, it's just an owie. However, if no one is there to comfort you, the experience is likely to become a trauma. Many years later, this trauma and its attendant feelings can be activated by a current or recurring conflict, and you'll be flooded with feelings.

You can always tell if this is happening by the intensity of your reaction to a current conflict. If you experience a sudden rush of feelings or energy that is greater than the current conflict should evoke, then you know you're in the throes of an old unresolved conflict or an old trauma prompted by the current conflict. If you have a partnership agreement to resolve conflicts at their source, you can ask your partner to help provide the comfort or support you need to turn the trauma back into just an owie.

THE BOTTOM LINE

- Persistent and intractable conflicts are the biggest barrier to intimacy.
- Many of the conflicts that erupt in close relationships are anchored in unhealed trauma from earlier in life that both partners brought to the relationship to heal.
- Most people either are not aware of the unhealed trauma until the relationship gets close, or are consciously hiding from this trauma, thinking it has magically disappeared.
- Both parties in a relationship must commit to acting as partners in learning and using skills to resolve conflicts.
- The most common way that people deal with conflict is to avoid it.
- Avoiding conflict in a relationship erodes the foundation of honesty, and conflict eventually erupts in destructive ways that can destroy intimacy and goodwill.

12. Pillow Talk
Sexual Communication

*On the stage[,] . . . masks are assumed with some regard to procedure;
in everyday life, the participants act their parts without consideration
either for the suitability of scene or for the words spoken by the rest of
the cast: the result is a general tendency for things to be brought to the
level of farce even when the theme is serious enough.*

— Anthony Powell

Sexual encounters for people with counter-dependency issues are typically quite different from those for people with co-dependency issues. While co-dependent people may cling to their partners and seek intimacy through the sexual part of the relationship, people who are counter-dependent want to be sexual but to avoid the intimacy aspect.

COUNTER-DEPENDENTS DO IT FAST

The bedroom is where the person with unmet counter-dependent needs may have his or her worst problems. Many people with counter-dependent behavior patterns have difficulty with the level of intimacy and closeness that ongoing sexual relationships require. As a result, these people have learned to be emotionally absent during lovemaking as a way to avoid intimacy. They may be able to handle the mechanics of lovemaking, but they're usually unable to handle the mechanics of intimacy that go with it. Separating sex and nurturing is also something that people with counter-dependent issues can't do. They're often interested in getting sex over with as quickly as possible so that they don't have to deal with their anxieties and fears.

COUNTER-DEPENDENT VERSUS INTERDEPENDENT SEX

The contrast between these two forms of sexual contact can be striking. People without counter-dependent issues are more capable of interdependent sex. We've listed the major characteristics of each form of sexual encounter:

Counter-dependent sex is

- performance-oriented, based on showing your partner how great you are;
- ritualistic and mechanical;
- used as an escape from problems;
- manipulative and controlling, requiring lots of effort;
- physically satisfying;
- comparative and competitive;
- followed by feelings of emptiness and loss; and
- used to avoid past problems.

Interdependent sex is

- communication-oriented, based on your taking charge of your own pleasure and asking for what you want;
- spontaneous and creative;
- a celebration of the resolution of problems;
- relaxed and effortless;
- physically, emotionally, and frequently spiritually satisfying;
- intimate and cooperative;
- followed by warm, connected feelings;
- used to work through past problems.

Part of the problem of sexual intimacy for people with unmet counter-dependent needs is caused by the way our society distorts sexual behaviors and the meaning of sex. Another part of the problem usually can be traced to some kind of unintentional or intentional sexual abuse in childhood. Let's first address the social causes of the problem.

THE SEXUALLY ADDICTED SOCIETY

We are bombarded with sexual hype in our culture. Sex is flaunted in television commercials, billboards, magazines, newspapers, books, videos, the Internet, and movies. We are assaulted daily by sexual messages that distort our notions about how sex should be. Collectively, we spend billions of dollars trying to look sexy, smell sexy, taste sexy, feel sexy, and act sexy. From dieting to surgical procedures to exercise, the focus is on how to look beautiful, thin, and attractive. Women are portrayed as sex objects in order to sell everything from soap to suntan oils, from automobiles to garage door openers! Sexy men are hawking shaving lotion, cologne, and clothing "that will drive her mad."

What people are actually being sold is not a product but a fantasy. The fantasy promises us that looking sexy is the formula for success. This is the perverted version of the American dream, in which people become successful through external means.

Many people with unmet counter-dependent needs have bought this one completely because looking good is what it's all about for them (the creation of a False Self). They hope that, *if* they can look sexy enough or confident enough or perfect enough, no one will ever suspect them of being the weak, insecure, uncertain, needy people they actually are. Because we live in a society obsessed with youth, sex, and looking good, it's easy for people with unmet counter-dependent needs to hide, at least until they find themselves in an intimate, emotionally close relationship. This can cause enough anxiety to make it difficult for men to get sexually aroused.

Many men who flee intimacy buy pornography or call women who will talk to them in sexual ways. This allows them to have a sexual relationship with a fantasy person without having to get involved in an actual relationship. They may masturbate and fantasize a sexual encounter, which appears to be safer than the real thing and therefore less anxiety provoking.

Excessive masturbation is a common way that people with unmet counter-dependent needs meet their sexual needs without risking intimacy. Children, particularly those who are molested while young, may turn to masturbation as an alternative way of experiencing good feelings that they yearn for. While people with unmet counter-dependency needs still try to get their nurturing needs met through sex, they often confuse their need for nonsexual nurturing with their need for sexual satisfaction or intimacy.

SEXUAL ABUSE AS A CAUSE
OF COUNTER-DEPENDENT BEHAVIORS

In addition to the sexual distortion inflicted on children by our culture, children who were sexually abused get an extra dose of it. As everyone knows, child sexual abuse is grossly unreported. Here are some of the most recent statistics on reported child sexual abuse:

DID YOU KNOW THAT...

- By age eighteen, one in every four girls and one in every six boys has been sexually abused.
- There are an estimated 39 million survivors of childhood sexual abuse in America today.
- A family member or someone outside the family who is known to and trusted by the child commits about 90 percent of all reported sexual abuse.
- Over 30 percent of children never disclose their abuse to anyone.
- Young victims frequently do not realize they were sexually abused.
- Almost 80 percent initially deny abuse or are tentative in disclosing it, indicating that they feel guilt or shame.
- The way a victim's family responds to abuse determines, to a large degree, how it affects the victim (owie versus trauma).
- Children who were sexually abused are more likely to have physical problems and school problems, be depressed as adults, have eating disorders, engage in alcohol and drug abuse, experience psychiatric disorders, get pregnant before age eighteen, get involved in teen prostitution, be sexually promiscuous, suffer sexual dysfunctions, go to prison, or become serial rapists themselves.[1]

Sexual abuse may be intentional or unintentional. The statistics listed in the sidebar "Did You Know That..." apply almost entirely to intentional sexual abuse. If you add in the unintentional sexual abuse and the sexual neglect that rarely gets reported, you have what amounts to a national disgrace.

Modeling unhealthy or inappropriate sexual behavior, withholding accurate sexual information, and referring to sex as "dirty" or "bad" are forms of unintentional sexual abuse or neglect. "Intentional sexual abuse" refers to deliberate acts of sexual violence and abuse. People with unmet counter-dependent needs may not have any memories of sexual abuse or neglect from their childhood, and so may have no idea that their adult struggle with intimacy may be related to a traumatic incident or series of childhood incidents involving unintentional or intentional sexual abuse or neglect.

There are several explanations for this memory loss, which is similar to the memory loss experienced by Vietnam veterans who were in combat and later could not remember what happened. People who experienced either combat or childhood sexual trauma suffer similar symptoms, such as disturbed sleep, nightmares, phobias, addictions, and other obsessive-compulsive behaviors.

This loss of memory is now recognized as post–traumatic stress disorder. Trauma therapy often helps people recover their memories of traumatic events and helps them express repressed feelings that are part of the original trauma. For many adults, the memory of childhood sexual abuse may not return for twenty or thirty years. In a landmark case, two daughters won a large damage suit against their father, who had sexually abused them almost forty years earlier. The memory of this abuse remained hidden from these women until they sought therapy for sexual dysfunctions.[2]

When childhood sexual abuse involves a parent or trusted adult, children have an even greater tendency to repress the memory. Research shows that parents, other adult relatives, older siblings, priests, and other trusted adults do most of the intentional sexual abuse of children. During the first six to eight years of life, children have a natural need to see their parents and other adults as perfect. This provides them with the sense of security they need to grow up. Without this, they fear they won't survive. When sexual abuse occurs before the age of eight or ten, children tend to blame themselves for the abuse rather than see their parents or other adults as not perfect. These children believe that they must have done something bad and must deserve bad things that happen to them.

To protect themselves, sexual perpetrators often threaten children with messages such as "I'll kill your little sister if you tell," or "You're a bad boy, and you'll go to hell if you tell anyone about this." This causes children to develop symptoms of counter-dependency and become adults who believe they are bad, worthless, unlovable, and disgusting. This distortion causes people who have been sexually abused or neglected to hide these memories from themselves. This also helps them maintain the belief that their parents were perfect, which keeps their security blanket intact. They believe they need this security blanket because they are flawed and unworthy and, as a result of the experience, incapable of changing who they are.

Sexual neglect is different from sexual abuse but has similar outcomes. There are subtle forms of inappropriate sexual behavior, including giving your child no information about sex or distorting the information with your own moral or religious biases. This kind of subtle sexual abuse and neglect may be unintentional or intentional, depending on the adults' awareness and motives. Many religions also heap moral judgments on children who even think sexual thoughts by labeling this sinful and damning them.

We have seen clients who didn't remember any incidents of intentional sexual abuse in their childhood, but who suffered either from the lack of information, or from wrong information, or from having subtle sexual energy directed covertly at them by a parent. The developmental traumas caused by repeated exposure to these forms of sexual abuse and neglect can create the same kinds of sexual dysfunctions in adults that are caused by intentional sexual abuse and neglect.

We have some anecdotal data from our therapy practice suggesting that some gays and lesbians were victims of intentional or unintentional sexual abuse or neglect, and that this abuse or neglect may have affected their sexual preference. A daughter who was unintentionally or intentionally sexually abused by her father when she was a child may be afraid of men and turn toward females for intimacy. Sons who were invaded sexually by their mothers may have trouble being close to women and may choose intimacy with men as a solution. However, there are also healthy reasons why people might be gay or lesbian. The important point is that it may be a reaction to the early abuse or neglect. More research must be conducted to determine all the factors that influence sexual preference before definite conclusions can be drawn.

In addition, it's clear from our clinical experience that sexual abuse and eating disorders are closely connected. If you are a compulsive eater or dieter, then likely you experienced some form of childhood sexual abuse or neglect. Susan Mendelsohn's book *It's Not about the Weight: Attacking Eating Disorders from the Inside Out* is an excellent resource on this topic, as is Marion Woodman's classic, *Addiction to Perfection*.[3]

SEXUAL ABUSE AND NEGLECT

Part of the process of unraveling the complex denial and repression that follow sexual abuse and neglect is to seek out accurate information about what constitutes sexual abuse and neglect. Frequently, those who were abused don't recognize the acts of unintentional sexual child abuse or neglect that they experienced, even though they still suffer from the effects.

There are two categories of sexual abuse and neglect we'd like to examine in more detail. First is unintentional sexual abuse or neglect by parents who are ignorant of what constitutes sexual abuse or neglect. This unintentional form is common. Second is intentional sexual abuse or neglect, in which the parent or other adult knew that he or she was abusing or neglecting children but could not, or would not, stop. Let's look more closely at each category.

Unintentional Sexual Abuse and Neglect

The following list was developed by consensus by therapists and other experts in the field of child abuse and neglect.[4] To help you recognize whether you experienced childhood sexual abuse and neglect, place a check mark next to any items that happened in your family. We've taken items for this list and the following one, on intentional abuse or neglect, from similar lists in Carla Wills-Brandon's excellent book *Is It Love or Is It Sex?* See her book for further information.

_____ Parents did not give you age appropriate information or talk to you about human sexuality while you were growing up.

_____ Parents did not give you specific information or talk to you about menstruation or normal sexual development in adolescence.

_____ Parents gave you false information about masturbation, where babies come from, or the role of sex in a relationship.

_____ Parents refused to answer your questions about sexual development.

_____ Parents invaded your privacy while you were in the bathroom or your bedroom (not knocking on your closed door before entering or asking permission before entering).

_____ Parents used religion to shame and condemn any of your sexual curiosity.

_____ Parents gave you very little appropriate nonsexual touching or hugging.

_____ Parents had you bathe or sleep with them after you reached school age.

_____ Parents exposed you to pornographic magazines or materials when you were a child, without any information.

_____ Parents exposed you to crude sexual jokes and sexual remarks.

_____ Parents forced you to sleep or bathe with your older opposite-sex siblings after you reached school age.

_____ Parents walked around the house nude or wearing only underwear and/or skimpy negligees.

_____ Parents encouraged you to assume a surrogate spouse role by confiding in you about their adult sexual problems, talking to you about the details of their own sex life, and/or discussing the sexual problems they were having.

_____ Parents shamed you if they caught you masturbating or exploring your genitals.

_____ Parents called you degrading sexual names like "whore," "slut," "hot number," or "sleaze."

_____ Parents made fun of your sexual development or teased you for having breasts or for growing hair around your genitals.

Unintentional sexual abuse can also lead to or be part of another form of abuse that is common when the parents' relationship is weak or a parent is missing. Children caught in the dysfunctional drama triangle, for example, are often "parentized." They're encouraged to act as an adult partner to one of their parents and, in turn, may be given special titles such as "Daddy's little princess" or "Mama's little man." This behavior is considered covert incest, since it entails no actual intercourse or inappropriate touching but does involve the presence of active sexual energy. With parentizing, it's common for the parent to control the sexual life of the parentized child. When girls get older and are ready to start dating, fathers will try to over-control them and prevent any dating. Boys may not feel free to date, or may find their mothers examining their underwear or grilling them for details of what happened on a date.

Intentional Child Sexual Abuse and Neglect

Many people experienced intentional acts of child sexual abuse and neglect that they haven't identified as such. We've compiled a list of the more common intentional acts to help you identify those you may have experienced in childhood. As you read this list, place a check mark next to any items that you remember, and any items that you have no conscious memory of but have a "feeling" or intuition about.

_____ A parent or other adult gave you wet or open-mouthed or lingering kisses on your mouth.

_____ A parent or other adult touched, washed, or stimulated your genitals while giving you a bath or while dressing or undressing you.

_____ A parent or older sibling watched you dress or undress, or watched you take a bath, after you reached school age.

_____ A parent or other adult forced or encouraged you to be sexual with siblings or other children.

_____ You had your genitals or breasts touched or tickled by a parent, older sibling, or other adult while engaged in horseplay or roughhousing.

_____ You were forced to watch while another child was molested or raped.

_____ You were masturbated by a parent, older sibling, or other adult.

_____ You were forced to masturbate a parent, older sibling, or other adult.

_____ You were forced to watch while a parent, older sibling, or other adult masturbated himself or herself.

_____ You were forced to strip down or stand naked in the corner under the guise of punishment.

_____ You were spanked on your bare bottom or spanked while lying nude on a bed after you reached school age.

_____ You were massaged by a parent or other adult in or around your genital area and/or breasts.

_____ You were requested to sit on a parent or other adult's lap while that person rubbed against or touched your breasts or genitals, and you felt this person get an erection or you saw this person stimulate himself or herself.

_____ You were permitted to watch parents bathe and/or were allowed to see them stimulate themselves or each other sexually.

_____ You were forced to have oral, anal, or vaginal intercourse with a parent, older sibling, or other trusted adult.

Taking Inventory of Your History of Sexual Abuse or Neglect

The following is a short inventory of adult behaviors related to childhood sexual abuse and neglect.[5] Read each statement and check those that apply.

_____ I have a fear of going crazy.

_____ I have large gaps in my childhood memories.

_____ I am more than fifty pounds overweight.

_____ I was physically abused as a child.

_____ I have sexually abused someone else.

_____ Sex turns me off.

_____ I have trouble maintaining an intimate relationship.

_____ I am ashamed of my body.

_____ I sexualize relationships even when I don't want to.

_____ I regularly experience migraines, gastrointestinal disturbances, or genitourinary disturbances.

_____ I have a general sense of depression that I can't shake.

_____ I freeze in certain situations, such as when I encounter an authority figure or in certain sexual situations.

_____ I am afraid of having children or afraid of being around them.

_____ I am accident prone.

If you checked off *two or more* of these statements, you may have experienced sexual abuse as a child. If you have these symptoms but no memory, you can read accounts of how others remembered their own childhood abuse, talk to other people who experienced sexual abuse as a child, or enter psychotherapy for help in exploring this possibility.

CASE EXAMPLE

Sharon called for an individual appointment with Janae to work on a problem of frigidity that she was experiencing in her relationship with Gary. When she came to therapy, they had not had sex for almost six months. Gary was impatient with Sharon's problem in the bedroom and wanted her to get it fixed. Rather than starting to work directly on Sharon's sexual dysfunction, Janae decided to find out more about her childhood.

Sharon's alcoholic parents had separated when she was about nine years old, and she spent the next four years shuttling back and forth between them. She remembered going along with her father to the bar he frequented and being present when he entertained his cronies at poker games at his house. In both situations, her father would invite his drinking buddies to notice how pretty Sharon was and would encourage them to "get friendly" with her. As she matured, their friendliness turned into seductiveness. By the time she was twelve or thirteen, her father was offering her sexually to his friends as a favor.

Shortly after her fourteenth birthday, Sharon's father died, and she went to live with her father's brother and his wife. They had two younger children and expected Sharon to help with the housework and child care. Her aunt related to her mostly as if she were hired help, while her uncle alternately criticized her and teased her in sexual ways. By the time she was fifteen and well-developed physically, her uncle began accosting her in secluded areas of the house.

He would rub up against her breasts, pat her buttocks, and make suggestive remarks about how sexually appealing she looked to him. That was followed by attempts to get her to undress and to touch his erect penis. His insistent pursuits began to frighten her so much that she started staying out with her friends. Sharon found places where she could stay overnight, and failed to return home two or three nights a week. Sometimes she took drugs and drank beer with her friends. When the boys in the group began to make sexual advances toward her, she would return to her aunt and uncle's house for several days.

One night when Sharon was sixteen, she was out dancing at a western bar and met Gary. He was big and strong-looking, though kind of quiet. He bought her a drink and they sat and talked. She liked Gary's quiet strength and began spending more time with him. Eventually, she began to stay overnight with him with the understanding that they were just friends.

Sharon spent less and less time at her uncle's house by splitting her time between staying with Gary at his place and hanging out with her friends. Her prolonged absences began to irritate her uncle. One evening, he followed her to a friend's house. After watching for a while outside, he burst in. He was furious when he found several of her friends using drugs; and he exploded in a fit of anger at her. He called her names and accused her of being a "doper" and gave her one day to get her belongings out of his house.

At the age of seventeen, Sharon had few options about where to move. She told Gary about her eviction and asked if she could stay with him for a few days while she decided what to do. Gary said it would be fine with him if she wanted to move her things there for a while. Her stay turned into weeks, then months.

During this time, she slept on the sofa in Gary's living room and continued to be his friend. One night when they went out dancing and drinking at a bar, Gary got drunk. Sharon had to help him into the house. He passed out on the sofa and fell asleep, so she decided to sleep in his bed. Near morning he woke up and came into his bedroom and got into bed. He curled up with her and held her for a while. After a while their closeness turned into sex.

During the next few weeks their relationship became very sexual and intense. Gary, a few years older than Sharon, decided he wanted to get married. Sharon, thrilled that someone finally wanted her, accepted his offer, and they were married when Sharon turned eighteen.

Sharon had managed to finish high school with good secretarial skills, and she found a job soon after marrying Gary. The first year or two they had a wonderful time being together, especially Sharon. It was her first experience of permanence and stability with a person who cared about her. She reported to me that her sexual relationship with Gary was great, up until about the end of the second year of their marriage.

At that time, she began to notice things about Gary she had not seen before. He tended to be messy at home and not look very attractive. He also lost his full-time job and began working temporary positions. The time between his temporary positions grew longer and longer. He would stay at home drinking, watching television, or playing on his computer. Sharon began providing most of their financial support as Gary worked less and less. She even cooked and cleaned when she came home, despite the fact that he had been home all day not working.

After a period of this discontentment, Sharon began to feel herself growing repulsed by Gary's behavior and appearance. She started pulling away when he made sexual overtures and often avoided sex if she could. Her distancing behavior provoked Gary into drinking more, either at home or at a bar. During drunken episodes, he would pursue her and try to force her to have sex. After several months of this, Gary finally exploded and told her that if she wasn't willing to have sex with him, she was to get out of his house.

This frightened Sharon, for it reminded her of her uncle throwing her out of his home. In desperation, Sharon began to talk to her friends at work about her problems with Gary. It was through them that she found counseling with Janae.

Once Janae heard her story, she suggested that Sharon's background of sexual abuse might be the source of her sexual dysfunction. She also suggested that Sharon ask Gary to come with her to counseling, so that he could learn how to support her while she healed the wounds caused by her father's and uncle's abuse. Gary was reluctant to come for therapy, insisting that he was not sick and that the problems were all Sharon's. However, he did agree to come for one session with the understanding that the therapy would focus on Sharon.

When they arrived, Janae spent some time discussing with the two of them how childhood sexual abuse creates difficulties in adult sexual relationships. She also described the approach she used in treating couples where one of the partners has been sexually abused, and encouraged them to see their problem as treatable. Once Gary had this overview, he agreed to come with Sharon to a series of six sessions over three months. During that time he would try out Janae's approach and see if it helped.

We work together when we see couples, so Barry joined the therapy sessions. We've found that each person often needs an ally during conflicts. We began by helping Gary see that Sharon had never developed a sense of ownership about her body, and that she'd been routinely exposed to sexual innuendos by her uncle and her father's friends. They also affirmed the positive aspects of their relationship by acknowledging that it was now safe enough for her issues of abuse to surface. We helped them both see that Sharon's unmet developmental need was to learn to set appropriate boundaries for her body. She could learn to do this by being in charge of their sex life during the next three months. She was to say when, where, and how she wanted sex. Gary groaned at the idea. We reminded him that he couldn't be much worse off than he was now, since he'd been without sex for nearly six months. Finally, he agreed to cooperate.

They were sent home with the sexual communication exercise at the end of this chapter and encouraged to not have sex for a week. They could only cuddle and hold each other. After the second session, sex was permitted at Sharon's initiation. For another two weeks, Sharon made absolutely no sexual advances toward Gary. In therapy, he complained that she wasn't learning much, and said he felt she would never want to have sex again. He was encouraged to stick with the contract and keep allowing Sharon to be in charge. With the support Sharon got in therapy, she began to grow stronger and be more assertive. When she finally did approach Gary for sex, they both were excited. Gary liked being pursued, and Sharon liked being the initiator.

Toward the end of their six sessions, the tension between the two of them began to decrease. Each time they came for a session, they appeared happier and more playful, like the young people they were. By the end of the three months, Gary decided the experiment was working and wanted to stay married to Sharon. At their termination session, they created a new three-month contract for their sex life. During this period, they could approach each other for sex, and either of them had the right to say no. If Sharon didn't feel sexual, Gary was to surrender to her need for boundaries and safety. Gary hardly ever said no to Sharon, so that was not really a problem. They were warned that healing sexual abuse requires a lot of patience and caring, and that they should give themselves at least a year to get beyond the awkwardness of the appropriate boundaries that Sharon had set.

Barry also helped Gary see how his invasive, self-serving attitude of wanting Sharon to be sexual on demand was not supporting intimacy between them. Janae continued to encourage them to keep talking about their feelings for each other and about sex.

SELF-QUIZ

Barriers to Sexual Intimacy

DIRECTIONS: Place a number in the blank before each statement to indicate the degree to which the statement is true for you.

1 = Never   2 = Occasionally   3 = Frequently   4 = Almost always

_____ I have difficulty asking for what I want sexually from my partner.
_____ I'm afraid to feel my sexual feelings fully and completely.
_____ I'm afraid to let my partner know what I enjoy about sex.
_____ I find that my enjoyment of sex largely depends on my partner's enjoyment.
_____ I'm afraid that my body will not be attractive to my partner.
_____ I'm afraid that my partner might be overwhelmed by my sexual feelings.
_____ I secretly wish my partner would pay more attention to me while we are making love.

_____ I experience sex as mainly a physical release.

_____ I'm afraid I won't be able to satisfy my partner.

_____ I find sex to be very hard work.

_____ I feel sad and lonely after having sex.

_____ I use sex to try to smooth over arguments with my partner.

_____ I'm jealous when my partner pays attention to other men/women.

_____ I get scared when my partner initiates sex with me.

_____ I'm afraid to initiate sex with my partner.

_____ I'm afraid that I will lose control while making love.

_____ I'm afraid that my partner will disapprove of what I'm doing or feeling sexually.

_____ I don't find masturbation enjoyable and satisfying.

_____ I'm afraid to explore my body and what gives it pleasure.

_____ I'm afraid to be myself when I'm making love.

_____ Total score

SCORING: Add up the column of numbers to find your score. Use the following guidelines to interpret it.

20–40 Very few barriers to sexual intimacy. No effect on sexual functioning.

41–60 Some barriers to sexual intimacy. Possible effect on sexual functioning.

61–80 Many barriers to sexual intimacy. Major effect on sexual functioning.

SKILL-BUILDING EXERCISE:
COMMUNICATION EXERCISES FOR THE BEDROOM

Communicating about sex in a *healthy* way involves clear, direct communication so both partners can get closer to each other and meet their wants and needs — an "everybody wins" situation. In this circumstance, total intimacy develops and people feel completely free to share sexual enjoyment and pleasure. This helps the couple develop an interdependent sexual relationship like the one we described earlier in the chapter.[6] The following exercises, which come from another of our books, will help you strengthen your skills in communicating about sex.[7]

DIRECTIONS: Take turns reading each communication rule to the other person. The discussion of each rule proceeds as follows:

1. Each person, in turn, explains the rule in his or her own words — for example, "I think this rule means _____."
2. Each person, in turn, gives an example of his or her use or misuse of the rule — for example, "This morning, I said _____ instead of _____."
3. If you agree or disagree or want to add a comment, state your point of view — for example, "I will agree with only part of that rule, and my question is _____."
4. Follow these directions for each of the rules.

Apply the ideas from each rule when discussing other rules. Also, if your partner misuses any rule during the discussion, point it out: "I think you just misused rule 2. Will you go back and reread that rule?"

RULE 1. *When you're expressing your thoughts and feelings, use "I" instead of "one," "they," "you," or "people."* Say, "I'm afraid to get close to you," instead of "People are often afraid to get close to each other."

RULE 2. *Use eye contact and speak directly to your partner.* This demonstrates genuine interest in your partner. Also, maintain eye contact while your partner is talking to you. Avoiding eye contact is a way of avoiding intimacy.

RULE 3. *Avoid interrupting your partner while he or she is speaking.* This is an indication that you're not listening and may be already planning your response instead.

RULE 4. *When sharing your thoughts and feelings, be specific.* Provide the necessary information in addition to asking for what you want, so your partner can respond to your thoughts and feelings — for example, "I'm angry because you seem to rush through having sex, and I want to take more time. Will you agree to spend more time while making love?" A common error is to omit the request for what you want, which then pressures your partner to guess at what you want.

RULE 5. *Make sure that your verbal and nonverbal communication is clear.* Ask your partner to restate in his or her own words the essence of your message. For example, "Will you repeat what I just said?" or "What I heard you say was that you like your breasts touched softly. Did I hear you right?"

RULE 6. *Avoid asking questions unless you really need information.* Many times questions are statements in disguise: "Don't you think we ought to turn off the lights?" or "Don't you feel afraid that we are making too much noise?" Your communication will be much clearer if you make a statement about your own thoughts and feelings: "I would like to turn off the lights. Is that all right with you?"

a.   "Why" questions are often meant to interrogate and, as a result, can contribute to defensiveness. For example, "Why do you always have to be in such a hurry?"

b.   "How" questions are generally more appropriate: "How are you feeling?" or "How long do you want to take tonight when we make love?" Though these "how" questions are better than "why" questions, even some "how" questions can seem critical and may create a defensive reaction or negative situation.

RULE 7. *Comparative and competitive statements can lead to power struggles.* One person may act as if his or her thoughts or feelings are more important than the other person's. Or that person may put himself or herself down and act as if the other's thoughts and feelings are more important. For example, "You've had more sexual experience than I have had."

a.   Assert yourself by saying, "No, I won't," or "I don't want to," instead of saying "I can't." Or say yes, when you actually want to.

b.   If your partner asks a question, respond with a direct, clear answer, or say, "I'm not willing to answer that question." People often avoid answering questions they don't want to answer. Also do not say, "I don't know," when you do know. In this case, "I don't know" really means "I won't tell myself" and/or "I won't tell you."

c.   Consider your partner's needs and the situation when making requests. For example, if you want a lengthy lovemaking experience, don't wait until a late hour when you or your partner may be too tired.

RULE 8. *Being unassertive with your partner is an ineffective way of solving problems.* It indicates an unwillingness to take responsibility for your own thoughts, feelings, and behavior. For example, you may not let your partner know what you like and dislike in sex, and may expect him or her to be able to guess or figure out what you want. Assertiveness means you're willing to take responsibility for getting your needs and wants met without ignoring the stated needs and wants of your partner.

a.   The best way to get your wants and needs met is to ask directly. For example, say, "What I want is for you to tell me what you like about me while we're making love. Are you willing to do that?" ("If not, what are you willing to do about my request?") If you're afraid to ask for what you want, admit it.

b.   If you agree to do something that your partner asks you to do, be sure it's something you want to do and/or are willing to do. For example, "Whatever you say, dear!" as a response to something you don't want to do is being unassertive and misleads your partner. You can say no without losing your partner's love and respect. If you don't want to do what's requested, be clear about what you do want and are willing to do.

c.   When you're quiet, be sure it's because you choose to be quiet and not because you're afraid to speak. If you're afraid, you can say, "I'm afraid to ask you for what I want, because my fantasy is that you might get angry and/or reject me." Then ask for reassurance: "Will you tell me that it's fine for me to ask you for what I want, and that you won't reject me for asking for it?"

d.   If your partner is quiet and does not communicate his or her needs or wants to you, ask about them. If your partner says, "I don't know," it generally means "I don't want to think about it," or "I won't tell you or tell myself." You can ask your partner to think about what he or she wants and tell you later.

e.   Avoid blaming your partner for causing your feelings. Don't say, "You make me angry," or "You make me happy." Both statements are inaccurate. It's important that you take ownership for your feelings: "I'm angry that you ignored my request to have sex tonight," or "I'm happy with the way we make love."

f.   Avoid using the words "I'll try" or "I'll work at that" when you agree to do something. "I'll try" usually means "I won't do the best I can, because I don't really want to do it anyway." Saying "I will do it" communicates that you are committed to following through to the best of your ability. If you don't want to do it, saying no is more assertive and effective in solving problems.

g. Don't say "I guess," "probably," or "maybe" when you have a definite opinion or point of view — for example: "I guess oral sex is all right with me." If you aren't sure, admit it: "I'm not sure if I like oral sex; let me talk about my reservations." If you are sure, say so: "I really like oral sex."

RULE 9. *When expressing your thoughts or feelings, avoid exaggerating or understating.* This is an ineffective way of drawing attention to yourself and is a way of defending your point of view rather than a way of solving your problems.

a. Avoid exaggerations such as "I always" or "You never." Instead of saying, "You never tell me you love me anymore," be specific and speak from your own experience: "I don't remember you telling me that you love me in the past two days. Will you tell me now?"

b. Don't act helpless when you're not. "I got so excited, I couldn't wait for you to have an orgasm." The truth is that you decided not to wait.

RULE 10. *Avoid rescuing your partner.* Rescuing, in this context, means doing something for your partner that he or she can do for himself or herself. This also applies when your partner needs or wants something from you and is not asking for it. Rescuing means taking responsibility for something that's not legitimately yours (not your territory); this leads to conflicts and confusion in the relationship.

To avoid being rescued means to be willing to ask for what you want or need 100 percent of the time. For example, Mary wanted more physical caressing before intercourse, but she was unwilling to tell Sam. Sam wasn't sure what to do, so he assumed that Mary wanted to move directly to intercourse. As a result, he hurried through foreplay in order to please Mary — he was rescuing Mary. Mary, not wanting to hurt Sam's feelings, decided to go along when he hurried to intercourse — she was rescuing Sam. In this case, neither Mary nor Sam was really asking for what each wanted, and each ended up with unexpressed, angry feelings.

Mary could have avoided rescuing by asking Sam to caress her more before initiating intercourse, and Sam could have decided what he wanted and asked for that. If their wants conflicted, they could have decided on a solution that was agreeable to both and, therefore, avoided further conflicts in that area.

RULE 11. *Avoid interpreting the behavior, feelings, or motivations of your partner.* For example, avoid saying, "You refuse sex with me because you're mad at me!" or "What you're really thinking is…" or "When you say nice things to me, you really mean…" Sometimes interpretations are ways of saying your own thoughts or feelings and acting as if they belonged to the other person. For example: "The reason you're frowning is because you don't like what I'm doing." Instead of interpreting your partner's behavior, do the following:

a. Describe your partner's actions without analyzing them: "When you put your arm under my neck like this, it pulls my hair."
b. Describe how *you* feel without telling the other how he or she feels: "My head hurts when you do that."
c. If you have an impression of what's motivating your partner, do a perception check and ask him or her if your thoughts are accurate: "Are you angry with me?"

THE BOTTOM LINE

- Intentional or unintentional sexual abuse or neglect of children is very common and can lead to counter-dependent defenses and serious intimacy problems in adults.
- Because you grew up in a sexually addicted society, you likely developed distorted ideas about the role of sex in relationships. You must examine and revise these ideas in order to create an intimate relationship.
- It's useful to consider unintentional or intentional sexual abuse as a cause of counter-dependent behaviors.
- Learn to identify any barriers to sexual intimacy you may have developed.
- You may need to learn healthy communication tools to create a more satisfying sex life.

Part 3
BEYOND COUNTER-DEPENDENCY
PATHWAYS TO PARTNERSHIP

13. Creating Partnership Relationships

Love does not consist of gazing at each other,
but in looking together in the same direction.
— Antoine de Saint-Exupéry

The idea of using your relationships to free yourself from your co-dependent and counter-dependent behaviors seems like a no-brainer to us. We discovered, however, that this is a radical idea to most people — at least, doing it consciously is. Very few professionals ever recommend it. In fact, most of them discourage couples from doing this kind of work together, saying it's too difficult for people to sort out their own unfinished business in an intimate relationship. It may, in fact, be useful or necessary for couples to have outside resources to help them unravel the old relationship patterns, especially if either partner has a history of severe abuse or other traumas. Sometimes individuals in relationships need to work separately on their issues in therapy for a while or even live separately for a period of time.

We believe, however, that it's necessary to integrate the breaking-free process into intimate relationships, which is where things break down to begin with. Because counter-dependent and co-dependent behaviors are anchored in relationships, they can best be healed in relationships.

UNRAVELING CO-DEPENDENT/COUNTER-DEPENDENT RELATIONSHIPS

There are four stages of relationship, and there are essential developmental processes that must be completed in each stage. Since most people have not completed these processes from the co-dependent and counter-dependent stages of development, they bring them to their intimate relationships. Most couples struggle with the healing process because they don't understand it and don't recognize it as an important source of intimacy in their relationship.

> A committed, conscious relationship is a powerful tool for breaking free of counter-dependent behaviors.

In order to better understand our cooperative framework and the benefits of using it, complete Partnership Exercise 5, "Resolving Intractable Conflicts at Their Sources," presented at the end of chapter 11 (page 229). It provides a step-by-step tool for healing relationship conflicts and issues anchored in early childhood.

In this chapter, you will also find a chart to help you identify symptoms of incomplete developmental processes and developmental traumas that may be present in your current relationships. The chart also provides suggestions on how you and your partner can work cooperatively to heal these traumas.

Committed, conscious relationships provide the safety, the motivation, the intensity, and the sustained contact necessary to bring up unmet needs and unresolved issues so you can work cooperatively to transform them, and so you can both finally meet your developmental needs. The true purpose of relationships is to help us become whole and fully functioning human beings. Relationships are the richest environments for "wholing" that we know of. Part of the wholing process in committed, conscious relationships is the creation of social and organizational support for new forms of partnership relationships. We need new visions, new tools, and new community

THE STAGES OF COUPLE RELATIONSHIPS, WITH THE ESSENTIAL DEVELOPMENTAL PROCESSES NEEDED TO FACILITATE COUPLE EVOLUTION[1]

Stage of Development	Developmental Processes in Couple Evolution	Experiences for Completing These Processes
Co-dependency (Harmony)	• Bonding with each other • Establishing primal trust in the relationship • Establishing an identity as a couple	• Establishing friendship as a valued quality of the relationship • Recognizing and acknowledging each other's spiritual essence • Exchanging nurturing touch and talk • Respecting and validating each other's needs and feelings • Giving and receiving unconditional love • Exploring common interests, values, beliefs, and goals
Counter-dependency (Conflict)	• Separating psychologically from each other • Resolving internal conflicts between needs of self and needs of other	• Exploring interests outside the relationship • Separating nurturing touch from sexual touch • Establishing individual goals, values, and beliefs within the relationship • Establishing and receiving respect for individual boundaries • Identify self-needs versus other-needs • Negotiating directly to get needs met

THE STAGES OF COUPLE RELATIONSHIPS, WITH THE ESSENTIAL DEVELOPMENTAL PROCESSES NEEDED TO FACILITATE COUPLE EVOLUTION (*continued*)

Stage of Development	*Developmental Processes in Couple Evolution*	*Experiences for Completing These Processes*
Independence (Resolution)	• Mastering self-sufficiency within the relationship • Establishing an equal, egalitarian form of autonomy within the relationship	• Achieving object constancy as a couple • Achieving financial, professional, educational, and spiritual equality in the relationship • Achieving a balance between individual needs and interests and the couple's needs and interests • Maintaining individual goals, values, and beliefs within the relationship • Experiencing object constancy with each other in spite of conflicting needs and/or wants
Interdependence (Partnership)	• Partnering with each other • Developing an experience of synergy in the relationship	• Utilizing the couple's synergy in service to the community or world • Using win-win conflict resolution methods • Building and sustaining a spiritual dimension in the primary relationship • Utilizing the relationship as a tool for individuation and mutual spiritual evolution • Mutually affirming each other's spiritual values and goals and acting in accordance with them • Identifying situations where the couple's devotion can be extended to others outside the relationship

structures to build a partnership society. As we each reach new levels of co-operation and partnering in our primary relationships, we will no longer be satisfied with anything less in all other areas of our lives, including our work, schools, churches, and communities.

IDENTIFYING COUNTER-DEPENDENT RELATIONSHIP PATTERNS

In order to get beyond the battle of the sexes and move toward partnership relationships between men and men, women and men, and women and women, people must break free of their counter-dependent relationship patterns. We've identified the following four common couple relationship combinations involving counter-dependent behaviors.

A Male with Counter-dependent Behaviors and a Female with Co-dependent Behaviors

This is the most common form of relationship pattern. In this combination, the male who has unmet counter-dependent needs, tries to appear strong, secure, successful, independent, and self-centered while dominating and invading his partner. The female with unmet co-dependent needs tries to appear weak, helpless, insecure, unsuccessful, and dependent as she invites domination and invasion from him, hoping he will eventually meet her unmet needs. Their sexual relationship is set up primarily to meet his sexual needs. Relationship combinations with obvious or subtle one-up, one-down power arrangements usually have little genuine intimacy.

A Female with Counter-dependent Behaviors and a Male with Co-dependent Behaviors

The reverse pattern is present in this combination but with some important differences. Usually in this coupling, the sexual relationship is much less prominent and may even be absent, as the female often has a history of childhood sexual abuse or severe trauma that makes her want to avoid repressed feelings. The male with co-dependent behaviors often feels controlled, one down, and may be or gradually become sexually passive or impotent. He may be depressed and may hold his feelings inside, rather than expressing them clearly. He may wait to dump them on other people while playing the victim role in the drama triangle.

A Male with Counter-dependent Traits
and a Female with Counter-dependent Traits

This pattern is popular among young, urban professionals who have two-career relationships in which both people work long hours and accumulate a lot of material goods. Striving to reach certain career goals leaves little time or energy for intimacy. Their relationship may become a legitimate, socially sanctioned way of avoiding intimacy. In many such relationships, there is infrequent sexual contact, perhaps only a few times a year. The overriding emphasis in this relationship combination is usually on incessant activity and avoiding deeper intimacy.

Couples in this combination may have a compulsive need to wear the right clothes, have the right degrees, have high-profile jobs, drive the right cars, have the right friends, and take the right vacations. The emphasis is also on looking as though they have a successful relationship, even if it isn't emotionally satisfying. They hope that others will be impressed and will approve of their lifestyle and choice of mate and, therefore, approve of them. This attempt to earn the approval of others can lead to a life of quiet desperation.

Partners with Both Counter-dependent
and Co-dependent Behaviors Who Switch Roles

This combination is also very common. The co-dependent partner pursues the counter-dependent partner, who is running away or avoiding intimacy. At some point, the co-dependent partner tires of the pursuit, gives up the quest for intimacy, and pulls away. This triggers the fear of abandonment in the counter-dependent partner, which causes him or her to flip and become the pursuing or co-dependent partner. At this point, the person who began as the co-dependent role becomes revengeful, decides that he or she doesn't want to be intimate with the other person, and makes a complementary flip. So, they switch roles in a relational pattern that we call "the dance of intimacy." It keeps the relationship churning with drama and chaos enough of the time to prevent intimacy in both relationship combinations. At some point in the dance, however, one or the other may give up the dance and seek out a relationship combination in which both people act out their counter-dependent behaviors.

A fifth form of relationship, which is not as widespread as one might think, is between two predominantly co-dependent people. This book does not specifically address this pattern. To learn more about it, consult our book *Breaking Free of the Co-dependency Trap*.[2]

A NEW VISION OF RELATIONSHIPS

From a historical perspective, the desire for an emotionally, psychologically, and spiritually committed relationship is still relatively novel. During the last twenty-five years, this vision of relationships has emerged because of advances in psychology and our expanded consciousness. It has probably also emerged out of a desire to meet our unmet needs from childhood.

In the early twentieth century, marriage was considered to be more of a political or material contract. In that era, the focus was primarily on survival, and marriage helped to support political and economic alliances. This was done not only at the national and international levels but also in the villages and countryside. Marriages were often based on some economic affiliation between the two families involved.

During this time, the extended family was still the primary support system for most marital relationships. As industrialization spread, the extended family began to fragment. Children moved to cities to work, and the two world wars turned soldiers into world travelers.

By the 1950s, the nuclear family system had replaced the extended family system. In this evolutionary process, we see the developmental model at work. The extended family system of the early 1900s functioned more as a co-dependent system, in which members were enmeshed. By the postwar 1950s, the nuclear family functioned more as a system that supported counter-dependent behaviors. Children growing up in families during the 1960s and 1970s attended college away from their hometowns, married strangers, and took jobs in other parts of the country.

By the 1980s, many of this culture's young people had emancipated themselves; were participating in the sexual, gender, and racial revolutions; and were experimenting with higher consciousness through drugs, music, and alternative religions. As the baby-boom generation approached midlife, these forays into independent lifestyles provided them with a comfortable lifestyle and optimal personal freedom. Unfortunately, they also experienced isolation and loneliness. Becoming a cog in the industrial machine, moving from one unsatisfactory relationship to another, losing parenting relationships because of divorce, and facing the realities of epidemics of sexually transmitted diseases, like AIDS, confused and scared many men and women.

The personal growth and individual freedom movements of the 1970s and 1980s changed into the "relationship movement" of the 1990s, as people moved toward new levels of self-actualization. In this emerging movement, people wanted to create more stable and functional family life experiences for children, to end the battle of the sexes, to create long-term love relationships, and to integrate psychological, emotional, and spiritual values into relationships. These were signals of a new awakening of consciousness among people in the developed countries of the world.

This emerging consciousness was frequently expressed as a growing desire for intimacy, often described as a special kind of closeness, a communication that is deeper than what can be achieved physically, a sharing that goes beyond material partnership, and a spiritual connection that touches the heart and soul of the beloved ones.

Such relationships are possible only when there is a deep commitment between partners to help each other break free of co-dependent and counter-dependent behaviors and to use the healing process as a springboard to a more spiritual relationship. The biggest obstacle blocking this new vision of relationship is the competitive, one-up, one-down model that exists in almost all relationships.[3] When couples develop committed relationships based on equality, cooperation, and mutuality, a whole new culture based on partnership values emerges.

MOVING FROM COMPETITION
TO COOPERATION AND PARTNERSHIP

The primary source of competition in relationships is the belief that there isn't enough of something to go around. This belief in scarcity enters adult relationships from experiences in childhood in which children experienced a shortage of unconditional love, nurturing, mirroring, positive support, food, or clothing to meet their developmental needs.

Most all our values and beliefs are formed in childhood as a result of developmental traumas. When we become adults, we still carry these beliefs and find they are still controlling our behavior. Barry gives an example from his life:

When I was growing up, my family was very poor and there was often just enough food for us at dinner. We all knew that the first one to finish eating got a chance for second helpings. I developed "the fastest fork in the East" while vying with my younger brother to see who would get to the second helping, because there was usually only enough for one. This often left me with indigestion, and it gave me a pattern of eating fast. As an adult, even when there was enough food, I would still find myself finishing first. I had to change this habit in order to avoid indigestion.

When you work on your responses to the first three segments of the "Troubleshooting" sidebar on the next page, it may be best to do so in therapy, where your inner child has emotional support and can safely explore painful childhood events. Changing the last belief in the list is one that only you can do. It requires creating a network of supportive people around you who are available to meet your needs — people you can make contracts with and ask directly for what you want. Once you have this network in place, you won't need to compete, because you'll have many resources available for meeting your needs. When we work with individuals and couples, creating this supportive network is an important step in the journey to independence, interdependence, and abundance.

Creating this kind of network may provide you with a new form of extended family. People willing to cooperatively work together on healing the unfinished business of their childhood become emotionally and spiritually bonded and are able to create a partnership at its most primal level.

Much of our own ability to work as professional partners has come from our personal partnership in helping each other heal childhood traumas. The depths to which we have gone in revealing ourselves and our wounds to each other has created a base of trust and safety that allows us to take risks, be spontaneous, and be creative. In working with other couples, we've noted the

TROUBLESHOOTING

How to Change Your Belief in Scarcity

- Review any childhood experience(s) in which you learned to believe in scarcity of some kind. (For example, "I remember when we did not have much to eat.")
- Identify the core beliefs you took away from those experiences. ("There isn't enough for everyone.")
- Express any unexpressed feelings related to your experience(s) of scarcity. ("I felt sad that this happened so often in my family.")
- Review any old beliefs that you learned from the experience(s) to see if they are still valid in your current relationships. ("I'm in a new family with new opportunities.")
- Create a new reality of abundance based on new beliefs. ("There is enough of what I need in this family.")
- Establish new goals to live according to a set of beliefs in abundance. ("I'll ask for what I need and want and negotiate with others so we all meet our needs.")

same outcomes among many of them as well, for what most people seek is an emotional and spiritual partnership. From this partnership, the mental and physical levels of partnership often emerge. This doesn't mean that all couples should become professional partners the way we have. But they still can be more supportive of each other in the personal aspects of their lives.

DOMINATION VERSUS PARTNERSHIP IN RELATIONSHIPS

The emerging partnership form of relationship is distinctly different from the dominator form of relationship. The dominator form could also be called the counter-dependent form, because almost all the behaviors used to maintain that form of relationship are dysfunctional attempts by counter-dependent individuals to meet unmet needs. Partnership relationships support interdependent actions based on unity, mutuality, and cooperation that are characteristic of an interdependent relationship. The chart "Differences between Dominator and Partnership Relationships" compares the two types of relationship.

DIFFERENCES BETWEEN
DOMINATOR AND PARTNERSHIP RELATIONSHIPS

Dominator Relationships	Partnership Relationships
• use force or threat to enforce domination	• use the vision of higher consciousness to encourage linking for the common good
• create inequalities in power and decision making	• create equal opportunities for money and use knowledge as shared power for joint decision-making
• value violence and exploitation	• value nurturing qualities such as compassion and nonviolence
• enforce rigid sex roles	• permit fluid gender roles
• are competitive	• are cooperative
• use fear to create separation	• generate hope and high ideals to create unity
• are materially oriented	• are spiritually oriented
• see women and children as property	• see women and children as equal, unique individuals
• support co-dependent and counter-dependent behaviors	• support interdependent behaviors and intimacy
• follow a path of fear and protection	• follow a path of learning and discovery
• use control, manipulation, and deception in communicating	• use truth, empathy, and directness in communicating
• value either the needs of the relationship or the needs of the individual	• value both the needs of the individuals and the needs of the relationship

From this comparison, we can see the differences in the philosophy and practice of these two models of relationships. Many couples come to us for help in creating a partnership relationship with each other and with their children. They tell us how difficult it is for them to live in partnership on a daily basis. Until our culture supports partnership relationships, those with partnership ideals must band together in support groups and small communities to help hold firm to their vision.

COMMON ELEMENTS OF PARTNERSHIP RELATIONSHIPS

As we have worked on our own relationship, and have helped many other couples work on theirs, we have found a number of characteristics inherent in partnership relationships:

- a mutual understanding that unmet developmental needs from childhood create dysfunctional behavior patterns that each individual brings to the relationship
- a commitment to help each other heal the childhood wounds and change the dysfunctional behavior patterns
- a commitment to stay together during periods of conflict in the healing process, when partners are likely to project and to blame each other for problems
- a commitment to the path of learning, to self-discovery, and to revealing each person's True Self
- a commitment to learning contracting, negotiating, conflict resolution, self-awareness, and reflection skills
- a commitment to partnership principles that support equality in power, opportunity, and responsibility
- a commitment to tell the truth about behavior, feelings, and needs 100 percent of the time
- respect for each other's personal boundaries
- a new definition of intimacy in relationships that includes the "downs" as well as the "ups"
- a willingness to use prayer, meditation, affirmations, visioning, couples retreats, and other spiritual tools such as yoga and tai chi chuan to support the self-actualizing aspects of the relationship

CREATING A PARTNERSHIP RELATIONSHIP

In the previous section, we briefly noted the common elements of partnership relationships. The following is a more complete discussion of each of the elements.

Recognizing the Unfinished Business

This is a key component of partnerships. So many relationship conflicts are caused by dysfunctional behavior patterns that each person brings into the relationship, especially patterns involving unmet developmental needs. Until this fact is clearly acknowledged and addressed, a relationship cannot move to a partnership, or interdependent, stage. When both partners are willing to look at the sources of their current conflicts and to identify their unmet developmental needs, it's possible to meet their needs and heal their wounds. No longer do partners in relationships need to pretend they have it all together when they don't. They can be truthful about their unmet developmental needs and use them as a source of bonding and intimacy in the relationship.

While these are characteristics of partnership-type relationships, each relationship is unique. One of the contemporary joys of being in a relationship, whether it's a love relationship, a parent-child relationship, or a relationship between two friends, is the opportunity for creating something unique that really meets the needs of the individuals. With the old, rigid roles in our society fading, it's now possible to have new forms of male-male, male-female, female-female, and adult-child relationships. We now have many choices in relationships that can help us find safe and appropriate ways to meet our mental, emotional, spiritual, and physical needs.

A Commitment to Heal Childhood Wounds

When a couple makes a commitment to help each other heal their childhood wounds and meet their unmet developmental needs, they have made the most important shift necessary for creating a partnership. This commitment transforms the relationship's competitive, scarcity framework to a cooperative, abundance mode. This commitment also paves the way for a deeper level of intimacy to emerge in the relationship. The real reason that two people establish a relationship in the first place — but one often not recognized — is to heal their wounds from childhood. When this reality is verbalized, the unspoken dream of the relationship can become conscious and be realized.

A Commitment to Stay Together

In order to make a relationship safe enough to do the deep healing work, there must be a commitment to stay together and work out the old unfinished business. When people expose their childhood wounds to each other, they feel vulnerable and scared. They're afraid they will be abandoned because of their weaknesses. In fact, this is exactly what happened to them in childhood. As children, we were emotionally and/or physically abandoned, usually with no understanding of why it happened. We're afraid this will happen again, so we hide our wounds and our needs from our partners until we know they won't abandon or reject us.

When we work with couples in therapy, we ask them to make contracts to stay together for three months, six months, or one year while working on their deeper issues. They agree to stay together during this period no matter what happens, unless there is physical abuse. They agree to work cooperatively on their relationships using the tools we give them. They also contract to participate in an agreed-upon number of therapy sessions, workshops, or support groups, and to evaluate their progress at certain key points. They can agree to extend the time period if they feel they need more time. The length of time needed depends on how old the wounds are, how long the partners have been together, and how hard they are willing to work on their issues.

Some couples make it through this period quite well, and some don't. We emphasize at the beginning that we do not focus on saving the relationship. Our primary role is to help them become clear about why they are together. We also focus on finding out whether they really want to help each other heal the wounds of their inner children. If they choose not to help each other, then we help them make their separation as clean and clear as possible so that they both leave from an "I'm okay and you're okay" position. We help them to leave with dignity and to use the divorce or separation process as an opportunity to become more aware of their own issues and patterns. This conscious separation helps them recognize their patterns earlier in their next relationships and address them earlier.

We've worked with a number of couples whose relationships actually improved *after* they went through a divorce. It was clear to us that they were each moving from the counter-dependent to the independent stage of development. It was not always clear to them, unfortunately.

There are often good reasons why some couples decide not to stay together. Sometimes they've created a reservoir of ill will so deep that they cannot tolerate the hurt from the deep wounds they keep triggering in each other. Some people don't seem to like each other enough to be willing to work cooperatively on their old issues, and other couples seem convinced that they got into the relationship for all the wrong reasons. They often simply want out of the relationship when they discover the truth. They're too scared to work it out with each other and will have to work it out in other relationships.

A Commitment to Learn about Each Other

It still surprises us that many people who've been together for some time actually know very little about each other. Most adults have developed masks to hide their real feelings and thoughts. In a partnership, both people commit to removing their masks and being as authentic as they can be with each other.

This commitment and authenticity also involves reclaiming what they've projected onto each other, which allows partners to see each other the way they really are. For instance, partners commonly project positive images onto each other, such as "perfect parent," "perfect mate," or "perfect person," or negative images such as "critical parent," "controlling parent," or "rejecting parent." Sometimes these projections are so strong that they prevent any real understanding of the other person beyond the projection. Reclaiming these projections allows us to see our partners as the people they really are, and not see them as people who remind us of someone from our past.

In partnership, both people must be willing to take back these projections and to test their perceptions to see if they are based on the projections. This takes a lot of work and awareness, but it does lead to more self-discovery and discovery of the other person's essence.

To identify a projection, we ask couples to watch for times when they have a reaction to something their partner said or did that seems out of proportion to the actual situation involved — a fifty-cent reaction to a dime issue. This kind of reaction signals that they are projecting, even though they may not know the nature of the projection. These situations call for a perception check. For example, you can say to your partner, "I'm perceiving you as angry at me for some reason. Is this true?" We also remind clients that when they are projecting they are not upset for the reason they think. Almost any conflict is based on an old hurt or unmet need from childhood.

A Commitment to Use Partnership Conflict Methods

It's very important that couples agree to eliminate "dirty fighting" techniques and instead develop effective, responsible partnership skills for resolving conflicts. These skills help build and maintain trust in a relationship. It's been our experience that very few adults have *ever* witnessed or been part of a partnership resolution in solving conflicts. Mostly people have been exposed to the "Four Horsemen of Conflict Resolution": domination, intimidation, manipulation, and exploitation. So when a conflict occurs, people automatically assume there must be a winner and a loser. Since no one likes to lose, the game becomes to win at all costs. No one can create or maintain a partnership under such conditions.

Partnership conflict resolution tools also help deepen intimacy. Rather than seeing conflict and problems as something to avoid, people in partnerships learn to welcome conflict as an opportunity for growth.

A Commitment to Create an Equal Relationship

Creating a relationship equal in power, equal in opportunity, and equal in responsibility is easier said than done. There are numerous subtle and not so subtle ways that people prevent equality in their relationship. We ask couples to give up using power plays to get what they want. Common power plays include threats of violence, refusing to resolve the conflict, threatening a divorce, blaming the other person, and becoming verbally abusive. We also ask them to avoid rescuing, a subtle power play that lets one person feel superior to the other. When you do something for your partner that he or she could do for himself or herself, *and* you don't ask first if it is okay, and he or she didn't ask you to do it, you are rescuing. This sets the stage for all kinds of problems. As one male client stated it, "My wife does things for me that I don't ask her to do and sometimes don't even want. Then she expects me to be grateful to her for what she did and to do something for her in return."

We also ask couples to be *willing* to ask for what they want or need 100 percent of the time. This prevents rescuing and requires each to take full responsibility for meeting their needs. In order to help couples become more aware of rescuing, we ask them to go "cold turkey" with each other: they cannot do anything for the other person unless that person asks for it directly. They also cannot expect their partners to do anything for them unless they ask. During this exercise, many couples discover examples of how they rob their partners of power.

A Willingness to Tell the Truth

At first glance this seems easy. We can testify that it's not. We both grew up in families where there were big secrets and no one ever told the whole truth. The message was that truth is taboo. Unless we are conscious of these kinds of influences, we may have difficulty telling our partners the truth about our thoughts, our feelings, our needs, our bodies, or our spiritual beliefs. If we are projecting a "critical parent" onto each other, this may make it difficult to tell the truth. We expect the other to judge us as our parents did, so we hide our essence from each other. Many people with unmet counter-dependent needs are afraid they'll be rejected if they show their partners how needy and insecure they really are.

Respect for Each Other's Personal Boundaries

Many people with counter-dependency issues invade their partners' boundaries without much thought. When it comes to boundaries in a partnership, it's a two-way street. Both people must identify their boundaries and take responsibility for communicating them to each other. Both must agree to respect these boundaries and develop a mutual process for addressing unintentional boundary violations. Respecting boundaries can help build trust or destroy trust faster than almost anything else can in a relationship.

Finding a New Definition of Intimacy

The old definition of intimacy focused on close, romantic, highly positive times in the relationship. A new definition of intimacy involves developing a sense of oneness, sharing, taking risks, and trusting each other at deep levels as well. Intimacy deepens as partners risk greater openness, become more emotionally present, and display a high degree of caring for each another.

While much of this seems to relate to sharing positive feelings, it can also involve dealing with "the stuff" in the relationship. Intimacy is like an instrument with many strings. The most satisfying relationship music comes from playing a full range of chords that includes both harmony and disharmony. A flow between harmonic chords creates a composition with variety and interesting movements.

Using Spiritual Tools to Support the Relationship

You have to be willing to put time and energy into a partnership, as you do with anything you value. If you want your relationship to flourish, add daily rituals and spiritual practices to help build deeper kinds of connections. These can be simple things such as taking walks together, scheduling a block of time each day to talk with each other about important happenings, and finding time to nurture each other with nonsexual touch, such as foot or back rubs. You can also use daily spiritual practices such as prayer, meditation, yoga, or tai chi that support the growth of a partnership.

FROM COUNTER-DEPENDENCY TO COMMITMENT AND INTIMACY

The shift from counter-dependency to commitment and intimacy can be a daunting process. We suggest going slowly and mastering it in incremental steps. Generally, each step builds on the previous one. You may find yourself skipping a step because you learned that step previously. This list provides you with a map for the breaking-free process, and we are fully aware that the map is not the territory.

The leap to commitment and intimacy is often terrifying for people with counter-dependent symptoms, so terrifying that most never commit, and those who do often retreat from it. We recommend a gradual move into commitment, which will provide the protection and safety that people with counter-dependency issues require. The stages in the commitment process are as follows:

- Determine if there are any primary incompatibilities, such as highly divergent spiritual or philosophical values and beliefs that will undermine intimacy in the long-term. We often use an intention-setting exercise to do this.

- Create a personal plan for each partner to work on unmet developmental needs.
- Make a short-term contract of three to six months during which the partners will help each other heal specific wounds or change specific behaviors.
- Agree not to end or threaten to end the relationship.
- Agree to return to counseling if you want to terminate or renew the contract. Most couples prefer to begin with short-term contracts to help them determine if they want a long-term contract.
- Create a long-term contract that articulates a mutual vision for the numerous aspects of their relationship. These can include financial, spiritual, recreational, educational, parental, familial, and occupational components.
- Create ceremonies to end and restart the relationship as new aspects unfold that allow you to let go of the old parts or phases and celebrate the new ones. Such ceremonies encourage personal transformation of the partners and of the relationship.

This approach can replace the serial monogamy (one relationship after another) so common in the last twenty years and encourage a new form of conscious, committed, cooperative long-term relationship.

HEALING DEVELOPMENTAL TRAUMA

The chart that follows identifies some common relationship issues anchored in developmental trauma. You can use it to help you identify issues recycling in your relationships, their source, and processes you can use to heal and clear them. To clear some of them, you might need the help of a therapist, particularly if they involve early abandonment and abuse.

SELF-QUIZ

Identifying and Healing Developmental Trauma[4]

DIRECTIONS: Place a number in the column under the heading "Degree Present" to indicate the degree to which the issue is present in your life.

1 = Never   2 = Occasionally   3 = Frequently   4 = Almost always

Common Issue	Degree Present	Incomplete Developmental Process from Childhood	Suggested Processes for Healing Developmental Trauma
Fears intimacy		Experienced emotional, sexual, or physical abuse or invasion of boundaries by caregivers	Use "empty chair" technique to help release feelings with a therapist serving as a protector.
Has anxiety or compulsive behaviors		Experienced possible abuse or neglect of basic needs, and shame-based discipline	Learn relaxation and meditation techniques. Ask your therapist to do them with you.
Is passive; lets others lead		Had little support for independent thoughts and/or actions	Ask your therapist to role-play parents and give supporting messages for independent thoughts and actions.
Fears trying new things		Received more "no" messages than "yes" messages	Ask your therapist to role-play your parents and give you "yes" messages.
Fears touch, combined with compulsive eating		Experienced sexual abuse and/or physical abuse	Identify possible perpetrators and have your therapist witness you express feelings (express them on a pillow). Ask for nonsexual touch from your partner.
Is easily bored, externally motivated		Experienced lack of support for exploratory behavior; may have been a "playpen baby"	Ask your therapist to give you support for exploring new ideas and activities.
Rejects help from others		May have experienced shame-based discipline in learning limits	Ask your therapist to help you express your feelings about being shamed.
Strives for perfection		Experienced shame and/or other abusive methods of discipline used to control and set limits	Ask for unconditional messages of acceptance from your therapist.

Common Issue	Degree Present	Incomplete Developmental Process from Childhood	Suggested Processes for Healing Developmental Trauma
Is unable to admit mistakes		Was severely punished for mistakes, either with shame or by hitting	Have your therapist role-play a parent and be understanding when you make another mistake. Ask for positive messages about mistakes being the way to learn.
Is unable to follow through with agreements		Was not effectively taught self-management skills; personal boundaries not respected	Create written agreements with your therapist. Each person decides on a consequence for breaking an agreement and then implements it.
Is unable to handle time and money effectively		Lacked support for self-care	Explore the relationship between "mother" and the material world. Invest in a time-management tool where all time is structured. Hire a financial counselor to teach you how to manage your finances.
Uses intimidation or manipulation to resolve conflicts		Not allowed to make own age-appropriate decisions; had "helicopter" parents	Create and enforce a "no-power-plays" contract with your therapist. Learn to express feelings of shame directly.
Overpersonalizes conflicts and other issues; is moody		Manipulated with shame and guilt to prevent development of independent ideas or actions	Use journaling to recover early memories of trauma. Contract with your therapist to witness the feelings and to role-play any unfinished conversations.
Has difficulty in giving and receiving compliments		Lacked support and positive feedback for efforts to be independent	Contract with your therapist to give you a specific kind and amount of positive feedback every session. Write positive affirmations.

Common Issue	Degree Present	Incomplete Developmental Process from Childhood	Suggested Processes for Healing Developmental Trauma
Has low tolerance for frustration and/or ambiguity		Was sabotaged either overtly or covertly during efforts to become separate; was punished for failures	Sign up for a wilderness experience or ropes course to develop risk-taking skills.
Is unwilling to be responsible for actions		Lacked effective limit-setting; raised with permissive discipline	Use goal- and limit-setting structures in your life (time, money, energy) to structure realistic goals and limits.
Follows direction of others instead of trusting own wisdom and intuition		Received messages that it was not safe to be a separate person; attempts to separate were punished or ignored	Take a public speaking or leadership development class. Explore some new activity outside your comfort zone that pushes you to take more risks.
Fears the future; fears being left behind; feels inadequate; has low self-esteem		Possibly experienced unprocessed birth trauma or early abandonment when bonding needs were not met	Use breath work with your therapist. Ask your therapist to affirm you by offering unconditional love.
Has difficulty relaxing; has chronic body tension		Experienced early tactile deprivation and a lack of constant care as an infant	Get massages for nurturing, nonsexual touch.
Experiences compulsive eating, smoking, drinking, or sex		Deprived of nourishment and/or love; basic needs may have been neglected	Ask your therapist to give you nurturing messages and support.
Feels unconnected to others or isolated in the relationship		Abandoned early by caregivers	Ask your therapist to role-play a parent or caregiver providing you with nurturing messages.

Common Issue	Degree Present	Incomplete Developmental Process from Childhood	Suggested Processes for Healing Developmental Trauma
Is suspicious of others' motives		Experienced birth trauma and lack of attention to needs at birth	Ask your therapist to put you under a blanket in a quiet room filled with soft lights and soothing music. Have your partner lead you on a trust walk.
Feels unloved by partner		Received insufficient loving messages from parents and/or other caretakers; socialization taught through criticism rather than praise	Ask your therapist for reassurance in a time of doubt or fear. Identify all the things you wish your parents had said and done during childhood, and then ask your therapist to say them to you.
Is unable to define wants and needs; expects others to know how these needs should be met		Had hovering parent(s): needs for feeding, affection, and diapering were anticipated and met before appropriate cues were supplied	Ask your therapist to role-play your parents and give you permission to identify your needs and affirm your right to get them met. Contract to ask directly for things you want and need.
Is unwilling to negotiate to meet needs		Subjected to win/lose methods of conflict resolution; interpreted negotiation as "losing"	Enroll in a class in conflict resolution and learn win-win methods for conflict resolution. Express past feelings about situations where loss was experienced and have them affirmed.
Is unable to shift from oneness to separateness without great difficulty		Raised in rigid atmosphere where everything was either "black" or "white"; experienced some trauma between the ages of one and two	Identify instances of trauma or repression and ask your therapist to witness your expression of feelings about these experiences. Learn to identify the "gray area" in situations.

Common Issue	Degree Present	Incomplete Developmental Process from Childhood	Suggested Processes for Healing Developmental Trauma
Avoids intimacy through workaholism or other compulsive activities		Had an abusive, invasive, or neglectful relationship with an adult during childhood that made intimacy unsafe	Identify instances of abuse or invasion and ask your therapist to witness your expression of feelings about these experiences.
Resists developing spiritual practices		Experienced spiritual traumas between the ages of four and twelve; experienced religious abuse	Identify instances of spiritual trauma and ask your therapist to witness your expression of feelings about these experiences.
Fears abandonment		Removed from mother too soon at birth and taken to nursery; had abrupt or extended separation from mother during the first year of life, reinforced by later experiences of traumatic separation	Contract with your therapist for "I'm leaving now and I'll be back at ____" messages at times of separation; do inner-child work to validate and release the feelings of loss and trauma during early childhood.
Breaks and/or forgets relationship agreements		Had unpredictable parents; broken agreements, sadness, and anger about broken agreements	Create a commitment contract with your therapist about keeping agreements, with consequences for breaking them. Process feelings.
Is unwilling to accept that past conflicts are the source of current conflicts		Has unprocessed rage from abusive and/or shame-based discipline and limit setting	Identify instances of abusive and/or shame-based discipline and ask your therapist to witness your expression of feelings about these experiences.

Total score _____

SCORING: Add up the column of numbers in the "Degree Present" column to find your score. Use the following guidelines to interpret it.

30–62 Little evidence of unhealed developmental trauma from your childhood.

61–80 Some evidence of unhealed developmental trauma from your childhood.

62–100 Moderate evidence of unhealed developmental trauma from your childhood.

100–124 Strong evidence of unhealed developmental trauma from your childhood.

CASE EXAMPLE

Sandy had decided to leave her husband, a highly successful physician who was also a cocaine addict. During the sixteen years of their marriage, Sandy had learned how to be the strong one, supporting her children almost single-handedly. Before the divorce, she had worked intensely on herself for two years in individual and group therapy and had learned a lot about herself and her life patterns. With the divorce behind her, she was finally able to create a stable financial base for herself and her children.

As her children grew into their teen years and began to develop interests outside the family, Sandy began to yearn for male companionship. After her divorce and her inner-child work in therapy, she realized she was emotionally still a teenager herself. She wished for a male friend with whom she could just have fun. About that time, Lyle appeared in her life.

Lyle was also divorced and was still paying a lot of child support and alimony to his ex-wife. He felt financially encumbered and decided he needed a few years to work on himself, so that he wouldn't create another unhealthy relationship. Lyle was attracted to Sandy because of her playful attitude and girlish enthusiasm for life.

Their common experiences in individual therapy had taught them that a relationship was the best place to activate and heal old patterns and unfinished business. With their common painful experiences of divorce still so fresh, they mutually decided to create a "committed friendship" contract. Without any long-term expectations, they agreed to do recreational and religious things together on a regular basis. They hoped that, as their friendship matured, they would find opportunities to work on conflicts that emerged — with the assumption that their conflicts would have their old business at their source.

After about three months of seeing each other, they were able to identify that they were each projecting their unfinished business with their mothers onto each other. They were each able to look for what hadn't been completed with their mothers and to consciously contract to role-play each other's mother for short periods of time. Over a period of another two months, they found themselves moving deeper into their mother projections with each other. Eventually they found themselves so deep in old pain that they had difficulty in taking their mothers' faces off each other. At that point they sought therapy with us.

We helped Sandy and Lyle identify their respective roles in the relationship. Sandy's childhood history was one of extreme physical abuse, while Lyle's was one of physical and emotional neglect. Lyle had counter-dependent behaviors characteristic of most men but had flipped into co-dependency issues as the result of the trauma of his divorce. Sandy was currently playing out the counter-dependent role in their relationship. As Lyle got more in touch with his dependency needs and began to approach Sandy with them, it brought up all her fears of intimacy. She continued to see Lyle as a potential abuser and began to pull away from her friendship with him.

Sandy confronted Lyle in therapy about the contained violence and rage that she felt in him, saying it reminded her of how it felt to be around her mother as a child. Lyle, a rather mild fellow, was stunned by Sandy's feedback. He experienced a quick flash of anger, which he quickly extinguished. When we asked him where the anger came from, he responded that Sandy sounded like his mother. We then suggested they create a corrective-parenting contract.

Lyle asked Sandy to play his mother so he could tell her how angry he was with her criticism. As he got into his anger, we quickly put our vinyl beanbag and old tennis racquet in front of him. He picked up the racquet and began smashing the beanbag with all his fury. He cried, cussed, ranted, and raved about the losses in his relationship with his mother, emptying himself of fifty years' worth of old resentments and anger. Then he moved into feeling rage at his father for abandoning him at the age of three. For another ten minutes he alternately sobbed and raged about the losses in his relationship with his father. After about twenty minutes of raging, he collapsed exhausted in a heap on the floor. In a few minutes, he caught his breath and began to sob quietly. He looked tentatively at Sandy and asked if she would hold him. Without words, she held out her open arms. He crawled over and curled into a little ball in her arms.

This session helped Lyle see that he still wasn't emotionally separate from his mother, so he contracted to do a "Completion Process with Your Parents" exercise with Barry. (This exercise can be found at the end of chapter 10.) He emerged from this session saying that he felt as though a weight had been lifted off him.

As Sandy witnessed Lyle's rage during the therapy session, it brought up her own old anger at her mother. She then decided that she needed to do some more work with her mother related to the abuse she had experienced from her. Sandy decided to do this work without Lyle. She felt that he had helped her get in touch with it, and was grateful to him, but that she could complete her work in therapy without his presence. This fit Sandy's need to maintain her counter-dependent behavior as a safety valve against intimacy in the relationship and also honored the fact that they were not currently on a "committed intimate" relationship track.

Sandy was able to release her rage at her mother in therapy and then went through the "Completion Process with Your Parents" exercise. For a couple of weeks Sandy and Lyle did not see each other, though they talked on the telephone several times. They felt a need to let things settle a little bit before they got back together. Eventually they decided that this was a "transitional" healing relationship for each of them, and that neither was ready to have a more permanent relationship. They decided to remain friends and support each other's growth.

THE BOTTOM LINE

- Being in a committed relationship is the most powerful and effective way to heal your developmental traumas and meet your unmet needs.
- Creating an intimate partnership requires the ability to identify the symptoms of developmental trauma and unmet needs that each of you brought to this relationship.
- Creating a partnership requires working cooperatively with your partner to heal your developmental traumas and help each other meet important developmental needs.
- By doing this work together, each of you will evolve in ways you never thought possible. This soul work creates deep love and intimacy.

14. Creating the Partnership Society

The only thing that will redeem [hu]mankind is cooperation.
— Bertrand Russell

In chapter 5 we described human development from a systems perspective, showing that all human systems go through a counter-dependent stage of development: intimate relationships, family relationships, religious groups, political institutions, and national and international structures. From this broader, evolutionary perspective, you can better understand your own counter-dependency issues. It would have been impossible to grow up in this culture without having some developmental trauma and counter-dependent behaviors.

This larger perspective also reveals how important it is for you to break free of your counter-dependent behaviors. By moving forward in your own development, you also help humanity to evolve. In chapter 5 we also discussed how counter-dependent behaviors in each human system are contributing to a world crisis that may imperil the very survival of the human race. After reading this chapter, you might want to review that chapter to

> Humanity, as a species, is stuck in the counter-dependent stage of development.

better understand the big picture of where we are in our human evolution.

Crisis *is* often the catalyst for growth opportunities. Erik Erikson writes that each stage of individual development is heralded by a crisis.[1] In the bonding stage, for instance, the infant has a crisis of trust with the mother that must be resolved in order to separate during the counter-dependent stage. The severity and number of crises currently facing humankind may provide the impetus we need to move forward in our evolution. Making this evolutionary leap can be a little frightening, because some of the few humans who reached interdependence, such as Jesus and Joan of Arc, were deified and then killed. These individuals were seen as deities because they demonstrated psychological and emotional interdependence. In more recent times Abraham Lincoln, Mohandas Gandhi, John Kennedy, and Martin Luther King reached a similar level of evolution and were subsequently martyred. Other highly evolved humans, such as Joanna Macy, Thomas Berry, and Andrew Harvey, have managed to avoid this fate and provide us with inspiring examples of individuated living.

When Buddha's followers asked him who he was, they were astonished by his answer. They asked him, "Are you a god or a saint or an avatar?" He replied, "No, I am awake." He had transcended his individual identity and lived from a mystical, more aware state that he described as "waking up." When we achieve our psychological birth, we become more awake and aware of the larger patterns that exist in our lives and the world we live in. At that point, we can often choose to live our lives based on broad universal principles imbedded in our wisdom traditions rather than according to local, family, and cultural norms.

This chapter is our attempt to describe the healing process that is trying to happen at all levels of human systems. The process for healing individual developmental traumas can be applied to all human systems. Applying it this way does involve a more complex way of thinking, but there are many parallels between individuals and larger human systems.

In this chapter we use communication guidelines that we supplied in our discussion of the functional family triangle in chapter 3 to show you how to break free of dysfunctional counter-dependent behavioral patterns that exist at all levels of human systems. These complement the "Guidelines for Completing the Individuation Process" we presented in chapter 3.

BREAKING FREE OF COUNTER-DEPENDENCY ISSUES IN RELATIONSHIPS

This chapter elaborates on the chart titled "The Stages of Couple Relationships, with the Essential Developmental Processes Needed to Facilitate Couple Evolution," in chapter 13, to help you better understand how couple relationships parallel the development of other human systems. When the desire for individuation occurs in an intimate relationship, and one of the partners wants to explore the world through new activities or wants to develop friendships outside the relationship, it's important to frame this as a positive event. If both partners understand that the need for emotional separation and individuation is a normal and important developmental need, the conflicts over oneness and separateness are easier to handle. In order to provide emotional support for your partner during this process, you must understand the dynamics of the separation process. The process is complex because it involves a replay of efforts to complete the psychological birth during childhood.

The separation process often appears to create a triangle made up of the two bonded partners and an outside "attraction." At this point, the partners must look at what's right about it and identify the unmet developmental needs that might be surfacing in each person. Using the communication guidelines summarized in chapter 3 can help make the separation process easier.

If one partner uses destructive methods to help him or her separate, such as having affairs, complaining, or developing addictive behaviors, it's important to frame these as mechanisms for coping with the emergence of repressed emotions and as "unskilled behaviors." Remember, both partners are doing the best they can. It's also important for partners to define their relationship as a sacred place for healing developmental traumas without shame or blame. When both partners work cooperatively to heal developmental traumas and meet unmet developmental needs, the relationship becomes a crucible for deep intimacy rather than something to flee.

If either partner becomes afraid and the separation process breaks down, the couple may need an impartial third party to support them and get them through this important developmental process. This third party, who may be a skilled friend, a therapist, a minister, or a group, should follow the guidelines listed in chapter 3. By using an outside resource to help resolve separation issues in intimate relationships, you can create the functional family triangle in your relationship.

BREAKING FREE OF COUNTER-DEPENDENCY ISSUES IN FAMILIES

Virginia Satir, a noted American author and family psychotherapist, once said, "If you heal the family, you will heal the world." In the chart "Stages of Family Development," you can see that families go through the stages of development and developmental processes that parallel those of the individual and the couple. The third column of the chart lists processes that families can use to help them complete each stage of development.

STAGES OF FAMILY DEVELOPMENT		
Stages of Development	*Essential Developmental Processes of a Family*	*Processes for Meeting Developmental Needs of Family Members*
Co-dependence	• Establish a bond between parents and children • Establish primal trust in the family • Establish family identity	• Establish a constant environment for parenting the children • Recognize and acknowledge each other's spiritual essence • Exchange nurturing touch and talk between parents and children and between siblings • Give and receive unconditional love between parents and children and between siblings • Create common interests, values, beliefs, and goals for family members

	STAGES OF FAMILY DEVELOPMENT (*continued*)	
Stages of Development	*Essential Developmental Processes of a Family*	*Processes for Meeting Developmental Needs of Family Members*
Counter-dependence	• Create healthy emotional separation between parents and children • Resolve conflicts between needs and wants of parents and needs and wants of children	• Parents and children individually explore interests outside the family • Recognize the unique talents and life paths of each child • Build appropriate boundaries between parents and children • Identify parents' needs versus children's needs • Seek win-win solutions to conflicts between parents and children
Independence	• Encourage individual initiative • Develop models of individual and couple autonomy • Achieve object constancy as a family	• Provide children with independence training in managing time, money, school, and extracurricular activities • Develop a consequence-based method of disciplining children • Maintain boundaries between adult activities and interests and parenting activities • Achieve a balance between the needs of adults and of children • Experience constancy of family relationships and structures during times of stress and/or conflict
Interdependence	• Build consensus decision-making strategies • Develop equitable and equal relationships • Develop each member's fullest potential as a human being	• Manage family affairs through family meetings • Value and maintain healthy agreements between family members • Distribute power equitably between adults and children • Provide a high level of physical and spiritual resources for all members

Up to this point in human history, most families have not effectively healed the individual and couple separation issues related to incomplete developmental processes left over from the counter-dependent stage of development. Because most parents have not completed their own psychological births, they often become frightened when their children or spouses want to become more emotionally separate. Children's desire to separate almost always stirs their parents' anxieties about separation and evokes feelings of failure, abandonment, and rejection. Parents may give indirect messages to their children, conveying that it's not okay for them to become too independent. They may cling to the children or become critical of their attempts to separate. When this happens, the children's drive to separate often intensifies, causing them to become more rebellious.

Rebelliousness is much more difficult to cope with once children reach adolescence. They will have upgraded the separation process of their two-year-old selves and increased in complexity. By this time, they are bright, articulate, and fairly experienced at playing adult games that will test parents' patience to the limits. And limits are exactly what adolescents need to help them clear away remnants of omnipotence, grandiosity, euphoria, and entitlement. Adolescence is a last-chance opportunity to help children move out of counter-dependency and into independence.

It is important to cocreate contracts with adolescents that clearly identify what's permissible and what's not. When children help set their own limits, they are often stricter than their parents. Giving them input about limits also allows children to have personal power and prevents them from resorting to oppositional behavior and rebellion in order to feel powerful. At the time any agreements are jointly created, adolescents should be asked to define the explicit consequences they want if they do not keep the terms of the agreements.

Family meetings are ideal places for members to express feelings, get their experiences validated, resolve conflicts, make agreements, and create consequences. Here, children can learn firsthand about participatory democracy, see appropriate communication skills modeled effectively, learn cooperation, and take progressive steps toward autonomy and collaboration. You'll find guidelines for creating effective family meetings at the end of this section.

When an agreement is broken, it is the parents' responsibility to see that children take primary responsibility in administering the consequences. This supports the development of personal integrity and helps them see that the agreement is with themselves rather than with some external authority, which also helps them develop a conscience. Putting the child in charge of monitoring the terms of the agreement and enacting the consequences takes the parents out of the role of police officer. This diffuses many situations that can become power struggles over who is in charge. Giving children a sense of personal power, inner integrity, and individual responsibility are important parenting tasks that help them move into the independent and interdependent stages of development.

By placing family conflicts and disagreements in a developmental context, all family members recognize that they are in a growth process. Children need to hear permission statements that support their emotional separation such as, "It's okay for you to have your own beliefs, your own feelings, and your own dreams. I will still love you when you become your own person."

Family separation will also activate the parents' unfinished business. This can be seen as a gift for adults, as they often have difficulty in remembering their own childhoods. Parents need to be able to separate their own unfinished issues from those of their children. One way to know if your old issues are contaminating a current conflict with a child is to look at the size of the issue and at the size of your reaction to it. If the reaction is greater than the situation calls for, this indicates that your old issues are getting triggered.

It's essential, even critical, for parents to resolve separation issues in the family that are anchored in the counter-dependent stage of development. Parents often find they are reparenting themselves at the same time they are parenting their children. This can be complex and require outside help to separate parental issues from the issues of the children.

A family is also a system made up of different subsystems: individuals, the parents as a couple, and the family group as a whole. The adults, who make up the system's core level, must be committed to keeping their own relationship clear and must work diligently to resolve any conflicts between themselves. Anything not resolved between them will spread into the children's level of the system and create a family conflict. One child in a family often plays the "agitator" role and acts out anything that is unresolved, unspoken, or unaddressed in the system.

This child often becomes the "identified patient," or the "problem child," and is blamed for things that go wrong in the family. This child is often the one who is taken for counseling or who gets into trouble with authorities at school or in the community. In family systems theory, this child is seen as the carrier of all the unresolved problems in the family. From a family systems perspective, the whole family needs therapy.

Parents often project parts of themselves that they don't like onto their children to avoid dealing with their own unresolved issues. They may abuse, neglect, punish, or discriminate against a child who personifies and reflects back their own undesirable aspects. In such instances, parents may need psychological help in order to separate their issues from those of their children and learn to take back what they have projected onto their children.

Parents also need "cheerleaders" to empower them and validate the importance of this complicated work, as it's not currently highly valued by society. This work is essential for us as a species if we are going to evolve to interdependence. A knowledgeable therapist or parent support group can play a vital role in this healing process. When children are able to leave the family, and both they and the parents feel "I'm okay and you're okay," then the children can move toward the interdependent stage of development with a minimum of unfinished business. This means that their adult relationships, and ultimately their relationships with their own children, will be free from much of the dysfunction and difficulties that have plagued humanity for thousands of years.

When people experience functional ways of living and relating in their families, they will carry them out into the community. They will want their schools and workplaces to be as functional as their families. Functional individuals, couples, and families will help create functional institutions, nations, and eventually, a more functional world.

GUIDELINES FOR CONDUCTING EFFECTIVE FAMILY MEETINGS

1. Start slowly. It's best to initiate family meetings at a time when there are no crises in the family. Begin with short (fifteen- to thirty-minute) meetings and hold them at times convenient for everyone, such as during dessert after dinner. Start with fun and easy issues such as planning a family outing. Stick to agreed-upon time limits

and eliminate outside distractions such as TV, music, and telephone calls (agree not to answer the phone during the meeting). Do not make the meeting a big production.

2. Give equal time to everyone. Ask everyone to contribute something to the discussion, even if it's only: "I don't have anything to add at this time." The parents should encourage full participation by suggesting that each person propose an issue for discussion.

3. Focus on solutions. Avoid using meetings as gripe sessions. Present only problems and conflicts that cannot be worked out without full family input. Balance the presentation of problems with the recognition of positive accomplishments by family members, or with positive issues, such as planning menus for the coming week, planning where to go on a family vacation, and planning for birthdays and family celebrations.

4. Be flexible about meeting times. It's more important to have the whole family present at a family meeting than to have it at the same time each week. Ask family members to make meetings a high priority, or rotate meeting times to match their schedules if it's difficult to get everyone together at the same time.

5. Set clear ground rules. Everyone needs to know the agenda of the meeting, how long it will last, and what's expected. Follow basic communication ground rules: each person is heard, feelings are acknowledged and accepted, and no interrupting, put-downs, or name-calling. Stick to issues and concerns that affect the entire family or several family members. If possible, avoid taking time for individual issues ("Can I go over to Joey's house on Saturday?"). These can be taken care of after the meeting.

6. Avoid rescuing. Rescuing is very common in families and can be avoided in family meetings by having each person ask directly for what he or she wants. If everybody is aware of this rule, it'll be easier to support one another.

7. Avoid using meetings as a soapbox. Parents may be tempted to use family meetings to vent pent-up feelings or resentments or to assert their authority in the family. This can undermine positive outcomes.

8. Break bread together. A good way to make family meetings special is to serve popcorn, dessert, or other treats.

BREAKING FREE OF COUNTER-DEPENDENCY ISSUES
IN RELIGION

In *The Different Drum*, M. Scott Peck identifies four stages of spiritual development and describes how this developmental process breaks down in organized religions. He calls stage 1, that of undeveloped spirituality, "chaotic and antisocial."[2] This stage, which include Peck's self-serving "people of the lie," parallels the co-dependent stage, in which the child lacks boundaries and internal limits. These people live unprincipled and disorganized lives and end up in jail or in other kinds of social difficulties.

During stage 2, the "formal and institutional stage," people try to leave the chaos behind through allegiance with some kind of external authority, such as a church, a twelve-step recovery group, a spiritual group, a guru, or the military, that provides them with structure, rules, and consequences for breaking the rules. In more extreme cases, people whose lives have become extremely chaotic may "choose" jail time to help them move out of chaos and into more orderly lives. In our model, this stage parallels the co-dependent and counter-dependent stages of development.

Stage 3, the "skeptic and individual stage," begins when people start questioning the rules of the source of authority — the church, spiritual leader, group, or military — and they voice doubts about the rigid structure or contradictory beliefs they've encountered. They may become actively skeptical, ask truth-seeking questions, or even rebel against the external authority in some way. This stage parallels our counter-dependent stage of individual development, in which children try to understand the truth about their world. People often make the church or group into the enemy and leave feeling angry and disgruntled. This keeps people spiritually arrested, because it's not possible to mature while making people into villains. This behavior parallels that of two-year-old children, who say, "I'll show you I don't need you," but who are not yet psychologically grown up.

According to Peck, people go back and forth between stages 2 and 3 as they integrate their church's beliefs with their personal beliefs in an effort to build an "internal" church. This vacillation is similar to that of the child who ventures back and forth between oneness and separateness during the counter-dependent stage in an effort to become a separate individual.

An individual in stage 4, the "mystical and communal stage," sees life as a mystery. People in this stage are able to empty themselves of preconceived notions and prejudices. From this empty place, they seek the larger patterns of life in which everything is connected. They may be able to continue as members of established religious organizations or may find their own sanctuaries within. These people create their own sets of principles to guide their lives and do not rely on external rules or institutional dogma to direct their spiritual thinking. In the mystical stage, religion often becomes redefined as spirituality. This stage of spiritual development has parallels with the independent and interdependent stages of individual development. Once people develop some degree of emotional and psychological independence, they are able to remain in this mystical stage for the rest of their lives.

Peck says that the place where the process of spiritual development typically breaks down is in the third stage, when a devout church member begins to doubt and question the party line. At this point, church leaders should support and encourage the questioning process. Unfortunately, most seekers are instead criticized, told to stop their search for their personal truth, and even threatened. Church officials should listen to the skeptics and treat their concerns seriously. The message should be: "It's great that you are searching for a personal religion and questioning the beliefs of the church. How can we support you in finding the answers you're searching for?"

If people entering Peck's third stage of spiritual development were given this kind of support, they probably would not have to leave the church in order to take the next steps in their spiritual growth. Peck says that most organized religions drive people away at this third stage of development by not permitting their skepticism and not supporting their quest for personal truth.

As a result, many religious institutions are simply failing to meet their parishioners' needs for spiritual growth. Instead, their unsupportive practices and policies encourage people to stay stuck in co-dependent and counter-dependent behaviors, which block their psychological development. The viability of many religious institutions is now in serious jeopardy, particularly after the sexual abuse scandals that have rocked both the Catholic and the Protestant churches. Their survival as institutions requires wise leaders who recognize that their members are replaying and acting out their psychological issues within the church. Visionary leaders can create ways to support members' developmental processes in ways that help both the individuals and the institution to evolve. Only when this happens will the churches become part of the evolutionary solution rather than part of the problem.

BREAKING FREE OF COUNTER-DEPENDENCY ISSUES IN NATION-STATES

By looking at large systems such as nation-states from a developmental perspective, it's possible to identify where they're stuck and the incomplete developmental processes that prevent them from moving to the next stage of evolution. The following chart shows these four developmental stages.

DEVELOPMENTAL STAGES OF NATION-STATES

Stages of Development	Developmental Processes of a Nation-State	Methods for Completing the Developmental Processes
Co-dependency	• Build trust with the citizens • Create a national culture and identity • Provide for the basic needs of all citizens • Build national pride • Provide a foundation for the rule of law	• Provide meaning through a national history • Identify common values and beliefs • Provide and protect basic human rights • Provide for the welfare of the poor and disabled • Provide equal education for all • Protect the rights of minorities • Utilize group songs, dancing, and rituals to unify and inspire
Counter-dependency	• Identify unique characteristics of the nation in an international context • Resolve conflicts concerning needs and wants, between cultural groups and between the nation and other nations	• Encourage creativity in expressing values and beliefs • Establish freedom of the press and of speech • Offer freedom of choice in work, religion, and residence • Establish laws to protect the rights and property of all people • Permit freedom to travel and study without undue restraint • Guarantee the right to vote and to petition the government • Offer conflict-resolution training to all citizens

DEVELOPMENTAL STAGES OF NATION-STATES *(continued)*		
Stages of Development	*Developmental Processes of a Nation-State*	*Methods for Completing the Developmental Processes*
Independence	• Create a national culture that honors diversity, initiative, responsibility, and individual freedom • Provide opportunities for cultural groups to celebrate their uniqueness within a national context of cultural diversity	• Create forums to encourage the interfacing and interweaving of diverse expressions of values and beliefs • Create laws protecting minorities and cultural subgroups • Acknowledge and honor the presence of cultural subgroups • Teach divergent and convergent thinking • Encourage direct communication between members of cultural subgroups
Interdependence	• Build interdependence between cultural groups and between nations • Support full development of all citizens • Develop a transnational perspective and a planetary culture	• Identify common goals and visions through collective processes • Utilize subgroup interactions for learning experiences • Create humanitarian nongovernmental organizations that provide needed services to all

The political system of the United States is designed for people who are prepared to function psychologically at an interdependent level of development. Unfortunately, most Americans still function largely with a combination of co-dependent and counter-dependent behaviors. Americans, like co-dependent children still working on trust issues, want security and safety by means of government programs that will take care of their needs for jobs, money, medical care, and retirement benefits. Like counter-dependent adolescents working on issues of separation and autonomy, they also rebel against laws that interfere with their freedom.

Most Americans still define freedom as freedom from outside authority, which keeps people from becoming responsible for their own needs and from looking at how their own behavior is part of a larger problem. The current political system has become more authoritarian because most Americans still do not exercise their political power by voting and actively participating in the democratic system. Until our leaders, and we as individuals, recognize that the problem lies in stunted psychological development, our country will limp along, ineffectively serving its constituents. What we need from American leaders is the kind of wisdom and foresight Thomas Jefferson had when he wrote,

> Some [humans] look at constitutions with sanctimonious reverence and deem them like the ark of the covenant, too sacred to be touched. They ascribe to the [humans] of the preceding age a wisdom more than human, and suppose what they did to be beyond amendment. . . . I am certainly not an advocate for frequent and untried changes in laws and constitutions. . . . But I also know that laws and institutions must go hand in hand with the progress of the human mind. As new discoveries are made, new truths disclosed, and manners and opinions change with the change of circumstances, institutions must advance also, and keep pace with the times.[3]

If Jefferson were alive today, he would probably be a family therapist rather than a politician. He would call a family meeting in the form of a "constitutional convention," where the "children" (senators, representatives, and citizen activists) could come to air their grievances, be heard, have their feelings supported and their experiences validated, and hear their "parents" (government leaders) tell the truth. Skilled "therapists" (developmental process consultants or planetary psychologists) would assist this process by making sure that communication followed the model of the functional family triangle, described in chapter 3. After all grievances were aired, the group would begin to work together cooperatively to determine the next steps in governing our national family. In this step, many ideas could be discussed, refined, and then brought to all the American people for discussion and action.

Through a family-meeting type of constitutional convention, Americans might learn how to effectively cooperate and actually use our democracy, which empowers and preserves the rights of each individual while supporting the collective welfare. In order for this to happen at a national level, we would begin with "family" meetings at the local and state levels, where people would become trained to tackle national problems and issues.

BREAKING FREE OF COUNTER-DEPENDENCY ISSUES IN INTERNATIONAL RELATIONS

On our first trip to the former Soviet Union, we had many opportunities to meet with Soviet men, women, and children to discuss the similarities and differences between our two countries. We also met with Soviet psychologists and discussed the psychological differences that seemed to exist between us. Frequently we were struck by the chemistry that existed between our two cultures. We seemed to mirror each other in so many ways that each seemed to fill some void in the other that was both individual and cultural. The interaction produced a personal alchemical reaction that everyone recognized but had difficulty articulating.

Some of it was sparked by natural curiosity between members of two countries that had been separated because of political ideologies. It seemed to go much deeper, however. The Soviet system was a heavily co-dependent system that tried to maintain central control of all aspects of daily life. The Communist Party ruled the country as if it were an authoritarian, enmeshed family. The system provided jobs, medical care, subsidized food and housing, and a monthly salary for everyone. However, it did not provide consequences for those who failed to show up for work and earn their benefits and salaries. It also failed to provide incentives to support individual initiative.

We observed in the former Soviet Union, after the introduction of perestroika (restructuring) and glasnost (openness), that the people and cultures moved individually and collectively into the counter-dependent stage of development. These people may be attracted to Americans now because they are looking to us as models for how to become more separate. They see that our lifestyle is driven by individual initiative, achievement, self-actualization, and reward, things that were missing in their system.

Americans, on the other hand, are attracted to the collective and cooperative nature of the people of the former Soviet Union. In maintaining their sense of self in a totalitarian system, the latter developed a deep soulfulness that seems missing in Americans.

We see the following polar characteristics, among others, in the two cultures:

United States	*Former Soviet Union*
Masculine orientation (Uncle Sam)	Feminine orientation (Mother Russia)
Counter-dependent	Co-dependent
Materialistic	Humanitarian
Decentralized government	Centralized government
Wedding ring on left hand	Wedding ring on right hand
Hot water faucet on left side	Hot water faucet on right side
Individual initiative	Group or collective initiative
Transcendent search for paradise	Search for paradise in present time
Men perform manual labor	Women perform manual labor
Extroverted	Introverted
Self-reflective	Nonreflective, no need for Self
Rigid	Adaptive
Controlling; direct use of power	Manipulative; indirect use of power
Verbal	Nonverbal
Visually oriented	Auditorily oriented
Cognitive	Emotional
Optimistic	Pessimistic

After the fall of Communism, the drive for separation and autonomy in the former Soviet Union began so fast that it quickly turned into something that looked like sibling rivalry between some of the smaller republics. The long history of oppression and domination by the central government of the Communist regime had created a reservoir of anger, rage, resentment, and suppressed violence in response to the loss of individual freedom and opportunity for self-expression, which these smaller republics are still processing.

Because there is no identified person at whom they can direct their anger and resentment, they project these feelings onto Russians or other racial, religious, or ethnic minorities. The process of recognizing the cultural differences between the countries offers an enormous opportunity for the Western nations and eastern European nations to begin a dialogue about how they can cooperate to create a planetary culture that meets the needs of all countries involved. This process is accelerating as a result of the Internet and other global communication systems now in place. We have more global contact than ever before in the history of the world, and it is leading us toward the establishment of a true planetary culture that incorporates and respects our multitude of differences, in new and creative ways.

ADDRESSING THE
GLOBAL COUNTER-DEPENDENCY CRISIS

We find the prospect of humanity working together to resolve the challenges of its unhealed developmental traumas and counter-dependent behaviors both frightening and exciting. On one hand, we could blow ourselves up and destroy the whole human race; on the other hand, we could leap into global cooperation and work collaboratively to solve the many crises facing us.

Our experiences in traveling in Russia, Ukraine, and Slovakia confirmed that the path to personal enlightenment and evolution lies in nurturing the tendrils of friendship and love that these people are extending to us. In our cross-cultural ventures, we have opportunities to teach each other. We learned a lot about collective initiative and cooperation from our relationships with these people. We also appreciate eastern Europeans' deep grounding in the "mother" archetype and the balance it provides for our own more masculine cultural heritage.

After training psychologists and family life educators in Ukraine from 1990 to 1994, we helped one of our colleagues found ROZRADA, a humanitarian and practical psychology training center in Kiev. This center initially worked with survivors of the Chernobyl nuclear disaster. After the fall of the Soviet Union, the center's mission expanded to help Ukrainians make the shift into post-Soviet life and cope with the rise of social evils, such as drugs and prostitution, in their culture.

In 1992–1993, we lived in Bratislava, Slovakia, where we helped establish the Bratislava International Center for Family Studies. This center was designed to offer programs during the United Nations' International Year of the Family and to provide training in family life education in eastern Europe.

In these cross-cultural environments, we learned more about the strength of eastern European families and their emphasis on consistent care for young children. From us, they learned about individual initiative and how to help people to separate emotionally from their families. In the alchemy between the East and the West lies both the hope and the reality of a more functional global family and the emergence of a rich planetary culture.

THE BOTTOM LINE

- There are common developmental processes in all human systems.
- All human systems are collectively stuck at the same place: the counter-dependent stage of development.
- Human beings work most effectively at the levels where we have the most control over the outcome, which is at the individual, couple, and family levels.
- The more we help microsystems evolve, the faster the more complex macrosystems will evolve.
- The planet cannot sustain itself much longer against our collective counter-dependent behaviors that are rapidly destroying all its ecosystems.
- The future of the human species literally depends on our individual, couple, and family work and the extension of that work to the planet's macrosystems.

15. How We Created a Partnership Relationship

*I don't know what your destiny will be, but one thing I know:
the only ones among you who will really be happy are
those who will have sought and found how to serve.*

— Albert Schweitzer

JANAE: After my first marriage ended in 1984, after nineteen years, I wanted to get back out into the world and find some larger meaning for my existence. After playing out my "mousewife" script and finding myself anticipating death as the marriage ended, I knew the last half of my life had to have some spiritual significance. These urges took me Dr. Jean Houston's first Mystery School.

My thirst for freedom and my yearning for spiritual meaning in my life forced me to take new risks: driving into Chicago, flying to New York alone, finding my way to a conference center in upstate New York, and mixing with 140 strangers for a year in a new program to study the esoteric teachings of the world religions. The year 1984 was exciting for me, and I felt like I had burst out of my cocoon and was becoming a butterfly.

Halfway through my year at the Mystery School, my friend Jane introduced me to Barry. It was three months, however, before we would meet again, this time on the dance floor as we were doing free movement during a

Mystery School weekend. Barry accidentally hit me in the chest as we danced past each other. This "accident" opened up a conversation between us that led to letter writing and his eventual invitation to visit him in Colorado.

A series of synchronistic events made me sure that I should indeed take him up on his invitation. Within the space of one day, I received three messages to visit Colorado, convincing me that there must be something important about going to Colorado. When I arrived there for a ten-day visit, I found him teaching a class at the university, called "The Possible Human," based on Jean Houston's work. I went with him to the class, intending to sit quietly in the back and observe. Part of the way through the class, however, he pulled up a chair beside him and motioned for me to join him up front. I went into shock. I couldn't imagine him wanting a recovering mousewife as a teaching companion, but his students were all watching me and I didn't want to look foolish. So I took the risk and went up to sit beside him. This vignette became a metaphor for our relationship as it matured. From the very beginning, he did everything he could to partner with me.

After only four days visiting with Barry in Colorado, I knew. My heart and soul and mind and spirit opened up, and I was filled with a deep sense of harmony that I had never known before and had only dreamed of. At that point, I was faced with a dilemma. I knew that entering into a new relationship so quickly would be a great challenge for me. Moving from Illinois to Colorado would mean leaving my support system behind and beginning again in a strange place. These were things my head said when I thought about my options. When I let my heart speak, however, there was no dilemma. I returned to Illinois, packed my belongings and headed for Colorado, pulling my U-Haul trailer and dragging my unfinished business behind me.

BARRY: During the year and a half after the death of my wife, Barbara, and before meeting Janae, I gradually rebuilt my life. Several seemingly unrelated events led me to finally meet Janae. In the fall of 1983, I attended a weeklong seminar in Chicago led by Jean Houston. One of the main themes of the seminar was finding the beloved within, which helped me complete another part of my own sacred marriage (the marriage of my inner masculine and feminine aspects). Although Janae was at the same workshop, we didn't meet. I did, however, meet one of her friends, Jane.

When I signed up for Jean Houston's Mystery School in New York, which started in February 1984, I didn't know that Janae had also signed up. From February through September of 1984, one weekend per month, we both traveled to upstate New York. There seemed to be a veil between us, and we spoke only briefly at the June meeting when Jane introduced us. When we finally connected, it was so powerful that we both acknowledged later we probably could not have handled it had it occurred any earlier.

On Friday evening of the September weekend, I was doing some free-form dancing and accidentally hit Janae in the left breast with my arm when I spun around. I offered an apology and continued my dancing. The next morning, I saw Janae and apologized again. We hardly spoke to each other again all weekend, but I felt a strong attraction to her. So, on Sunday afternoon as we were preparing to leave, I walked up to Janae and gave her a hug and told her I was attracted to her. I said, "I would like to get to know you better, and since these weekends are so full of activity, is there any chance you might be coming to Colorado any time soon?" She responded cautiously, "No, but you never know about these things."

On the plane trip back to Colorado that evening, I reflected on my uncharacteristic boldness. I decided to write Janae a letter telling her that, since Barbara's death, I had been in a "go for it" mode, and I was willing to take more risks and say what was on my mind. Fortunately, I received a reply to my letter in a week, telling me she was coming to Colorado the next month to do a vision quest and wanted to spend some time with me.

She had planned to spend ten days in Colorado that October. However, after four days together, we decided to get married. What I experienced was an unbelievable connection between our physical, emotional, intellectual, and spiritual bodies that was undeniable. We made plans for Janae to move to Colorado in November and to get married at Thanksgiving. Only in retrospect did we realize how shocked our families and friends must have been. To us there was no doubt in our minds and our hearts. This is how we began our incredible journey together.

IDENTIFYING OUR UNFINISHED BUSINESS

JANAE: Had I known how much unfinished business I brought with me in my U-Haul, how many unmet developmental needs and developmental traumas, our early days together would have been much easier. So we started from where we were with the tools we had and kept moving toward our mutual dream of partnership. At that time we didn't know we would use our journey to help create a map for other individuals and couples on their journeys to wholeness and partnership.

Much of the first year we spent bonding with each other. Sometimes this was easy for me, and sometimes it was difficult. When our intimacy involved peak experiences, I did fine. When intimacy involved getting in touch with old feelings, I didn't do so well. With my history of my mother's and first husband's emotional unavailability, I had difficulty believing Barry was really present for me and for our relationship. I repeatedly tested him to see if he really was going to stay present for me.

Many times when I got into the old feelings, I felt an overwhelming urge to run away. Sometimes my counter-dependent urges would win out. Several times I got out of bed in the middle of some conflict to go sleep in another room. In these instances, I felt tremendous confusion about my conflicting needs for getting through the old feelings and my fear of going deeper into them. I really wanted to heal my pattern of loss and abandonment and meet my bonding and separation needs. Struggling with this conflict has been some of the most difficult work I've ever done.

Barry's earlier reparenting therapy became a guide for helping me heal my early bonding breaks. The fact that he had repaired so much of his own early childhood traumas made it possible for him to be more available to me. He held me a lot and was sensitive to my fears when I wanted to escape. He served as a solid base that I came to count on, helping me to develop deep trust and a sense of safety. Gradually, I surrendered more and more of my inner self to the relationship, risking that I might get hurt again. And sometimes I was. This time, however, I had someone with whom I could work through the hurt.

We had been married five months when I began my first separation process with Barry. I entered a doctoral program that required a ten-day residency in Virginia. While those were some of the longest days of my life, I also found myself stretching out into the world again. I loved mixing with the diverse group of people, my fellow new learners, who came from all over the country and the world. I could feel myself stepping into an identity that allowed for an expansion of vision, of experience, of possibilities.

I found myself going back and forth between Barry and my newly found world and, like a two-year-old, having a love affair with both. This became a pattern of growth for me. The more I bonded with Barry, the easier it became to go out and explore the world. As a result of this process, I gradually began to develop both personal and professional object constancy. I felt more secure in my relationship with Barry, and I felt more confident in my growth as a therapist and teacher.

Many times Barry played the "good parent" I never had. This required us to keep the healing work we did between us in a context separate from our love relationship. I didn't want to become another "daddy's girl," and he didn't want a child as a wife. Keeping these two dimensions of our relationship separate helped us both define more clearly who we were and what we wanted. The vision between us was always "partnership." By the time we had been married a year, we had established a strong foundation of safety and security between us. Little did I know how this foundation would be severely tested in the years ahead.

BARRY: When we got married, I knew I still had a lot of unfinished grieving to do over Barbara's death. I felt a bit ashamed about this at first, but Janae gave me permission to talk openly about my loss and was willing to hold me and comfort me as long as I needed it. This provided me with an important opportunity to bond with Janae, as I allowed myself to openly grieve with her. Barbara's death also brought aspects of my early developmental traumas to the surface. I felt the abandonment and loss that had accompanied my first bonding break with my mother, when I was one week old. Janae helped me break free of both the adult grief and the childhood grief that I had never expressed fully.

Our relationship grew very close during our first three months together. I found out that the letting go and surrendering I had learned to do near the end of my relationship with Barbara had stayed with me. I found it relatively easy to take back my projections and to receive Janae without resistance.

We had our share of conflicts, but we knew how to get through them very quickly, usually in an hour or less. We made a commitment to find partnership ways to resolve the conflicts that occur between us. We don't put conflicts aside, even if they happen at an inconvenient time.

We also made a strong commitment to help each other heal our wounds and complete the unfinished business we each brought to the relationship. This commitment has helped us experience more intimacy than I ever thought possible.

We both agreed that we wanted a partnership relationship and a partnership lifestyle. We agreed to live, work, and play together, and we are with each other sometimes for days at a time, although we also enjoy spending time by ourselves or with others. We feel free to act in consciously co-dependent, counter-dependent, independent, and interdependent ways with each other. When we seem to want different things or have different needs, we are secure enough as individuals to resolve any conflicts and find a way to get what we want or need.

HEALING OUR LIFE DRAMAS

Janae: During the winter semester of 1986, Barry took a sabbatical from his teaching at the university. We had decided to go to Switzerland for six months to live and study. The plan was that Barry would write a book, I would write part of my dissertation, and together we would study with a Jungian analyst there. We both were attracted to this analyst and his innovative approach to therapy. The foundation of his theory seemed similar to that of my self-directed, process-oriented doctoral program at the Union Graduate School. So I anticipated the two blending quite well.

During the six months of intermittent training and therapy with this analyst and his group, we attended many classes and workshops. Our last training activity was a six-week-long period of intensive training using his approach. I anticipated that during this intensive training I would be able to learn this approach in a self-directed way. My research in learning styles told me that everyone learns in his or her own unique way. By this time, I knew quite a bit about my own learning style and saw this training as a place where I could learn naturally by following my own process.

By the time we were halfway through this training period, it was pretty clear that I was the only one who valued this way of learning. At that time, the classes were taught in a very traditional European manner, with the teachers lecturing and structuring the classes in authoritarian ways. This didn't work for me, for I needed more personal involvement in my learning. I preferred more interaction, experimentation, and activity-oriented methods that supported my way of learning. The more I tried to express my need to learn in my own way, the more resistance I met, especially from the male teachers. The more I spoke out in class about my learning needs, the more resistance I met. I eventually found myself engaged in a power struggle with one of the trainers — one that I would not win.

One morning I went into one of my classes and asked for time to talk with the group. I told them that I was leaving the class to study on my own because I could not get my learning needs met in the class. The teacher passed judgment on me for leaving, and he made the problem seem to be all mine. I also proceeded to drop out of all other classes where I was not permitted to follow my own process as a learner. The ensuing free time I used for independent study and a tutorial with one of the advanced female students, who taught in a way that was compatible with my learning style.

While my action took care of meeting my learning needs, it also triggered something deep and dark inside of me. I began to feel ostracized by other students who seemed to have no trouble learning in this traditional atmosphere. None of them seemed to want to address the quality of the learning environment to see if it really served them. Mostly they seemed to identify me as the only problem in the system. I felt as though I had been shot down by them.

I began to feel intense pain, grief, sadness, despair, and death move over me. Little by little I fell into an intense state of depression in which there seemed to be no bottom. I just kept falling, falling. Deeper and deeper I went inside. Barry got frightened when I would say that I felt like I was dying, as it stirred up his old feelings about Barbara's death. Several times I lay down on our bed and closed my eyes and surrendered myself to death. Each time I descended into a deep state where I had only my own inner resources.

Here in isolation, I felt the pain of the early abandonments at the core of my developmental traumas, and all of the layers of emotion contained there. My suffering, now substantial, required that I experience the truth of these events. I could no longer just act counter-dependent, deny my feelings, and armor myself to look good. I felt like an uncooked egg that had been dropped on the floor, scattering my insides into a puddle.

At this point, the pain was so intense that I looked for another way of dealing with it. I had already surrendered myself to death and found myself still alive. The only other option I could find was to go crazy. I remember the day when the pain became unbearable, and I decided I would find a place deep inside myself where the pain couldn't follow. My body began to feel more and more stiff. My eyes started glazing over and I stopped responding to people. I was becoming catatonic.

At the end of that day's classes, Barry and I headed to our car. He led me gently, seeing my pain and catatonia and not knowing what to do. Just as he opened the car door to help me in, I looked down the road. There I saw our good friend Adam, from Hawaii, whistling his way toward us. In that moment, he appeared as an angel to me. He was the only person I knew who was not involved in our intensive training and not coping with these challenges.

When Adam saw my pain and got brief input from Barry about what I was experiencing, he quickly responded as an ally. He went back to our apartment with us and spent the evening just sitting with us. In his quiet way, he supported us emotionally and helped validate our experience. He helped me reach out again. After a couple of days, I began to regain my equilibrium.

In the next weeks, I began piecing myself together again. I felt fragile and sometimes disoriented. I still have some of the dyslexia that appeared at that time. After we returned from Switzerland, I completed my doctoral dissertation, and we built a new home and created our nonprofit institute. These external creative activities helped me simultaneously restructure my inner world. After this breakdown, my brain began to work much better, my thinking capacities increased markedly, and my sense of personal power surged.

It took me several years to identify this experience as an "inner-child breakdown" and to understand how the group in Switzerland had helped me replay a family-of-origin developmental trauma. As I healed this old trauma, I began to draw clients who had similar issues. With my own experience as a resource and reference, I was able to be present in their experiences in a supportive way, which helped them not feel so frightened or crazy.

I also found descriptions of experiences similar to mine in Native American writings about shamanic experiences, particularly the "death walk" of Don Juan described in books by Carlos Castaneda and the spiritual emergence described by Stan and Christina Grof.[1] I also began to correlate this kind of breakdown with traumatic breaks in bonding during my early childhood. With a larger frame of reference about such breakdowns, and my own experience in helping both myself and clients get through them, I began to understand how important this process was for me.

In retrospect, I see that this experience took me into a place in my own depths that I now recognize as a place of strength. In this void, I've learned to access some deeper parts of myself that provide wisdom, guidance, and grounding — places where I can shed old, used-up parts of myself so that new ones can emerge. I know this place of "inner death" now as a source of renewal and transformation. It's a place where I can find my own deepest nature and give it a voice as I continually weave and reweave my Self. This experience was my first real knowing of my Self and my own deep feminine.

My experience in Switzerland also really helped me understand how the universe operates as a large, interactive system. I was able to understand even in the middle of my breakdown that my experience with the group was bringing up an unresolved family conflict.

Using a systems approach helped me gain an understanding of how the inner world and the outer world are always in relationship, helping to create each other. When the reactor at Chernobyl exploded, and when Americans flew in during the night to bomb Libya during 1986, I began to see the world as a dysfunctional family. Barry and I decided we must become part of the solution to global conflicts when we returned to Colorado.

BARRY: In the first year of our marriage, as we got closer to each other, I found myself dealing with new and unexpected issues related to my life drama. After getting married in late November, we went, in January, to Greece and Egypt on a belated honeymoon, along with a group of our Mystery School friends led by Jean Houston. This was an intense experience for both of us that seemed to bring us even closer together on a spiritual level. When we returned, we also participated in a five-day Native American dance ritual called the Long Dance, which opened us up spiritually even more.

Late that spring, I began to feel ill. I experienced low energy and pain in my left side. I finally went to the doctor and found out I had early-stage colon cancer. I was totally shocked and terrified. To me, cancer meant death, a slow horrible death.

As I began to recover from the shock and looked at my treatment options, I was determined to get to the source of the problem using a body-mind approach. With Janae's support, I elected to start with the least invasive physical treatment I could locate. This meant that drastic changes in diet and nutritional balancing were first. Next, I began to work on the unfinished business related to the cancer. Because the cancer was on the left side, at the top of the descending colon, I looked at the feminine side of my unfinished business. (The left side of the body is often associated with the feminine, and the right side with the masculine.) Several contributing factors immediately became apparent.

I was under tremendous stress at the university because I had been appointed as the faculty advocate for a female junior colleague who was applying for reappointment. In the process of meeting with various personnel committees and administrators, I encountered what I saw clearly as a "killing of the feminine" aspect of faculty members, both male and female. The only things my colleagues were willing to focus on were the number of publications this female colleague had published, the quality of her publications, and what line of research she had developed in the less than three years she had been at the university. No one was interested in the fact that she was a single parent who had to spend a lot of time with two very sick children during her first two years at the university. Also, no one was interested in the fact that she was hired at a salary level below that of most male assistant professors, and that she had to teach extra classes in order to provide for her family. No one was interested in knowing that she received almost no mentoring from any senior colleagues in her department about what she needed to do to prepare for her personnel review. When all my attempts to present a balanced perspective fell on deaf ears — those of my colleagues who were sitting in judgment on this case — I finally began to understand. The university system is designed to kill the feminine aspects of its faculty members. It was killing the feminine in me as much as it would try to kill anyone who attempted to be a whole person.

I immediately resigned as chairperson of my department, but put off resigning from the university until after my upcoming sabbatical in Switzerland. I knew that, if I didn't get to the bottom of this problem, my resignation was inevitable.

I worked further with the theme of the "killer of the feminine" to see where else it had happened for me as I was growing up. Certainly I never felt any support for my feminine qualities. They were either ignored, killed, or put down. I loved to read, write poetry, and listen to classical music, and none of that seemed to be of value in my culture. In order to be "one of the boys" in junior high school, I pretended not to study or be interested in reading books. Instead, I became a jock and played basketball and baseball in high school so I could belong. All my adult life, I had been fighting to recover my feminine side. After Barbara's death, I worked very hard to reclaim it, only to find people trying to kill it again.

I had seen that Barbara's death symbolized the killing of my feminine ideal that I had projected on her. At this point I began to wonder if I had really taken that back completely. Finally, I did some more therapeutic work to uncover the source of this illness, and what I found blew my mind.

In my daily meditations, I began to get images of being killed by someone stabbing me with a long spear in my left side. The more I worked with these images, the more I realized that they were not from this lifetime. They were Egyptian in nature, and eventually, in a waking dream, the whole story came to me.

As the dream revealed to me, Janae and I had been part of an Egyptian Mystery School, and I had threatened the power structure of this school because I wanted to integrate the feminine and masculine aspects of the school's teachings. Specifically, I wanted to have more attention placed on the earth and on the shadow aspects, while those in power wanted the school to focus on the transcendent qualities of the light, not the dark, side of human existence. I wanted a balance between these two, and apparently they decided I was dangerous and had to be killed. Janae (who was a man in that lifetime) was selected to be my killer. What to do with this awareness would soon become apparent.

In early July 1985, we went to California to attend a weeklong therapy workshop with the Jungian analyst we were planning to study with in Switzerland the following January. By the end of the second day, I decided to work on this issue in the group and asked this therapist to help. He suggested I do a psychodrama so I could reenact the death scene and learn what wasn't finished in it that I might be trying to finish with the cancer.

I reenacted the whole scene with Janae stabbing me in slow motion with a fireplace poker. When she pressed the poker against my side where the colon cancer was forming, I fell to the floor and screamed in agony. I reexperienced the physical and emotional pain of being betrayed and abandoned by my friends and loved ones. The pain subsided after a while, only to be replaced by intense anger. I raged on the floor while eight or ten people held me down to protect me from hurting myself or others.

When this subsided, I got up and faced Janae. I knew there was something else to finish with her. I grabbed her, and we began to wrestle. I felt as if I were fighting for every man who had ever been betrayed and abandoned by a woman, and later Janae confided that she had felt she was fighting for every woman who had been attacked and dominated by a man. It was an intense struggle between two strong opponents. Finally, I wrestled her to the ground and ended up sitting on top of her. After a few moments, she looked up at me and said calmly, "Aren't you getting lonely up there?" Obviously I was, because all the fight immediately drained out of me. I rolled off her, and I knew what I really wanted was full partnership with Janae. We ended our battle of the sexes that July day in 1985 in California.

I still wasn't out of the woods with the cancer. With additional psychological and nutritional work, however, my cancer went into remission, and I was symptom-free by August 1985, and I have remained symptom-free since then. I've continued a mostly vegetarian diet and take various nutritional supplements, and I try to keep myself from being overstressed. In July 1989, after one of my periodic checkups, my nutritionist said to me, "I have some good news and some bad news for you." I said, "Give me the good news first." She said, "The good news is that your body is perfectly balanced nutritionally. The bad news is that you'll have to devote almost two hours a day to spiritual work to keep it balanced." What she was referring to was prayer, meditation, yoga, and just taking time to be with myself and do unto myself. She said she believed my next challenge was to focus on taking care of myself for a minimum of two hours a day.

My first thought was how easy and nice that would be for me. What I discovered in the ensuing months, however, was that this was the most difficult prescription I'd ever had to fill. It brought me up against my deepest beliefs about not being worthy of two hours a day devoted to myself. Now, after many years of dealing with these issues, I can report success only about 50 percent of the time. My oldest program of taking care of others first really is hard to shake. Now that I've retired from teaching at the university, I'm able to maintain my two-hour goal more consistently, but it's still a persistent problem area that requires constant attention.

INTEGRATING OUR NEW LEARNING

Our time in Switzerland brought profound changes for us. Besides having our worldview expanded greatly, we were "nuked" while walking the streets of Zurich after Chernobyl's explosion. We were also assaulted by Europeans' anti-American pronouncements after the bombing of Libya.

We returned from Switzerland even more convinced that we needed to become more a part of the solution and less a part of the problem. We built an ecologically sound, passive solar, earth-sheltered home and turned our efforts to finding new and active tools for resolving conflicts at all levels. We founded a nonprofit, tax-exempt institute called the Colorado (now Carolina) Institute for Conflict Resolution and Creative Leadership and organized two international conferences, in 1987 and 1988, devoted to the premise "What would happen if peace broke out?" The breakup of the Soviet Union seemed like the first wave of the outbreak of peace on earth. However, the second wave of nationalism in the Balkans and the Middle East brought on more turmoil and strife, which was followed by a wave of terrorism. These events, unfortunately, have not brought us closer to peace on earth.

In the late 1980s and early 1990s, we made plans to expand our institute and develop extensive programs and services, and found ourselves faced with another important lesson. Because of some old needs to caretake others, we had inadvertently created a co-dependent group. It was after the collapse of this group that we saw how our own unfinished business from our families of origin had helped create a dysfunctional group structure. Our unfinished business had spread outside of us and into our organization, where it became so big that we could finally see it. That was when we decided to write a book about our personal and professional experiences of treating co-dependent behavior. This book, *Breaking Free of the Co-dependency Trap*, examined the personal and cultural roots of co-dependent behaviors.

While we learned a lot from our experience in co-dependent relationships with the Colorado Institute for Conflict Resolution and Creative Leadership, we were not through. We had yet another similar experience to encounter. After our co-dependency lesson, we were cautious about getting into similar situations. However, one began to develop right under our noses. In our local conflict resolution workshops and our training groups, the theme of "family" began to emerge. A number of people began to create a family support system that eventually became the Family Training Center and a related support network. Again, we began planning a joint therapy practice with a group of these people. Again, a very similar result occurred. Some people in the group began to want us to support their unmet co-dependent needs. They wanted us to set up the center and refer clients to them so they would never have to establish their own professional identity. When we saw what was happening and refused to allow this, they became angry at us and left.

This also brought up many counter-dependent reactions in people, and before very long, the whole project had to be tabled. We saw, in retrospect, that others had viewed us as the "good mother" and "good father" who would provide everything necessary to get the center started. When they found out about the partnership aspects of the business arrangements, they withdrew, and we became the "bad mother" and "bad father."

We invited each person to come and talk to us about his or her feelings in order to resolve anything that was unfinished. At that time, we still had not identified the concepts of developmental trauma and the trauma drama, and did not have all the tools we now have. Several people in the group chose to resolve the conflict from a win-win place. Several others decided to remain angry at us and refused our invitation to work things out. Since the invitation was open-ended, perhaps they may yet decide to do this.

We understood people's attempts to complete their emotional separation, but we were unable to help them get through it in some cases. Perhaps the real purpose of trying to create the center was to help everyone involved to move closer to individuation. Some of those involved took big steps toward completing their separation process.

We learned how difficult it is to help facilitate the separation process with a group of people when we're in the middle of it and unaware that this is what's happening. In the process, we certainly learned more about how to provide positive emotional support to a group of people who are trying to change their co-dependent and counter-dependent patterns and move toward individuation.

THE RETURN TO PARADISE

JANAE: In the winter of 1990, a friend brought me a wonderful book, *Memories and Visions of Paradise*, by Richard Heinberg.[2] As I read Heinberg's cross-cultural review of paradise myths, the whole concept of paradise began to fascinate me. At one point, I began to see that the earth did not change when I felt paradise slipping away from me, when I fell into replaying old traumas. Only my internal reality changed. This flash of awareness helped me see that the way back to paradise involved working with my inner reality.

I began to see each day as a new day in paradise. I began to trust the flow of life and the cycles of life and death as part of the larger process. I began to tap into deeper realities of my being by spending more time in nature. I also began to truly believe that my relationship with Barry was real and long-lasting. I noticed that my fears of intimacy had been replaced with a joyous attitude about discovering his unknowingness. The frequent rounds of conflict between us caused by unfinished business eventually began to diminish, and I began to experience instead a deep glow of warmth and relatedness that now feels so good in my body that I know I really have returned to paradise.

It's wonderful to find a partner who's always right there with me, challenging me to new heights and depths that cause our relationship to remain in a constant state of renewal. Sometimes we find that we need to crash and burn the structure of our relationship so that, like a phoenix, it can rise again. This now happens in such a natural and spontaneous way that we experience renewal as a more even flow, without the extreme peaks and valleys of earlier days. My biggest challenge these days is to receive paradise.

BARRY: Over the past twenty years or more, I've become increasingly aware of returning to paradise again. Finally, I feel that Janae and I are equal partners in all the important areas of our lives. We continue to deepen our spiritual connection on a daily basis. I can experience long periods of intimacy with Janae now without being afraid I'll lose myself or be consumed by her. My boundaries are clear; I can set limits if I need to, and I know she'll respect them. I no longer feel I have to take care of her in any way. I know she is fully capable of taking care of herself; and, most important, my worth as a person does not depend on taking care of anyone but myself.

I feel a tremendous sense of personal freedom to be who I want to be and do what I want to do. Through my spiritual practices of prayer, meditation, and yoga, I keep in daily contact with the flow of my inner life. I use reflective thinking, perception checks, visioning, asking for what I want and need, boundary setting, and conflict resolution skills to help me stay in daily contact with the flow of my inner life.

Being in a relationship with Janae for over twenty-three years has brought me another dimension of paradise. There is such a flow of creative energy between us that it seems like making love almost all the time. We inspire each other and support each other in our separate endeavors, and we embrace each other when we are working together. In spite of this wonderful flow between us, there is still a sense of mystery and discovery in our relationship. We use the relationship to continue to open up new and unknown aspects of ourselves and share them with each other. In this way, our relationship serves as a holy garden on fertile ground where we can nurture new and emerging aspects of ourselves. We are constantly surprised by the newness and freshness we feel. Just when we think we are becoming "old married folks," we find a new and unexplored dimension of ourselves to explore in our relationship with each other. This may not be everybody's vision of paradise, but it sure is mine, and I'm certainly enjoying it.

Acknowledgments

First, we acknowledge our own belief in this book, as we self-published it for more than fifteen years. We particularly thank John Bradshaw, who was one of the few people who recognized the importance of our work on counter-dependency. This has meant a lot to us, as counter-dependency has been largely ignored in the addictions and recovery field.

We also thank the many clients, students, and colleagues who helped us refine the tools that we learned from our "laboratory" — our own relationship. We also acknowledge those who read previous editions of this book and gave us helpful editorial and conceptual feedback to make it a more effective mechanism for growth and change.

We also acknowledge the folks at New World Library, who are now bringing this book to a wider audience. We appreciate the supportive staff there who patiently helped shape the final version, including Associate Publisher Munro Magruder, Senior Editor Jason Gardner, and Managing Editor Kristen Cashman and our copy editor, Bonnie Hurd, whose kind and thoughtful comments helped articulate our work more clearly.

Notes

INTRODUCTION

1. M. Mahler, *On Human Symbiosis and the Vicissitudes of Individuation* (New York: International University Press, 1968).

CHAPTER 1

1. J. Weinhold and B. Weinhold, *Healing Developmental Trauma* (Swannanoa, NC: CICRCL Press, 2007).
2. B. Weinhold and J. Weinhold, *Conflict Resolution: The Partnership Way* (Denver: Love Publishing, 2000).
3. Ibid.
4. K. Magid and C. McKelvey, *High Risk: Children without a Conscience* (New York: Bantam, 1988); the quotation at the end of the paragraph is from Ken Magid, personal communication, 1992.
5. B. Perry, "Incubated in Terror: Neurodevelopmental Factors in the Cycle of Violence," in *Children, Youth, and Violence: Searching for Solutions*, ed. J. Osofdsy (New York: Guilford Press, 1996).
6. Magid and McKelvey, *High Risk*.
7. F. Cline, *What Shall We Do with This Kid? Learning Disorders and School Problems* (Evergreen, CO: Love and Logic Press, 1979).
8. J. Campos and K. Barrett, et al., "Sociomotor Development," in *Handbook of Child Psychology*, vol. 2, Infancy and Psychology, ed. M. Haith and J. Campos (New York: Wiley, 1983), 783–915.

9. J. Bowlby, A Secure Base: Clinical Applications of Attachment Theory (London: Routledge, 1988); M. Ainsworth, "Attachments Across the Life Span," *Bulletin of the New York Academy of Medicine* 61 (1985): 792–812.

10. R. Karen, *Becoming Attached* (New York: Oxford University Press, 1998).

11. American Psychiatric Association, *Diagnostic and Statistical Manual*, 4th ed. (Washington, DC: American Psychiatric Association, 1996), s.v. "conduct disorder."

12. F. Cline, *What Shall We Do with This Kid? Learning Disorders and School Problems* (Evergreen, CO: Love and Logic Press, 1979).

13. Perry, "Incubated in Terror."

14. A. Krause and B. Haverkamp, "Attachment in Adult Child–Older Parent Relationships: Research, Theory, and Practice," *Journal of Counseling and Development* 75 (1996): 75.

15. Weinhold and Weinhold, 2000.

16. W. Pollack, appearance on the "How to Raise a Better Boy: Crying Bullets" episode of *The Oprah Winfrey Show*, April 5, 1999.

17. Perry, "Incubated in Terror."

18. Weinhold and Weinhold, 2000.

19. M. Straus et al., *Behind Closed Doors: Violence in the American Family* (New York: Anchor Press, 1980), 148.

20. A. Miller, *For Your Own Good* (New York: Farrar, Straus, Giroux, 1984).

21. S. Forward and C. Buck, *Betrayal of Innocence* (New York: Penguin Books, 1978).

22. A. Sedlak and M. Broadhurst, *The Executive Summary of the Third National Incidence Study of Child Abuse and Neglect* (Washington, DC: National Clearinghouse on Child Abuse and Neglect Information, 1996), 6.

23. Ibid, 8.

24. Ibid, 8.

25. National Child Abuse and Neglect Data System, Summary of Key Findings from Calendar Year 2000 (Washington, DC: National Clearinghouse on Child Abuse and Neglect Information, U.S. Department of Heath and Human Services, 2002).

26. Sedlak and Broadhurst, Executive Summary, 8.

27. L. DeMause, "The Universality of Incest." *Journal of Psychohistory* 19 (1991): 123–64.

28. D. Daro and R. Gelles, "Public Attitudes and Behaviors with Respect to Child Abuse Prevention," *Journal of Interpersonal Violence* 7:4 (December 1992): 517–31.

29. Sedlak and Broadhurst, Executive Summary, 8.

30. Ibid.

31. Ibid.

32. B. Widom and M. Maxfield, *An Update on the Cycle of Violence* (Washington, DC: Office of Juvenile Justice and Delinquency Prevention, U.S. Department of Justice, 2001), 7.

33. S. Marcus-Mendoza, E. Sargent, and C. H. Yu, "Changing Perceptions of the Etiology of Crime: The Relationship between Abuse and Female Criminality," *Journal of the Oklahoman Criminal Justice Research Consortium* 1 (1994): 17. Available at http://www.doc.state.ok.us/offenders/ocjrc/94/940650B.HTM (accessed October 17, 2007).

34. National Institute of Justice, *The Cycles of Violence Revisited*: NIJ Research Preview (Washington, DC: U.S. Department of Justice, 1996), 2.

35. Weinhold and Weinhold, *Conflict Resolution*.

36. Weinhold and Weinhold, *Healing Developmental Trauma*, 54–55.

CHAPTER 2

1. M. Mahler, *On Human Symbiosis and the Vicissitudes of Individuation* (New York: International University Press, 1968).

2. M. Mahler, *On Human Symbiosis*; S. Johnson, *Humanizing the Narcissistic Style* (New York: W. W. Norton, 1987).

3. B. Weinhold, *Breaking Family Patterns* (Swannanoa, NC: CICRCL Press, 2006).

4. A. Miller, *Prisoners of Childhood* (New York: Basic Books, 1981).

5. A. Miller, *For Your Own Good* (New York: Farrar, Straus, Giroux, 1984), 97.

6. S. Hoeller, *Gnosticism: New Light on the Ancient Tradition of Inner Knowing* (Wheaton, IL: Theosophical Publishing House, 2002), 13–24. Margaret Mahler and others also use the term "individuation"; however, Jung has a different take on its meaning.

CHAPTER 3

1. T. Verny, *The Secret Life of the Unborn Child* (New York: Delta Books, 1981); T. Verny and P. Weintraub, *Nurturing the Unborn Child* (New York: Delacorte Press, 1991).

2. Verny, *The Secret Life of the Unborn Child*; Verny and Weintraub, *Nurturing the Unborn Child*; S. Grof, *Realms of the Human Unconsciousness* (New York: E. P. Dutton, 1976).

3. C. Violato and C. Russell, "Effects of Nonmaternal Care on Child Development: A Meta-analysis of Published Research" (poster presentation at the Canadian Psychological Association Convention, Penticton, BC, Canada, July 1, 1994).

4. D. Lero et al., *Canadian National Child Care Study: Parental Work Patterns and Child Care Needs*, catalogue no. 89-529E (Ottawa: Statistics Canada, 1992), 62.

5. S. Karpman, "Fairy Tales and Script Drama Analysis," *Transactional Analysis Bulletin* 7 (1968): 39–43.

6. L. Kaplan, *Oneness and Separateness* (New York: Simon and Schuster, 1978).

7. B. Weinhold and J. Weinhold, *Conflict Resolution: The Partnership Way* (Denver: Love Publishing, 2000).

CHAPTER 4

1. G. E. Vaillant, *The Natural History of Alcoholism* (Cambridge, MA: Harvard University Press, 1983), 106.
2. Ibid.
3. C. M. Weisner and R. Room, "Financing and Ideology in Alcohol Treatment," Social Problems 32 (1984): 167–84, quoted in S. Peele, *The Diseasing of America* (Lexington, MA: Lexington Books, 1989), 49.
4. L. Grinspoon and J. B. Bakalar, *Cocaine: A Drug and Its Social Evolution* (New York: Basic Books, 1985).
5. S. Peele, *Diseasing of America* (Lexington, MA: Lexington Books, 1989), 25.
6. Ibid.
7. S. Peele, "The Surprising Truth about Addiction," *Psychology Today* (May–June 2004): 44.
8. S. Rollnick and W. R. Miller, "What Is Motivational Interviewing?" *Behavioral and Cognitive Psychotherapy* 23 (1995): 325–34.
9. T. Maeder, "Wounded Healers," *Atlantic Monthly* (January 1989): 37–47.
10. P. Carnes, *Contrary to Love* (Minneapolis: CompCare Publishers, 1989), 234.
11. J. Bradshaw, *Healing the Shame That Binds You* (Deerfield Beach, FL: Health Communications, 1988).

CHAPTER 5

1. J. Weinhold and B. Weinhold, *Healing Developmental Trauma* (Swannanoa, NC: CICRCL Press, 2007), 138–39, 140–41.
2. G. Bateson, *Steps to an Ecology of Mind* (New York: Ballantine, 1972).
3. B. Lipton, *The Biology of Belief* (Santa Rosa, CA: Mountain of Love/Elite Press, 2005).
4. R. Eisler, *The Chalice and the Blade* (San Francisco: Harper and Row, 1987).
5. L. Brown et al., *Plan B 2.0: Rescuing a Planet under Stress and a Civilization in Trouble* (New York: W. W. Norton, 2006).

CHAPTER 7

1. C. Rogers, *On Becoming a Person* (Boston: Houghton Mifflin, 1961), 332.
2. R. Bolton, *People Skills* (New York: Simon and Schuster, 1979).
3. B. Weinhold and J. Weinhold, *Conflict Resolution: The Partnership Way* (Denver: Love Publishing, 2000), 43.

CHAPTER 8

1. B. Weinhold, *Breaking Family Patterns* (Swannanoa, NC: CICRCL Press, 2006), 17.
2. C. Rogers, *On Becoming a Person* (Boston: Houghton Mifflin, 1961).

CHAPTER 9

1. J. Bradshaw, *Healing the Shame That Binds You* (Deerfield Beach, FL: Health Communications, 1988), vii, viii.
2. R. Bly, "Your Spiritual Shadow," *Magical Blend* (July 23, 1989): 10–23, 96.

CHAPTER 10

1. J. Bradshaw, *Homecoming: Reclaiming and Championing Your Inner Child* (New York: Bantam Books, 1990), 192–93.
2. J. Masterson, *The Search for the Real Self* (New York: Free Press, 1988).
3. A. Miller, *Prisoners of Childhood* (New York: Basic Books, 1981).

CHAPTER 11

1. E. Berne, *Games People Play* (New York: Grove Press, 1961).
2. J. Paul and M. Paul, *From Conflict to Caring* (Minneapolis: CompCare Publishers, 1989).
3. B. Weinhold and J. Weinhold, *Conflict Resolution: The Partnership Way* (Denver: Love Publishing, 2000).

CHAPTER 12

1. Darkness2light, Statistics Surrounding Child Sexual Abuse, 2006, www.darkness2light.org (accessed on December 25, 2006).
2. H. Prankratz, "Sisters with Sex Lawsuit vs. Dad $2.3 Million Given for Years of Abuse," *Denver Post*, May 17, 1990.
3. S. Mendelsohn, *It's Not about the Weight: Attacking Eating Disorders from the Inside Out* (Lincoln, NE: iUniverse, 2007); M. Woodman, *Addiction to Perfection* (Toronto: Inner City Books, 1982).
4. C. Wills-Brandon, *Is It Love or Is It Sex?* rev. ed. (Deerfield Beach, FL: Health Communications, 2000).
5. B. Weinhold and J. Weinhold, *Breaking Free of the Co-dependency Trap* (Novato, CA: New World Library, 2008).
6. B. Weinhold and G. Andresen, *Threads: Unraveling the Mysteries of Adult Life* (New York: Richard Marek, 1981).
7. Ibid.

CHAPTER 13

1. J. Weinhold and B. Weinhold, *Couple Evolution*. Unpublished manuscript (Swannanoa, NC: CICRCL Press, forthcoming), 3.

2. B. Weinhold and J. Weinhold, *Breaking Free of the Co-dependency Trap* (Novato, CA: New World Library, 2008).
3. Ibid.
4. J. Weinhold and B. Weinhold, *Healing Developmental Trauma* (Swannanoa, NC: CICRCL Press, 2007), 190–92.

CHAPTER 14

1. E. Erikson, *Childhood and Society* (New York: W. W. Norton, 1963).
2. M. S. Peck, *The Different Drum* (New York: Simon and Schuster, 1987), 187–206.
3. S. K. Padover, ed., *Thomas Jefferson on Democracy* (New York: New American Library, 1939), 32, 67.

CHAPTER 15

1. S. Grof and C. Grof, *Spiritual Emergency* (Los Angeles: Tarcher, 1989).
2. R. Heinberg, *Memories and Visions of Paradise* (Los Angeles: Tarcher, 1989).

Bibliography

Ainsworth, M. "Attachments Across the Life Span." *Bulletin of the New York Academy of Medicine* 61 (1985): 792–812.

Alsop, R. "Drug and Alcohol Clinics for Patients." *New York Times*, November 14, 1988, B1.

American Psychiatric Association. *Diagnostic and Statistical Manual.* 4th ed. Washington, DC: American Psychiatric Association, 1996.

Andresen, G., and B. Weinhold. *Connective Bargaining: Communicating about Sex.* Englewood Cliffs, NJ: Prentice Hall, 1981.

Armstrong, L. *The Home Front.* St. Louis: McGraw-Hill, 1983.

Bateson, G. *Steps to an Ecology of Mind.* New York: Ballantine, 1972.

Berne, E. *Games People Play.* New York: Grove Press, 1961.

Bly, R. "Your Spiritual Shadow." *Magical Blend* (July 23, 1989): 10–23, 96.

Bolton, R. *People Skills.* New York: Simon and Schuster, 1979.

Bowlby, J. *Attachments and Loss.* Vol. 1. New York: Basic Books, 1969.

———. *Attachments and Loss.* Vol. 2. New York: Basic Books, 1973.

———. *A Secure Base: Clinical Applications of Attachment Theory.* London: Routledge, 1988.

Bradshaw, J. *Healing the Shame That Binds You.* Deerfield Beach, FL: Health Communications, 1988.

———. *Homecoming: Reclaiming and Championing Your Inner Child.* New York: Bantam Books, 1990.

Brown, L., et al. *Plan B 2.0: Rescuing a Planet under Stress and a Civilization in Trouble.* New York: W. W. Norton, 2006.

Campos, J., K. Barrett, et al. "Sociomotor Development." In *Handbook of Child Psychology.* Vol. 2, *Infancy and Psychology*, ed. M. Haith and J. Campos, 783–915. New York: Wiley, 1983.

Carnes, P. *Contrary to Love.* Minneapolis: CompCare Publishers, 1989.

Clarke, J. *Growing Up Again: Parenting Ourselves, Parenting Our Children.* Center City, MN: Hazelden, 1989.

Cline, F. *What Shall We Do with This Kid? Learning Disorders and School Problems.* Evergreen, CO: Love and Logic Press, 1979.

Darkness2light. *Statistics Surrounding Child Sexual Abuse.* 2006, www.darkness2light.org, accessed on December 25, 2006.

Daro, D., and R. Gelles. "Public Attitudes and Behaviors with Respect to Child Abuse Prevention." *Journal of Interpersonal Violence* 7:4 (December 1992): 517–31.

DeMause, L. "The Universality of Incest." *Journal of Psychohistory* 19 (1991): 123–64.

Eisler, R. *The Chalice and the Blade.* San Francisco: Harper and Row, 1987.

Erikson, E. *Childhood and Society.* New York: W. W. Norton, 1963.

Forward, S., and C. Buck. *Betrayal of Innocence.* New York: Penguin Books, 1978.

Grinspoon, L., and J. B. Bakalar. *Cocaine: A Drug and Its Social Evolution.* New York: Basic Books, 1985.

Grof, S. *Realms of the Human Unconsciousness.* New York: E. P. Dutton, 1976.

Grof, S., and C. Grof. *Spiritual Emergency.* Los Angeles: Tarcher, 1989.

Havinghurst, R. *Developmental Tasks and Education.* New York: David McKay, 1972.

Heinberg, R. *Memories and Visions of Paradise.* Los Angeles: Tarcher, 1989.

Hoeller, S. *Gnosticism: New Light on the Ancient Tradition of Inner Knowing.* Wheaton, IL: Theosophical Publishing House, 2002.

Johnson, S. *Characterological Transformation.* New York: W. W. Norton, 1985.

———. *Humanizing the Narcissistic Style.* New York: W. W. Norton, 1987.

Kaplan, L. *Oneness and Separateness.* New York: Simon and Schuster, 1978.

Karen, R. *Becoming Attached.* New York: Oxford University Press, 1998.

Karpman, S. "Fairy Tales and Script Drama Analysis." *Transactional Analysis Bulletin* 7 (1968): 39–43.

Krause, A., and B. Haverkamp. "Attachment in Adult Child–Older Parent Relationships: Research, Theory, and Practice." *Journal of Counseling and Development* 75 (1996): 63–75.

Kreisman, J., and H. Straus. *I Hate You — Don't Leave Me.* Los Angeles: The Body Press, 1989.

Lero, D., et al. *Canadian National Child Care Study: Parental Work Patterns and Child Care Needs.* Catalogue no. 89-529E. Ottawa: Statistics Canada, 1992.

Lipton, B. *The Biology of Belief.* Santa Rosa, CA: Mountain of Love/Elite Press, 2005.

Maeder, T. "Wounded Healers." *Atlantic Monthly* (January 1989): 37–47.

Magid, K., and C. McKelvey. *High Risk: Children without a Conscious.* New York: Bantam, 1988.

Mahler, M. *On Human Symbiosis and the Vicissitudes of Individuation*. New York: International University Press, 1968.

Masterson, J. *The Search for the Real Self*. New York: Free Press, 1988.

Mendelsohn, S. *It's Not about the Weight: Attacking Eating Disorders from the Inside Out*. Lincoln, NE: iUniverse, 2007.

Miller, A. *The Body Never Lies: The Lingering Effects of Hurtful Parenting*. New York: W. W. Norton, 2006.

———. *Breaking Down the Walls of Silence*. New York: Dutton, 1991.

———. *For Your Own Good*. New York: Farrar, Straus, Giroux, 1983.

———. *Prisoners of Childhood*. New York: Basic Books, 1981.

———. *Thou Shalt Not Be Aware*. New York: Meridian Books, 1986.

Miller, W. R., P. L. Wilborne, and J. E. Hettema. "What Works: A Summary of Alcohol Treatment Outcome Research." In *Handbook of Alcohol Treatment Approaches: Effective Alternatives*, ed. R. K. Hester and W. R. Miller, 13–63. 3rd ed. Boston, MA: Allyn and Bacon, 2003.

Mindell, A. *River's Way*. London: Routledge and Kegan Paul, 1985.

National Child Abuse and Neglect Data System. *Summary of Key Findings from Calendar Year 2000*. Washington, DC: National Clearinghouse on Child Abuse and Neglect Information, U.S. Department of Heath and Human Services, 2002.

National Council on Child Abuse and Family Violence. *Child Abuse Information*. Raleigh, NC: Prevent Child Abuse North Carolina, 2002.

National Institute of Justice. *The Cycles of Violence Revisited: NIJ Research Preview*. Washington, DC: U.S. Department of Justice, 1996.

Padov, S. K., ed. *Thomas Jefferson on Democracy*. New York: New American Library, 1939.

Paul, J., and M. Paul. *From Conflict to Caring*. Minneapolis: CompCare Publishers, 1989.

Peck, M. S. *The Different Drum*. New York: Simon and Schuster, 1987.

Peele, S. *Diseasing of America*. Lexington, MA: Lexington Books, 1989.

———. "The Surprising Truth about Addiction." *Psychology Today* (May–June 2004): 43–46.

Perry, B. "Incubated in Terror: Neurodevelopmental Factors in the Cycle of Violence." In *Children, Youth, and Violence: Searching for Solutions*, ed. J. Osofdsy. New York: Guilford Press, 1996.

Piaget, J. *The Child's Conception of the World*. New York: Humanities Press, 1951.

Pollack, W. *Real Boys: Rescuing Our Sons from the Myths of Boyhood*. New York: Random House, 1998.

Prankratz, H. "Sisters with Sex Lawsuit vs. Dad $2.3 Million Given for Years of Abuse." *Denver Post*, May 17, 1990.

Rogers, C. *On Becoming a Person*. Boston: Houghton Mifflin, 1961.

Rollnick, S., and W. R. Miller, "What Is Motivational Interviewing?" *Behavioral and Cognitive Psychotherapy* 23 (1995): 325–34.

Rosenberg, J. *Body, Self, and Soul*. Atlanta: Humanics, 1985.

Sargent, E., S. Marcus-Mendoza, and C. H. Yu. "Changing Perceptions of the Etiology of Crime: The Relationship between Abuse and Female Criminality," *Journal of the Oklahoman Criminal Justice Research Consortium* 1 (1994): 17.

Satir, V. M. *Peoplemaking*. Palo Alto, CA: Science and Behavior Books, 1972.

Schaef, A. W. *When Society Becomes an Addict*. New York: Harper and Row, 1987.

Sedlak, A., and M. Broadhurst. *The Third National Incidence Study of Child Abuse and Neglect*. Washington, DC: National Clearinghouse on Child Abuse and Neglect Information, 1996.

Straus, M., et al. *Behind Closed Doors: Violence in the American Family*. New York: Anchor Press, 1980.

Vaillant, G. E. *The Natural History of Alcoholism*. Cambridge, MA: Harvard University Press, 1983.

Verny, T. *The Secret Life of the Unborn Child*. New York: Delta Books, 1981.

Verny, T., and P. Weintraub. *Nurturing the Unborn Child*. New York: Delacorte Press, 1991.

Violato, C., and C. Russell. "Effects of Nonmaternal Care on Child Development: A Meta-analysis of Published Research." Poster presentation at the Canadian Psychological Association Convention, Penticton, B.C., Canada, July 1, 1994.

Weinhold, B. *Breaking Family Patterns*. Swannanoa, NC: CICRCL Press, 2006.

———. *Breaking Free of Addictive Family Relationships*. Walpole, NH: Stillpoint, 1991.

Weinhold, B., and G. Andresen. *Threads: Unraveling the Mysteries of Adult Life*. New York: Richard Marek, 1981.

Weinhold, B., and C. G. Hendricks. *Counseling and Psychotherapy: A Transpersonal Approach*. Denver: Love Publishing, 1992.

Weinhold, B., and J. Weinhold. *Breaking Free of the Co-dependency Trap*. Novato, CA: New World Library, 2008.

———. *Conflict Resolution: The Partnership Way*. Denver: Love Publishing, 2000.

Weinhold, J., and B. Weinhold. *Counter-dependency: The Flight from Intimacy*. 2nd ed. Asheville, NC: CICRCL Press, 2003.

———. *Couple Evolution*. Swannanoa, NC: CICRCL Press, forthcoming).

———. *Healing Developmental Trauma*. Swannanoa, NC: CICRCL Press, 2007.

Weisner, C. M., and R. Room. "Financing and Ideology in Alcohol Treatment." *Social Problems* 32 (1984): 167–84.

Widom, B., and M. Maxfield. *An Update on the Cycle of Violence*. Washington, DC: Office of Juvenile Justice and Delinquency Prevention, U.S. Department of Justice, 2001.

Wills-Brandon, C. *Eat Like a Lady: Guide for Overcoming Bulimia*. Deerfield Beach, FL: Health Communications, 1989.

———. *Is It Love or Is It Sex?* Deerfield Beach, FL: Health Communications, 1989.

Woodman, M. *Addiction to Perfection*. Toronto: Inner City Books, 1982.

Index

A

abandonment, 8, 23–26, 272
  and inner child, 202
  physical, 203
  and projections, 191, 192
  and rage, 204
abundance, 267, 268
abuse, 22, 28–29, 173
  See also child abuse; emotional
    abuse; physical abuse; sexual
    abuse
addictions, 14, 55, 81
  alcohol, 90–91
  and counter-dependent behav-
    iors, 82–83
  defined, 92
  developmental view of, 98
  as diseases, 93–95
  as identity, 95–96
  sex, 239
  treatment approaches, 95
  Weinholds' treatment approach,
    92–93
Addiction to Perfection (Woodman),
  242
adolescents, 292–93
aggression, 172
agitators, 293–94
agreements, effective, 176
alcohol addiction, 90–91
Alcoholics Anonymous, 142
anger, 172, 204–5
antisocial personality disorder, 25–26
attachment, 24–25, 32
authenticity, 273–74

B

Bateson, Gregory, 124
beliefs, 226–27
betrayal, 85–86, 192
birth, psychological. *See* psychological
  birth
birth trauma, 67

blame, 192, 197–98
Bly, Robert, 193–94
bonding, 6–7, 22, 49–50, 81, 113
    and co-dependency, 116
    developmental processes, 32,
        150–51
    and families, 120–21
    interruption of, 68
    relationship perspective, 119–20
boundaries
    appropriate, 172
    building, exercise, 179–85
    case example, 177–79
    emotional, 174–75, 183
    mental, 175–76, 182
    physical, 173–74, 181–82
    and protection, 184
    raising and lowering, 184–85
    respect for, 275
    setting, 144–45, 169–86
    spiritual, 176–77, 183–84
    touching and maintaining, 185
boys, 27–28
Bradshaw, John, 45, 190–92, 201
Bratislava International Center for
    Family Studies, 303
*Breaking Free of the Co-dependency
    Trap* (Weinholds), 19, 265, 317
Brown, Lester, 131
Buck, Craig, 29

C

Carnes, Patrick, 108
The Chalice and the Blade (Eisler),
    124–25
child abuse, 8, 28–30, 244–45
childhood wounds, 271–72
children, 25, 27–28
    and abandonment, 202
    developmental processes of, 25,
        27–28, 113–15, 292

development of, 36–38
    and drama triangle, 73–75
    and separation, 292
    what they need from parents, 61
client-therapist relationship, 171
Cline, Foster, 24
co-alcoholism, 91
co-dependency, 31, 97–98
    behaviors, 5
    and bonding, 113, 116
    breaking free from, 150–53
    and conflict, 218–19
    vs. counter-dependency, 4–6,
        19–47
    in couple evolution, 261
    developmental stages and
        processes, 32, 150–51
    and family development, 290
    and human development, 36
    major signs of, 19–20
    and nation-state development,
        298
    relationships, 260–63
    and sex, 237
    unresolved issues, 127–28
    and wholeness, 82
Co-dependents Anonymous (CodA),
    45
cognitive therapy, 102
Colorado/Carolina Institute for
    Conflict Resolution and Creative
    Leadership, 221, 317
Columbine massacre, 27–28
comfort objects, 54
commitment, 276–77
    and relationships, 45–46, 84,
        142–43, 271–75
communication
    and empathy, 156
    and intimacy, 144, 146
    between parents and children,
        78–81

perception check, 192–93
  sexual, 237–56
competition, 266–68
complete separation phase, 57–60
compulsive behaviors, 91
conduct disorder, 25–26
conflict
    and co-dependent behaviors, 218–19
    and counter-dependent behaviors, 219–20
    and intimacy, 217–35
    intractable, 229–31, 234
    limiting beliefs about, 217–18
    sources of, 228–29
    over values and beliefs, 226–27
    over wants and needs, 225–26
conflict resolution, 28, 221–22
    case example, 231–35
    and intimacy, 146
    and partnership relationships, 274
    Partnership Way, 222–31
Conflict Resolution (Weinholds), 146, 222
contracts, 104, 145, 206–9
cooperation
    and competition, 266–68
    developmental stages and processes, 35
    and interdependence, 115, 118
core beliefs, 159
core trauma
    and addictions, 92
    completing, 81–82
    healing, 72
    identifying, 85–86
    and infant development, 65–66
    as life pattern, 68–69
counter-dependency, 31
    and abuse, 28–29
    and addictions, 82–83

assumptions about, 42–44
behaviors, 4, 5, 9–11, 160–64
and boundaries, 170–72
breaking free from, 44–46, 100, 146–49, 150–53
causes in adults, 6–8, 22–23
changing behavior, 82–85, 141–44
characteristic behaviors, 20–22
vs. co-dependency, 4–6, 19–47
and conflict, 219–20
in couple evolution, 261
current crisis, 128–30
developmental stages and processes, 33
and developmental trauma, 159
and empathy, 158–59
and False Self, 188
and families, 290–94
getting stuck in, 65–87
global crisis, 303–4
and human development, 36–37
identifying relationship patterns, 263–65
vs. interdependent sex, 238
in international relations, 301–3
move to commitment and intimacy, 276–77
and nation-states, 298–301
overview, 19–30
parental influence, 38–39
and projections, 188
in relationships, 260–63, 289–90
and religion, 296–97
self-quiz, 46–47
and separation process, 114, 117
and sexual abuse, 240–42
and sexual encounters, 237–38
systems perspective, 119
understanding, 49–64
unresolved issues, 127–28
what it is, 3
and wholeness, 82

counter-dependent culture, 111–33
    case example, 130–32
    treating, 131–32
countertransference, 75
couple relationships
    common combinations in,
        263–65
    developmental processes, 113–15
    and individuation, 120
    stages of, 261–62

D

dance of intimacy, 264–65
defenses, 158
denial, 175
development
    of couple relationships, 261–62
    delayed, 104
    family, 290–91
    incomplete, 107
    individual, 32–38
    infant, 65–66
    macrosystems stages and
        processes, 116–18
    microsystems stages and
        processes, 113–15
    of nation-states, 298–99
    psychological, 128
    spiritual, 296–97
developmental needs, unmet. *See*
    unmet developmental needs
developmental permissions, 206
developmental process work, 9, 103–6
    and bonding, 150–51
    consultants, 103–6, 131–32
    incomplete, 42–43, 137–38,
        149–53, 206
    and therapy, 105
Developmental Systems Theory
    (DST), 9, 31–38, 112–26

developmental trauma, 7–8, 22, 26–28
    and counter-dependency, 159
    healing, 277–83
    identifying, 66–68
The Different Drum (Peck), 296
differentiation, 121–22
disease model
    and addictions, 94, 95
    of relationships, 89–110
    and sexual addiction, 95, 106–9
    and therapists, 109–10
    of therapy, 100–103
diseases, 93–94, 203
domination, 76–77, 268–70
dominator society, 125–26
drama triangle, 72–77, 244

E

early exploration phase, 52–53
early partnership society, 125–26
early separation phase, 55–57
eating disorders, 242
ego-reduction, 129
Eisler, Riane, 124–25
either/or thinking, 56
emerging partnership society, 125–26
emotional abuse, 8, 29, 30
empathy, 155–68, 220
    and counter-dependency, 158–59
    learning, 164–67
    training, 144
    what it is, 155–56
environment, 34, 130
equality, 274–75
Erikson, Erik, 288
evolution
    couple, 261–62
    individual, 32–38, 113–15
    psychological, 128
    soul, 14
evolutionary perspective, 124–25
exploration phase, 52–55

F

False Self, 50, 57, 62, 141
    and boundary setting, 171
    and counter-dependency, 188
    and empathy, 159
family, 77–78
    and bonding, 120–21
    breaking free from counter-
      dependency issues, 290–94
    developmental processes, 113–15
    relationships, 265
family meetings, 292, 294–95
Family Training Center, 317–18
fathers, 58–59
feelings, 92, 156–57, 174, 201–5
fight response, 191
Forward, Susan, 29
freedom, 122–23, 127–28, 299–300
full exploration phase, 53–55
functional family triangle, 77–78

G

gender, 39–42
gnosis, 62
God, 176–77
government, 127
group therapy, 142, 204
guilt, 96, 108, 190

H

Haeckel, Ernst, 124
Heinberg, Richard, 318–19
High Risk (Magid and McKelvey),
    23–24
Homecoming (Bradshaw), 201
Houston, Jean, 305, 307
human development, 31–38
human race, 116–18
human systems, 288

I

incest, 29
independence, 31
    in couple evolution, 262
    developmental stages and
      processes, 34
    and family development, 291
    and human development, 37–38
    mastery, 114, 118
    and nation-state development,
      299
individuation, 49–51
    and communication, 78–81
    and couples, 120
    developmental stages and
      processes, 33
    international perspective, 123–24
    See also psychological birth; sepa-
      ration
infants, 65–66, 68
inner child, 189
    bill of rights, 202
    healing, 199–216
    nurturing, 210
    shaming messages, 200
interdependence, 31
    and child development, 38
    and cooperation, 115, 118
    in couple evolution, 262
    developmental stages and
      processes, 35
    and family development, 291
    and nation-state development,
      299
    self-quiz, 132–33
    and sexual contact, 238
international perspective, 123–24
international relations, 301–3
intimacy, 12, 13, 146
    authentic, 138
    avoiding, 237
    barriers to, 250–51

intimacy (*continued*)
  and conflict, 217–35
  creating, 140, 144–46
  and feelings, 202
  move from counter-dependency
      to, 276–77
  new definition of, 139–40
  and partnership relationships,
      275–76
  and Partnership Way, 225–26
  recovering, 220–21
  search for, 138–39
intimidation, 76
Is It Love or Is It Sex? (Wills-Brandon),
    243
It's Not about the Weight (Mendelsohn),
    242

J

Jefferson, Thomas, 300
Johnson, Stephen, 51
journals, 176
Jung, Carl, 49, 62

K

Karpman, Steven, 72–73

L

life drama, 70–72
    authors', 310–16
life patterns, 69–72
Lipton, Bruce, 124
listening, 156, 165–67
loneliness, 212–13
love, unconditional, 176
love addiction, 98–99, 106–7

M

macrosystems, 116–18
Magid, Ken, 23–24

Mahler, Margaret, 50
Masterson, James, 203
mastery, 34, 114, 118
masturbation, 239
maternal-infant bonding, 50
McKelvey, Carol, 23–24
Memories and Visions of Paradise
    (Heinberg), 318–19
memory repression, 241
Mendelsohn, Susan, 242
microsystems, 113–15
Miller, Alice, 29, 60–61, 204
Miller, William, 97
Mindell, Arnold, 221
mirroring, 36, 60
mothers, working, 68
Mystery School, 305, 307

N

narcissism, 57, 60–61
nation-states, 116–18, 298–301
needs, 225–26
neglect, 8, 23–26, 29–30
    adult behavior related to child-
        hood neglect, 245–46
    intentional, 244–45
    sexual, 242, 243–44
    unintentional, 68, 243–44
negotiation, 35

O

object constancy, 58, 63, 76, 175–76
organizations, 116–18

P

paradise, 318–20
parenting, corrective, 145
parenting contracts, 206–9
parents, 23–26, 60–61, 215
partnership relationships, 142–43,
    259–85

authors', 305–20
    case example, 283–85
    common elements of, 270
    creating, 271–76
    and domination, 268–70
partnership society, 124, 125–26, 287–304
Partnership Way, 221–22
    conflict resolution, 222–31
path of learning, 220
Paul, Jordan and Margaret, 220
Peck, M. Scott, 296–97
Peele, Stanton, 96–97
perception check, 192–93
perfection, 159
permissions, developmental, 206
Perry, Bruce, 24, 28
persecutor, 72–73, 74, 76, 219
personality disorders, 25–26
physical abuse, 8, 173–74
political systems, 122–23, 299
Pollack, William, 27
post-traumatic stress disorder, 28, 73, 241
primal trust, 85, 192
projections
    and blame, 197–98
    case example, 194–95
    defined, 187
    reclaiming, 145, 187–98
    recognizing, 191
    and shame, 190–92
psychic agreements, 70–72
psychological birth, 7, 22, 49–51, 57, 61–63
    See also individuation
psychotherapy, 45
    See also therapy

R

rage, 204–5
Real Boys (Pollack), 27

rebelliousness, 292
rebirth, spiritual, 62
regression, 191
regression-progression, 51
relationships, 119–20
    breaking free of counter-dependency issues, 289–90
    committed, 45–46, 84, 142–43
    disease model of, 89–110
    domination vs. partnership, 268–70
    new vision of, 265–66
    See also partnership relationships
religion, 121–22, 296–97
rescue, 72, 74–76, 274–75
responsibility, 197–98
Rogers, Carl, 156, 175
Rollnick, Steve, 97
ROZRADA, 303

S

scarcity, 266–68
Self, 11, 58, 83
    See also False Self; True Self
self-hatred, 200
self-love, 176
self-nurturing skills, 209
self-parenting, 199–216
    case example, 209–14
separateness, 51
separation, 6–7, 22, 55–60, 114
    and children, 50–51, 292
    and communication, 289–90
    and counter-dependency, 117
    developmental processes and needs, 152–53
    developmental stages and processes, 33
    and family development, 121
    international perspective, 123–24
    political perspective, 122–23
    religious perspective, 121–22

separation (*continued*)
    subphases of, 51–60
    See also individuation
sex
    addiction, 98–99, 106–7, 108–9, 239
    barriers to intimacy, 250–51
    and communication, 146, 251–56
    counter-dependent vs. inter-dependent, 238
Sex and Love Addicts Anonymous, 98–99
sexual abuse, 8, 29, 177–78
    case example, 246–50
    childhood, adult behavior related to, 245–46
    as cause of counter-dependent behaviors, 240–42
    and eating disorders, 242
    intentional, 241, 244–45
    and neglect, 243–46
    unintentional, 243–44
shadow, 188–89, 196
    See also projections
shame, 96, 108, 176, 190–92, 200
sins of omission and commission, 63–64
society, partnership, 287–304
Soviet Union, 301–3
spiritual awakening, 177
spiritual development, 296–97
spirituality, 276
spiritual rebirth, 62
splitting, 56, 76
support groups, 45, 142
surrender, 160
symbiosis, 50, 119
systems perspective, 119

T

talk therapy, 102
terror, 176–77
therapists, 101, 109–10

therapy, 45, 142
    boundary work, 170–72
    characteristics of, 101–3
    developmental process work, 103–6
    disease model of, 100–103
    group, 45, 142
Third National Incidence Study of Child Abuse and Neglect, 29–30
touch, 99, 173, 185
transitional objects, 54, 55
trauma, 10, 23, 104
    See also developmental trauma
trauma drama, 70
True Self, 11, 62, 159, 188, 204
trust, 85, 192
twelve-step meetings, 142

U

Ukraine, 303
United States, 130–32
unmet developmental needs, 20, 42, 64, 83, 271
    authors', 307–10

V

Vaillant, George, 90
values, 226–27
victim consciousness, 72–77
violence, 22–23, 28

W

wants, 225–26
Weinhold, Barry and Janae
    changing personal counter-dependent patterns, 305–20
wholeness, 82, 260
Wills-Brandon, Carla, 243
Woodman, Marion, 242
working mothers, 68
wounds, childhood, 271–72

About the Authors

Between them, Doctors Barry and Janae Weinhold have served for over five decades as licensed mental health professionals and have almost sixty years' teaching experience. Barry is licensed as a psychologist, and Janae is a professional counselor. The cofounders of the Carolina Institute for Conflict Resolution and Creative Leadership (CICRCL) near Asheville, North Carolina, they specialize in the areas of developmental psychology, trauma, violence prevention, conflict resolution, cosmologies, and consciousness studies. Barry is professor emeritus and former chair of the counseling and human services program at the University of Colorado at Colorado Springs. He is also the founder and director of the Kindness Campaign, a nationally acclaimed violence prevention program in over six hundred schools and communities. Janae is a consultant in children's mental health and a former adjunct professor at the University of Colorado at Colorado Springs. Both have served as United Nations consultants and are trainers with a sister nonprofit in Kiev, Ukraine. They are the authors or coauthors of thirty-one books. Their website is www.weinholds.org.